What is Criminology About?

Since its inception, criminology has had trouble answering the question of what it is about. But although many consider the answer to this question to be self-evident, this book pursues the provocative possibility that criminology does not know what the object of its study is; it merely knows what it is called. Aiming to foster dissent among those who claim to know what criminology is about – and those who do not – writers from different schools of thought come together in this collection to answer the question 'What is criminology about?'. Building on a resurgence of interest in the nature of the object of criminology, their responses aim to deepen, and to expand, the current debate. This book will, then, be of considerable interest to contemporary proponents and students of criminology and law.

Don Crewe is based at Leeds Metropolitan University.
Ronnie Lippens is based at the University of Keele.

What is Criminology About?

Philosophical Reflections

Edited by Don Crewe and
Ronnie Lippens

LONDON AND NEW YORK

First published 2015
by Routledge
2 Park Square, Milton Park, Abingdon, Oxfordshire OX14 4RN

and by Routledge
711 Third Avenue, New York, NY 10017

First issued in paperback 2016

Routledge is an imprint of the Taylor & Francis Group, an informa business

© 2015 Selection and editorial matter, Don Crewe and Ronnie Lippens; individual chapters, the contributors.

The right of Don Crewe and Ronnie Lippens to be identified as editors of this work has been asserted by them in accordance with sections 77 and 78 of the Copyright, Designs and Patents Act 1988.

All rights reserved. No part of this book may be reprinted or reproduced or utilised in any form or by any electronic, mechanical, or other means, now known or hereafter invented, including photocopying and recording, or in any information storage or retrieval system, without permission in writing from the publishers.

Trademark notice: Product or corporate names may be trademarks or registered trademarks, and are used only for identification and explanation without intent to infringe.

British Library Cataloguing in Publication Data
A catalogue record for this book is available from the British Library

Library of Congress Cataloging-in-Publication Data
A catalog record has been requested for this book

ISBN 13: 978-1-138-24155-8 (pbk)
ISBN 13: 978-1-138-02540-0 (hbk)

Typeset in Garamond by
Servis Filmsetting Ltd, Stockport, Cheshire

Contents

Contributors   vii

   Introduction   1
   RONNIE LIPPENS AND DON CREWE

PART I
Elements

1   What is criminology about? Reflections on the image of the line   13
      RONNIE LIPPENS

2   To criminology and beyond! A polemic   31
      DON CREWE

3   Criminology as 'chaosmic' art: a jazz perspective   47
      CLAUDIUS MESSNER

4   The quantum holographic turn. "Normal science" versus quantized, holographic, affirmative nomadology   66
      DRAGAN MILOVANOVIC

5   Criminology: What is it about?   84
      RAFFAELE DE GIORGI AND LUCIANO NUZZO

PART II
Themes

6   Individuals and groups of individuals breaking laws   105
      ANTHONY AMATRUDO

7	What is criminology about? The study of harm, special liberty and pseudo-pacification in late-capitalism's libidinal economy STEVE HALL	122
8	Sartre on edgework JAMES HARDIE-BICK	141
9	Criminology and 'criminalisable' legal persons GEORGE PAVLICH	159
10	The pursuit of a general theory of crime and the indeterminacy of human experience DAVID POLIZZI	178
11	Critical realism, overdetermination and social censure COLIN SUMNER	195

Index 210

Contributors

Anthony Amatrudo is Reader in Criminology at Middlesex University.

Don Crewe is Senior Lecturer in Criminology at Leeds Metropolitan University.

Raffaele De Giorgi is Professor of the Philosophy of Law at the University of Salento.

Steve Hall is Professor of Criminology at Teesside University.

James Hardie-Bick is Lecturer in Criminology and Sociology at the University of Sussex.

Ronnie Lippens is Professor of Criminology at Keele University.

Claudius Messner is Associate Professor of the Philosophy of Law at the University of Salento.

Dragan Milovanovic is Professor of Justice Studies at Northeastern Illinois University.

Luciano Nuzzo is Research Fellow in the Philosophy of Law at the University of Salento.

George Pavlich is Canada Research Chair in Social Theory, Culture and Law and Professor of Law and Sociology at the University of Alberta.

David Polizzi is Associate Professor of Criminology at Indiana State University.

Colin Sumner is Professor of Sociology at University College, Cork.

Introduction

Ronnie Lippens and Don Crewe

Introductory words

Since its inception, criminology has had trouble answering the question of what it is about. One of the key reasons for this is that it has been taken by so many that the answer to this question is self-evident. Hence many take it that this question is redundant because the answer is obvious. However, as is so often the case with *doxa*, this apparent self-evidence or obviousness is nothing of the sort but is, indeed, evidence of a certain *lack* of understanding: it is pure mystification. Criminology, one could argue, possesses two extremes in this respect, i.e. those who know absolutely what criminology is about, and those who have no knowledge whatsoever of what it is about. The aim of this collection is to challenge both of these positions. It attempts to foster dissent among those who know what criminology is about *and* those who do not. It is hoped that the contributions in this collection will bring the former to know less and the latter (perhaps) to know a little more. The aim, in other words, is to sow doubt where there is certainty yet on the other hand offering more than purely nihilistic relativism.

It is, of course, always possible, upon hearing the question, 'What is criminology about?', to reach for what has by now become the standard reply, which is, roughly, as follows. Criminology is the systematic analysis of, and reflection upon: (a) the ways in which a particular set of behaviours or indeed groups come be defined as 'criminal', and made punishable by law; (b) the reasons why particular individuals or groups of individuals at times break these laws; (c) the ways in which they thus commit 'crime', as well as the nature, spread, distribution and impact of such crimes; and (d) the reasons and justifications for a whole variety of possible ways, both formal and informal, of dealing with criminal offenders, or indeed with 'crime' as such more generally. Undergraduate students in criminology or criminal justice will, in their freshman year, have stumbled across a similar reply to the above question in one or more of their textbooks. Of course there have been debates, within what could be called the criminological community, to tweak elements in this more or less standard definition (by now at least) of what it is that criminology is about. For example, is criminology really about 'crime' as such? Is it, in other words, really about law and law breaking, or, rather, about 'deviance' from or 'transgression' of the 'norm' or 'discipline'? Or is it about 'harm' and 'redress'? Or 'revolt' and 'control'? And so on. The tweaks and turns that the criminological community has been able to generate in this context are quite numerous, and, again, undergraduate criminology students are now routinely introduced to most of them almost from the day they first set foot on a university campus.

We could leave it at that and move on to the order of the day, only to discover that the original question will not go away. What is criminology actually about? Is it really about law and criminal offence? But is there any difference between law and crime to begin with, or between law and offence, or between law and violence, and so on? Does that difference – if there is any difference here at all – take the form of a sharp boundary? Where is the line that sharply divides the norm from its deviance? Is not transgression, at least to some extent, also discipline? Is not revolt also control? And is not control also revolt? And what is law, actually? What is transgression? What is violence? What is harm? What is redress? These questions are not just about mere semantics, they point towards the need to make an effort to think more thoroughly about the object of criminology. In other words, criminology could do with a more thorough engagement with philosophy. Indeed, philosophers have written about such questions. Just to give one well-known illustration here: the deconstructionist philosopher Jacques Derrida (1992), for example, has made a very serious attempt to think of law as violence.

Engaging with philosophy, however, is easier said than done. Where to begin? The field of philosophy is, simply put, vast. It comprises a variety of areas (e.g. ontology, epistemology, ethics and aesthetics), perspectives (from Anglo-American analytical philosophy to continental deconstruction and post-structuralism, from phenomenology and existentialist philosophy to pragmatism, and a tremendous lot in between and beyond), concepts (from Plato's *Ideas* to Wittgenstein's *meaning as use*, from Gramsci's *hegemony* to Sartre's *life project*, from Marx's *alienation* to Deleuze and Guattari's *body without organs*, and so on) and authors (from Hegel to Lacan, from Kierkegaard to Lefort, from Nietzsche to Sloterdijk, from Marx to Badiou, from Husserl to Heidegger, from Spinoza to Bergson, and so on). For reasons that shall be clear soon enough, it is neither feasible nor necessary to give a systematic overview here, let alone an exhaustive one, of the field of philosophy. It would simply be impossible to do so in a short editorial introduction to a collection that includes 'philosophical reflections' on criminology's object (or lack thereof).

Let us, for our purposes, again stress the need for criminologists to engage more directly and thoroughly with philosophy. Such an engagement is necessary, we believe, if one wishes to make an attempt to think through the issue of what it is that criminology is about. It should be said, however, that most criminologists are not strangers to philosophical reflection. One could do the test: pick up any criminology textbook and the chances are that somewhere in the book you will find its author engaging with a philosophical concept, idea, author or perspective. However, very few criminologists do so in a more or less sustained or systematic fashion. There are of course exceptions. One of the more recent attempts to engage with philosophy more systematically is to be found in the collection of essays (2006) edited by Bruce Arrigo and Christopher Williams, who asked a number of fellow criminologists to think about the ontological, epistemological, ethical and aesthetic dimensions of crime and criminology. Others have made sustained attempts to explore particular philosophical perspectives with an eye on mobilizing them to particular topics or issues in criminology and criminal justice. In his book *Justice Fragmented* (1996), George Pavlich explored post-structuralist and postmodern philosophy in order to rethink the complexities, in a very late twentieth century, of what has become known as restorative justice, for example. More recently, we find criminological explorations of philosophy in collections edited by Don Crewe and Ronnie Lippens (2009), and by Lippens and James Hardie-Bick (2011), whose contributors focused on phenomenology and existentialist philosophy. More recently still, Steve Hall (2013) has engaged quite substantially with the work of a number of recent continental philosophers and philosophical perspectives to produce a refreshingly novel and penetrating analysis of the violent, *pseudo-pacifying* condition of late, very late capitalism.

However, there have been very few works that deployed sustained philosophical reflection in an attempt to rethink the issue of just what it is that criminology is about. One of the pioneers, however, is Colin Sumner who, in a series of path-breaking works (e.g. 1979, 1994), and using neo-Marxist perspectives, offered a new outline of criminology's object: criminology, argues Sumner, is about social *censure*. Dragan Milovanovic and Stuart Henry (1996) delved into a variety of postmodern perspectives (as well as in complexity theories and structuration theory) in a bid to rethink criminology's object as proliferating constitutive cycles of harm. And, lastly, Don Crewe has very recently (2013) explored a wide variety of philosophical sources, which led him to read criminology's object as *constrained will*.

The contributions

It is at this point, however, that the collection wishes to contribute. Each of the contributors has engaged with philosophy in their previous criminological work. Some of them, as we have seen, have done so quite extensively. For the purpose of this collection, all were asked to reflect upon the question, 'What is criminology about?', and to make an attempt to answer it. They were of course left completely free to decide for themselves how to approach the task and where, in philosophy, to search for inspiration. Any other editorial strategy would have made little sense. The field of philosophy is, simply, too vast, and it is constantly on the move, constantly exceeding and spilling over what went before. It is impossible to systematize it. This collection's question is never going to be answered definitively, but the exercise as such is worth doing. Indeed, the effort may lead us to acquire a deeper insight into the *how* and the *why* of the often paradoxical shakiness of criminology's foundations.

Some of the contributors chose to focus largely on what could be called 'elements' of thought, while others made attempts to connect such 'elements' to more concrete problems and issues. In the first group are Don Crewe's chapter on the alien, Ronnie Lippens' on the image of the line, Claudius Messner's on the senses and aesthetics, Dragan Milovanovic's on quantum holography, and Luciano Nuzzo and Raffaele De Giorgi's on the circularity of 'objectivity'. In the second, more connected group (so to speak), are Anthony Amatrudo's chapter on intentionality and criminal groups, Steve Hall's on the libidinal economy and the pseudo-pacification process, James Hardie-Bick's on transcendence and edgework, George Pavlich's on the 'logos of crimen', David Polizzi's on objectivism and integrative criminology, and Colin Sumner's on over-determination and censure. We could, of course, also have chosen to group the contributions according to the philosophical inspiration of their authors (e.g. Marxist, phenomenological and existentialist, Lacanian, post-structuralist and postmodern, Luhmannian systems theory, or analytical philosophy), but that would have been an undertaking of significant arbitrariness since most authors tend to be quite prolific and sometimes even eclectic in their engagement with philosophy.

That said, let us repeat that all contributors were asked to think of an answer to the very simple question, 'What is criminology about?'. They were left completely free in their attempts to produce such an answer. No restrictions were imposed nor directions given (apart, of course, from the suggestion that the answers to the question should demonstrate an engagement with philosophy, or with philosophical writings). One could, then, do worse than allow the contributions to speak for themselves. We group the contributions into two parts. It should go without saying that there is no strict boundary between the parts. However, as said, some contributors chose to answer the question by exploring one or a few basic ideas or notions which one would not necessarily find within the usual 'criminological' discourse. These we have included in Part I: Elements. Others preferred to start from themes that many criminologists would be familiar with, but which they (i.e. the contributors to this collection) then proceeded to critically explore by means of philosophical reflection. Their contributions are to be found in Part II: Themes.

Part I: Elements

In his chapter, Ronnie Lippens argues that criminology, in a way, is about lines, i.e. the lines between 'legal' and 'illegal', or, more broadly, between 'in' and 'out'. Criminology, then, is about the imagination of lines or, as De Giorgi and Nuzzo (see below) would probably say, about differentiations. In this chapter, two philosophical perspectives on the imagination of the line are explored and contrasted. On the one hand, we have what could be called vitalist philosophy in its Spinozist and neo-Spinozist forms, and on the other hand, phenomenology and existentialism. In the former, the image of the line is the result of bodily affectations, originating in and stretching back into infinite and vacuum-less duration. In the latter, the image of the line is a constituted object made in the void of indeterminacy. But both agree on this: that the image is a line, and that the line is, if not image, then imagination.

Like Lippens, Don Crewe argues that that criminology is about its categories and the lines that divide them. The process of categorization, of division, is a process which in criminology by and large rests on the subject-of-modernity. This produces a criminology of a particularly unpleasant flavour, one that appropriates the subjectivity of others and re-forms it to its own ends. This is the *energeia* or force of criminology, its isness. In his chapter, Crewe examines this isness beginning from the foundation of the subject-of-modernity. He claims that 'what is' is an unsatisfactory state of affairs and examines a possibility that we might characterize as the *dynamis* of criminology, or 'what might be', beginning from what we might loosely call the phenomenological subject as expressed in Levinas. Crewe concludes that truly to do justice we must step *beyond* the tyranny of criminology.

Claudius Messner asks himself whether we can imagine aesthetic experiences and procedures as a fruitful ground for understanding criminology's 'aboutness'. He then proceeds to answer this question by contrasting the predominant scientific sense of criminology with an aesthetic sense. First, he argues that the modernist figuration of what he calls 'ordinary crime discourse' (i.e. the discourse about law, crime and punishment in which it is assumed that these elements are all part of a separate sphere of life – the sphere of rule, regulation and control) embodies a disregard for the aesthetic dimensions of law and justice, and creates certain pitfalls that cause criminology's perennial identity crisis and irresponsiveness. Messner then proceeds to draw upon reflections on art and aesthetics, exploring jazz as the contrapuntal form of today's world music, and as an 'aesthetics of imperfection'. As a model of what is called 'chaosmic' ethics, jazz is presented by Messner as a pioneering practice for the development of a different *sense* of criminology.

Dragan Milovanovic argues that doing criminology within a Newtonian-based ontology needs to be re-assessed. He suggests an alternative ontology, one based on quantum holographic theory as a basis for formulating questions, hypotheses and directions of inquiry. Accordingly, he suggests, after a quantized re-formulation of Delanda's Deleuzian-inspired comparison of, on the one hand, the more dominant contemporary 'axiomatic approach', with, on the other hand, a 'problematic approach', that an alternative rooted in the latter can be derived more in tune with inspirational scholarly investigations taking place in quantum holographic theory. In his chapter, Milovanovic develops some of the more salient concepts in this alternative ontology.

In their jointly written and highly reflective chapter, which shares some ground with Lippens' chapter, Raffaele De Giorgi and Luciano Nuzzo reflect on the fact that they were asked to address a question. There is nothing strange about that. The history of thought is the history of questions. Or of answers, depending on the observer: Socrates, Plato, the scholastics, up until Heidegger or Derrida, they have all formulated answers (or questions). De Giorgi and Nuzzo aim to answer the question whilst averting the temptation of asking and answering, of giving reasons and justifications, and avoiding the lure of ideology and explanation and the characteristically medieval temptation to doubt the question being posed. They also seek to avoid the characteristically modern temptation of looking for alternative theories and bases, because this would mean succumbing to the same circularity as that of whoever formulated the question. They argue that: (a) the question, 'Criminology: what is it about?' is already an answer, in the sense that it implies a theoretical perspective that justifies both the question as an answer as well as any other type of answer (with the exception, perhaps, of the one which both authors give); and (b) the question which has been asked is closely analogous with other questions, all of which have only one plausible answer. For example, the plausible answer to the question, 'Language: what is it about?' is, 'language'. As with the question, 'Law: what is it about?', the answer is, 'law'. Criminology is concerned with language and law and the analogy is, therefore, a useful one.

Part II: Themes

In his chapter on gangs and organized crime, Anthony Amatrudo, inspired by analytical philosophy, argues that collective action is necessarily a product of individual agency. This requires though that each agent is both free to choose the action they perform, that the agency of others is respected, and that all hold a belief of common knowledge (so long as agents believe that this common knowledge condition is met, then it is). Building on work by authors such as Michael Bratman, Amatrudo provides a rationale that can be used to distinguish genuine collective action from other forms and that, if applied to gangs or forms of what is often called 'organized' crime, may lead to a fairer assessment – fairer at least than in assessments that presuppose the existence of a 'plural subject' – of issues of individual responsibility.

Steve Hall argues how in the post-war era the radical wing of western criminology mutated into 'controlology', the study and critique of social reaction to acts regarded as deviant by a normative mainstream. This post-war liberal paradigm is now reaching the point of exhaustion. In the post-political era, it is no longer possible to accept the radical principle of redefining criminal acts as some form of misguided or 'imaginary' proto-political resistance. However, nor is it possible to follow the conservative and classical liberal mainstream and regard criminality as an individualised aberration in our current way of life. Thus we must return to the questions of aetiology and motivation. The renewal of criminological thought requires the return of critical theory in a substantially updated form to re-examine the relationship between harm and crime. Drawing upon conceptual resources provided by Slavoj Žižek, Adrian Johnston and others, this chapter introduces the new criminological terms *special liberty* and *pseudo-pacification* contextualised in the currently developing meta-philosophical position of *transcendental materialism*.

James Hardie-Bick writes about 'edgework'. Criminologists have found Lyng's (1990) concept of 'edgework' to be particularly useful for exploring how individuals negotiate the boundaries that separate life and death. In his chapter, Hardie-Bick explores Lyng's arguments by comparing 'edgework' to Csikszentmihalyi's (1975) research on 'flow'. He argues that Csikszentmihalyi's research should also be seen as offering important insights in relation to the pleasures of voluntary risk-taking. Using the philosophy of Sartre to examine some of the unacknowledged similarities between 'edgework' and 'flow', the overall aim of this chapter is to show the relevance of both perspectives and to widen the current focus of criminological research on high-risk behaviour.

In his chapter, George Pavlich explores how criminology, especially in administrative guises, is often regarded as a derivative discipline in the sense that it relies on criminal law to define key precepts, such as crime and criminals. Without disputing that claim, this chapter considers a counter-view that criminology has in turn helped to shape the historical cultures wherein criminal law defines which persons are legitimate targets for its gaze and force. The focus on legal persons is deliberate, for it alludes to a singular politics of recognition by which criminal law defines its object, and hence jurisdiction. In this regard, criminology has foundational attachments to criminal law, as indicated by, for example, the legacy of four influential images of 'criminalizable' persons deemed suitable for criminal law's interventions: unequal colonial creatures, rational beings of classical standpoints, the criminal types of positivist making, and the biometrically calibrated criminals of biopolitical horizons. The chapter analyses the different effects of such criminological visions on criminal law's jurisdiction and responses to crime, before exploring some key implications of the criminology-criminal law nexus when framing 'criminalizable' persons in historical context.

David Polizzi's chapter focuses on the desire, in some corners of the criminological community, to develop a general theory of crime. Since its inception, criminology has been driven to discover the underlying objective factors or causes linked to criminality. Fundamental to this project has been the hope of constructing a general theory of crime and criminal behaviour, but success toward this end has been elusive. However, rather than question the philosophical foundation of these failed Cartesian processes, greater focus has been given to quantitative innovation and insight, which has rendered much of the same results. The conclusion should be obvious: an objective approach to criminology will neither deliver a general theory of crime nor tell us what we need to know about crime construction. Crime and criminal behaviour, as a subjective and indeterminate enterprise, must be viewed from a theoretical frame of reference that is able to take up the subtle and nuanced realities of human existence. Kauffman's theoretical biology, Heidegger's philosophy of the phenomenology of human being/being and Agamben's re-formulation of Foucault's concept of the apparatus provide the appropriate vantage point for this discussion.

In his chapter, Colin Sumner makes a plea for critical realism in criminology. Crime, like so many other surface phenomena, cannot be taken at face value. Critical realism allows criminologists to pierce through the crust of the surface in order to explore the over-determined and over-determining complex of multi-layered conditions and dynamics that, often inextricably tangled but always moving, constantly generate censure and division on the surface of life. Inspired by the work of Roy Bhaskar, and writing within a broadly Marxist perspective, Sumner avoids the pitfalls of both extreme relativism and crude positivism. In its attempt to explore what lies behind surfaces, critical realism is both realist (it assumes that such explorations may ultimately lead to approximations of the generative processes that underpin censure) but also philosophical (it refuses to take the surface of life at face value).

Acknowledgement

The editors would like to express their thanks to the contributors to this book for their abstracts.

References

Arrigo, B. and C. Williams (eds) (2006) *Philosophy, Crime and Criminology*, Chicago, IL: University of Illinois Press.
Crewe, D. (2013) *Becoming Criminal: The Socio-cultural Origins of Law, Transgression, and Deviance*, Basingstoke: Palgrave Macmillan.
Crewe, D. and R. Lippens (eds) (2009) *Existentialist Criminology*, London: Routledge.
Csikszentmihalyi, M. (1975) *Beyond Boredom and Anxiety*, San Francisco, CA: Jossey-Bass.
Derrida, J. (1992) 'Force of Law: The "Mystical Foundations of Authority", in D. Cornell *et al* (eds) *Deconstruction and the Possibility of Justice*, New York: Routledge, pp. 3–67.
Hall, S. (2013) *Theorizing Crime and Deviance*, London: Sage.
Lippens, R. and J. Hardie-Bick (eds) (2011) *Crime, Governance and Existential Predicaments*, Basingstoke: Palgrave Macmillan.
Lyng, S.H. (1990) 'Edgework: A Social Psychological Analysis of Voluntary Risk-Taking', *American Journal of Sociology*, 95 (4): 851–86.

Milovanovic, D. and S. Henry (1996) *Constitutive Criminology*, London: Sage.
Pavlich, G. (1996) *Justice Fragmented*, New York, NY: Routledge.
Sumner, C. (1979) *Reading Ideologies*, London: Academic Press.
Sumner, C. (1994) *The Sociology of Deviance: An Obituary*, Buckingham: Open University Press.

Part I

Elements

Chapter 1

What is criminology about?
Reflections on the image of the line

Ronnie Lippens

Introduction

It would probably amount to kicking in open doors if one claimed that criminology is actually about lines, i.e. dividing lines in particular. Indeed, since its formal inception in the nineteenth century (let us perhaps, for the sake of argument, agree on this chronology), criminology has been the place where a number of questions were pondered. Each of those questions refers to lines. Why is it that some people cross 'the line'? Or, why is it that we always end up with such 'lines' in the first place? How is it that only a particular set of behaviours (or those persons and groups associated with those behaviours) have been prohibited (or excluded), placed *out of bounds* so to speak? Why them, and why not those others over there? And what should we do with those who decide to transgress the lines and bounds? Should they be quarantined behind this or that line? Or should attempts be made to bring them back this side of the line, back into the fold, as it were? Should we make efforts to prevent any such crossings of 'the line'?

All this may sound very banal, very *open-door-like*, and much of it has been explored elsewhere (e.g. in Lippens 2003) and should perhaps not be rehearsed here. However, there is one particular question which criminologists have posed only very rarely, i.e. can there be a human world without any dividing lines at all? Could we possibly imagine such a world? Many a criminologist may have silently cherished the hope that the answer to that question might be a wavering 'yes'; some may still do. Perhaps they accept only grudgingly, or at least reluctantly, Durkheim's deep insight that yes, even in the community of saints, there will be the inevitable dividing lines. It is hoped this chapter might be able to contribute to answering that particular question, in however small a measure.

The aim here is to explore the question from two perspectives which often find themselves at opposite sides of the philosophical spectrum. The first might be called Spinozism and it includes the work and thought of Benedict de Spinoza and a series of authors whose work could, arguably, be deemed to have neo-Spinozist characteristics (e.g. Henri Bergson and, more recently,

Gilles Deleuze and Félix Guattari). Let us, for the sake of brevity, use the acronym SP to denote this perspective. The second perspective consists of the twin perspectives of phenomenology (as conceived and developed by Edmund Husserl) and existentialism (Jean-Paul Sartre's in particular). We may perhaps be allowed to use the letters PE here by way of an acronym. The work of the aforementioned philosophers is explored with an eye on answering one of the most basic questions that criminologists could agonize over, 'Is a human world without dividing lines imaginable?'. The answer, in a nutshell, will sound something like this, 'no, for images are lines, and lines are images'.

As said, SP and PE tend to occupy opposite sides of the philosophical spectrum. This is so for a number of reasons and many are discussed below. Let us just mention one, arguably the most crucial point of irreconcilable difference. In SP, the idea of a vacuum is vehemently denied and opposed, whereas in PE the vacuum, or the void, is actually the starting point of philosophical speculation, if not analysis. In his *Ethics* (published posthumously in 1677), Spinoza was very adamant about this (Spinoza 1996: 12): there can be no vacuum in Nature or God (Spinoza used both terms interchangeably). Nature/God is of one substance (and one substance only). All that is in Nature/God is just a mode of this one substance. A vacuum would have to be just one particular mode of the substance of Nature/God. But that, of course, implies that it could then never be a vacuum. Consciousness too is only a mode of the substance of Nature/God. There is nothing really special about consciousness, but here is where PE would beg to differ. There is something special about consciousness, and philosophers such as Sartre, for example, maintained that it is a void. It is a vacuum. This means that there are, at the very deepest level of conscious existence, strict boundaries, indeed dividing lines that are of an absolute nature. The separation between the void of consciousness on the one hand, for example, and everything else that it is not, is absolute. These positions are irreconcilable and as we shall see, they are also very important.

Having said that, however, both SP and PE agree on this: that the world – the human world in particular – cannot but generate lines of division. Let us for the purpose of this chapter focus on the world at the point where it would include the thing that in the PE perspective would be called 'consciousness'. Indeed, authors within the PE perspective are only interested in the world in so far as it is a world that includes 'consciousness'. SP and PE will tend to agree: the world (the world that includes consciousness in particular) inevitably generates lines of division. There can be no escape here. To be more specific even: the *human* world, or human life and human existence, will inevitably generate lines of division, and with division will come, equally inevitably, opposition and conflict.

In SP, we thus have a perspective where it is accepted that from a condition that is marked by the total, absolute lack of separation and division (the *oneness*, if you wish, of the substance of the world) flow, unavoidably, division and separation. In PE, on the other hand, lines of division emerge from a condition which itself, at its very deepest depths, already carries the seeds of radical, absolute separation. All this may not bode very well for those remaining criminologists who are still secretly harbouring hopes for a world where all division has been *eradicated* (the use of words here is, of course, deliberate) and where human existence has transcended to a *state* (again a deliberate use of words) of total inclusion and 'oneness'.

This chapter includes explorations only of just two philosophical perspectives, i.e. SP and PE, and very incomplete explorations at that. It should go without saying that the reader may not hope to find anything in this chapter that goes beyond the mere scratching of the surface of both philosophical perspectives. There simply is no space available here to go into more depth. It is hoped, however, that this chapter is read as an invitation to take this line of exploration further or, as the case may be of course, to critically *disassemble and re-assemble* the dividing lines in it (here again the choice of words is significant, as we shall see).

Spinoza and neo-Spinozism

Affecting bodies

Spinoza's Nature/God may be of one substance, it stretches into infinity. The substance of the world modulates infinitely. Bodies are formed in it incessantly. Those bodies impact on each other in cause-effect chains that are infinite and that cannot be uncovered or traced by any of the bodies which are too finite and too limited. It is impossible for them to grasp the infinitely vast chains of causes and effects that affect (i.e. have an impact on) them, and which they are fully part of. As said above, according to Spinoza, there can be no vacuum in Nature/God, since the world, or Nature/God, is of one substance. '[...], it follows also', he states, 'that corporeal substance, insofar as it is a substance, cannot be divided' (Spinoza 1996: 12). And since there is no vacuum, there cannot be free will: 'In the mind there is no absolute, or free, will, but the mind is determined to will this or that by a cause which is also determined by another and this again by another, and so to infinity' (Spinoza 1996: 62). The 'mind' also is, of course, only a 'mode' of the substance of the world. This world knows no good or bad. It just is. It is an infinite substance in which an infinite variety of modalities impact on each other in infinitely complex cause-effect chains. However, there is also an 'ethics' in Spinoza's *Ethics*. The point is, claims Spinoza, to strive to increase the capacity of bodies to impact on other bodies, and to be impacted by them. In other words: if there is a 'good' then by that it is understood 'what we certainly know to be useful to us' (Spinoza 1996: 116). 'Useful' is 'whichever so disposes the human body that it can be affected in a great many ways, or renders it capable of affecting external bodies in a great many ways' (Spinoza 1996: 137). 'Good', then, is what increases bodies' 'power of acting' (Spinoza 1996: 70).

This 'ethics', it should be noted in passing, has of course obvious implications for social or criminal policy. Spinoza explores a number of ways in which the capacity of bodies to act could be increased. The foremost among them is, however, the application of reason, i.e. through a deeper understanding of the cause-effect chains that the world is made of. A deeper understanding of these chains, Spinoza surmises, should allow bodies to exercise a certain level of control over themselves and their life conditions. A lack of understanding in bodies only leads them to be merely impacted upon, i.e. to be a mere effect in cause-effect chains, and to be a victim of 'passions' (Spinoza 1996: 165). Another way to increase bodies' capacities to act is 'friendship', i.e. joint endeavours whereby all partaking bodies share one another's capacities and potential.

So, then, where is the 'line' in Spinoza's world? It is telling that Spinoza himself saw the infinite network of cause-effect chains as 'a question of lines, places, and bodies' (Spinoza 1996: 69). This is a phrase that would much later be evoked by neo-Spinozists such as Gilles Deleuze who considered the work of 'schizoanalysis' (i.e. the analysis of vital, productive, restrictive, but always clashing life forces) to be 'this analysis of lines, spaces, becoming' (Deleuze 1995: 34). But there is another sense in which the line appears in Spinoza's world. When bodies impact on each other they generate 'impressions', or 'traces', in each other. Those impressions are 'images of things', that is, images of bodies and objects. Those images, once formed, are then also objects or bodies that can be held by bodies, 'In just the same way as thoughts and ideas of things are ordered and connected in the mind, so the affections of the body, or images of things are ordered and connected in the body' (Spinoza 1996: 163). In other words, the world (or Nature/God) is an infinite complex of bodies impacting on other bodies whereby, in this very process of impacting, images are generated which in turn are stored and connected in bodies, making the infinite cause-effect chains even more complex. To increase bodies' capacity to act, or their 'power of acting', actually amounts to increasing their capacity to generate, store and mobilise (i.e. connect and disconnect) 'images of things'.

This, as we shall see, is a point that was to be built on by later vitalists such as Henri Bergson, but seriously criticised by existentialists such as Sartre. For our purposes, however, we could do worse than stress that, only very recently, a number of neuroscientists are beginning to make use of Spinoza's insights to make sense of their own empirical data. Antonio Damasio for example was struck by how Spinoza's insights – in particular his notion of the 'idea of a body' – can be brought to bear on the analysis of the workings of the human brain (Damasio 2003). The human brain (i.e. the human body), when experiencing the world (i.e. when experiencing 'impact' from other bodies in the world) incessantly generates images. In this process, the human brain/body also generates images of its own body (the 'idea' of its own body) as it is positioned spatially in the world, surrounded by impacting bodies that are external to it. If and when this occurs, the brain/body 'feels'. Thus, when the human brain/body experiences the world, it will 'feel' it at the point where an image of its own body-amidst-its-impacting-surroundings is generated. This image is one that is marked by a line, i.e. the line that traces the contours of the body in its surrounding space. Other writers such as Bernard Andrieu (2006) suggest that human thought (which works by 'reflecting' upon 'mental images') is, on the one hand, of course generated by and in the body but is, on the other, also 'relatively autonomous' from the mere matter of the body. 'Relatively' autonomous, for any autonomy rests upon an 'illusion'. 'Human thought', Andrieu writes, 'is produced by human bodies, but thought believes in its freedom because of the natural *illusion* of forgetting its relative autonomy. Yet this *illusion* has a real power over the body' (Andrieu 2006: 153; emphasis added).

Other neuroscientists have, in turn, expanded on Damasio's neo-Spinozist work. Gail and Richard Murrow (2013), for example, have used Damasio (and therefore, indirectly, Spinoza) to describe how the line around the image of the body-in-its-impacting-world is only the very deepest, basic form of a number of other imagined lines. The human brain/body not only has the capacity to generate images of its own body as it is being impacted upon, or as it impacts on other bodies, it does, upon impact, also, and constantly so, generate images whereby lines are drawn around potential (indeed: imagined) *collective* bodies. According to Murrow and Murrow – and this is their main thesis – it is precisely this capacity to imagine lines around collective bodies that is the origin of all sense of community, law or morality, however diverse and potentially infinitely varied, of course, all the thus imagined collective bodies may be. With all this in mind, one could say that to increase bodies' capacity to act would actually boil down to increasing their capacity to imagine lines around as many potential collective bodies as possible.

Images and fabulations

Henri Bergson's work – which itself would later thoroughly inspire Gilles Deleuze's – is indebted to Spinoza's but takes the latter's insights further. Bergson takes from Spinoza the idea that the world is an infinite, indivisible expanse of ultimately ungraspable impacts or 'affects'. But he adds to Spinoza's insight. The world is in constant flux. It is constant, indivisible change or *becoming*. It is constant, unstoppable evolution. The world's evolution, however, is not just adaptive, as a Darwin would have it. It is also *creative*, as Bergson argued in his *Creative Evolution* (1911; published originally in 1907). The world creates, and has done so particularly from the moment life – life that itself emerged in a creative process of evolution of course – appeared on its 'inorganic body'. It generates newness constantly. Bergson, then, is less deterministic than Spinoza. The question then of course arises, 'How is evolution creative?'. The world creates because it is fuelled by what

Bergson calls the 'élan vital' (sometimes translated as 'vital current'), a certain forward-thrusting momentum that tends to take matter (and bodies therein) forward, beyond themselves as it were. This *taking bodies beyond themselves* is an important point, crucial even, which has, as we shall see later, drawn the attention of phenomenologists and existentialists. However, let us not run ahead of ourselves.

The workings of this creative life force occur on three planes. This, it should be noted, is another point inspired by Spinoza, and developed in the late twentieth century by the *Deleuzoguattarians* (e.g. Deleuze and Guattari 1972, 1980). The first plane is the plane of immanence, where forces of pure intensity flow and clash. On this plane, forces are pure intensity, that is, they are formless. They are, so to speak, pure energy flowing, or indeed, pure *potential*. A Nietzsche might have said: these intensive energies are pure *will to power*. Deleuze and Guattari used the word 'desire' to denote this intensity. The flows of intensity (desire, will to power) do, however, clash and where or when they do, *virtual* nodes or *schemas* of possibility emerge. Here a second plane (i.e. that of the virtual) is created. Deleuze and Guattari used the phrase 'abstract machines' to describe these virtual nodes or schemas of possibility. In them, the particular constellation of clashing intensities has generated a particular assemblage of lines of desire out of the infinite ocean of pure intensive potential that is the plane of immanence. This assemblage is a 'machine', first, because, like an ordinary machine 'it is a product or fabrication, but also because in turn it will – again like a machine – produce a particular set of outcomes on the third plane, i.e. in the *extensive* world (the world of matter, the world of the senses). The 'virtual' or 'abstract' nodes are, in a way, 'diagrams' (as Deleuze called them, borrowing from Foucault) that have the capacity to generate or *actualise* certain outcomes if the particularly shaped or assembled flows of desire in them eventually travel through the extensive world of matter, impacting there on bodies (see Deleuze 1988).

Let us return to Bergson. On all three levels (i.e. the level of pure intensity and pure potential; the level of virtual possibility; and the level of extensive actualization), the nature of the 'vital current' could never be grasped. Only aspects of it could perhaps be sensed. The force of life, infinite in its 'duration', always moving forward, travels through all levels but only manifests itself very partially in any location which it traverses. Like Spinoza's 'substance', this force of life is infinite and indivisible. Its manifestations are only local effects, facets, aspects, indeed *images*. Its intensive flows of desire are only partial images of its infinity. So are the virtual nodes that it generates, or the actualised extensions that it assembles in the sensory world of matter. And so are the images that are generated in the bodies that live in and experience this world where they (i.e. the bodies imagining images) are incessantly taken beyond themselves. Those images, however (i.e. the images generated in bodies, including human bodies), are always very partial, never able to grasp the current of life itself. Our intellect '[...] present[s] to us things and states rather than changes and acts. But things and states are only *views*, taken by our mind, of becoming' (Bergson 1911: 248; emphasis added). Indeed, there is something 'cinematographic' about human life in particular: human thought seems to be a succession of images of states and things, the one after the other (Bergson 1911: 211). The lines that we inevitably 'see' around 'things and states' are thus problematic, erroneous even, since in the current of life 'there are no things, there are only actions' (Bergson 1911: 192).

The 'élan vital' thus produces an infinity of images, one after the other, which all in turn become part of its infinite duration. The things thus 'seen' or imagined will end up in the infinite duration of the 'vital current'. Mere 'cuts' in 'the flux of the real', they become 'endlessly decomposable' and re-composable (Bergson 1911: 193). They remain available as materials for the further production of images during the infinite travels of the life force. This Bergsonian insight is now gradually finding its way also into legal theory and socio-legal studies (see e.g. Moore 2013). Bodies, like anything else, are collections of images. That also applies to human bodies.

Just as Spinoza maintained that there can be no vacuum in the substance of Nature/God, so Bergson states that there can be no strict separation between bodies. Indeed, bodies are just collections of manifestations – or images – of the forward thrusting, infinite, indivisible life force, so how could they ever be ultimately separate? There can be no individual independence: 'the individual itself is not sufficiently independent, not sufficiently cut off from other things, for us to allow it a 'vital principle' of its own' (Bergson 1911: 42). However, there is some ambiguity here, in particular when human consciousness is concerned. Consciousness is generated in the vital current's 'need of creation'. It emerges 'as soon as the possibility of a choice is restored' (Bergson 1911: 201). Human consciousness, however (which is, of course, also a manifestation and an effect of the life force), has something like openness about it. The 'human intellect' has 'the tendency to [...] fabrication' (Bergson 1911: 126). This is an insight that would form the cornerstone in Bergson's final opus, i.e. *Les Deux Sources de la Morale et de la Religion* (1967; published originally in 1932; but see further in this chapter on this particular point). Already, however, in *Creative Evolution* this 'tendency to fabrication' takes centre stage. In the human life form the 'élan vital', always taking bodies beyond themselves, seems to have struck something akin to a gap that allows consciousness, in human bodies, to 'see' things, to imagine things, to trace lines and draw boundaries that are not really there extensively. In human bodies, consciousness is able to sense and see gaps (Bergson uses the word 'interval') between 'representation and action', or 'between potential and real activity' (Bergson 1911: 117). In human bodies consciousness *itself* is taken beyond itself. That is: a kind of gap opens up in it which allows it to see or imagine 'the *lines* which mark out the boundaries of real bodies or of their elements' (Bergson 1911: 126; emphasis added). This gap allows human consciousness to also see or imagine the 'lines that mark out the boundaries' of itself, of its body, and of 'their real elements'.

The gap or 'interval' in the human intellect also gives it 'unlimited powers of decomposing [the lines that mark out boundaries] according to any law and of recomposing [them] into any system' (Bergson 1911: 126).

The above can be put slightly differently. Life is itself infinite and indivisible, indeed it is pure creative potential, but in its contact with the sphere of the extensive (i.e. with matter) it becomes 'spatialized' and thus broken up in 'thousands and thousands' of aspectual, localised manifestations (Bergson 1911: 199), that is: images. Those images are then 'cut' into 'things and states', and divided by 'lines', and incessantly decomposed and recomposed by an inevitably localised 'human intellect' which itself is only an image, a very partial image at that, of the force of life. In this process, there can, says Bergson, referring to Spinoza, be no room for a vacuum or a void (Bergson, 1911: 213–29). The void or the 'Nothing' is only an image, a 'line' drawn or 'cut' by the human intellect between the moment of one image and the next. However, the very fact that in human bodies the image of the void does emerge is important. The image of the void, in Bergson, is a manifestation of 'desire and regret', and it emerges 'under the pressure of vital necessities'. The void thus stands for the 'absence of utility and not of things'. Human beings cannot but imagine voids (i.e. trace lines around something which they then deem to be void) because the 'élan vital' takes them constantly beyond themselves, whilst they still remember their past, and are thus able to imagine 'the possible'. This 'interval' is filled with 'desire and regret' and it is those that generate, in human bodies, the image of the void. 'Our life is thus spent in filling voids', Bergson writes, 'we are constantly going from the void to the full' (Bergson 1911: 229). It is this point that Bergson expanded on in his 1932 book *Les Deux Sources de la Morale et de la Religion* (Bergson 1967).

In this book, Bergson argues how in human bodies there is an incessant gap between their experiences on the one hand, and the 'fabulations' that they generate to fill those gaps in a bid to exert some control over their life. Human beings are constantly taken beyond themselves by a creative 'élan vital'. The resulting gap in experience leads to anxiety. In order to alleviate this anxiety the bodies produce fabulations (e.g. a religious idol or authority, a social norm or rule, a scientific explanation, and so on) that almost instantaneously fill the gaps. The fabulations are only temporary. They are bound to dissolve under the pressures of the unrelenting 'élan vital' that, in human bodies, will keep on taking consciousness beyond itself, producing new gaps in the process, and forcing it to 'fabulate' time and time again. This process is unrelenting and unstoppable. The process follows a 'bodily logic [...] that is at play well before intelligence is able to find a conceptual form [for the fabulations]' (Bergson 1967: 175; translation by author). The fabulations serve a number of functions: they allow the individual to regain a certain level of imagined control, but, as objects that carry communicable meaning, they also serve to bind individuals to one another. They have, in other words, the capacity to produce 'society'.

Although fabulations result, they too, from the creative force of the 'élan vital', usually they consist of mere compositions (decompositions and recompositions) of materials that are readily available in the sphere of the extensive. Real, genuine creation occurs only exceptionally and only at particular locations (Bergson calls those locations 'genius'). 'Genius' (i.e. that which *generates*) is the location where the pure potential in the sphere of the intensive is accessed directly. When that happens, connections between deep, intensive flows of potential are formed which in turn will generate genuinely new virtual possibilities, and, eventually, real newness in the sphere of the extensive as well. One way of achieving this is by 'mystically' (Bergson's Buddhist-inspired word) attempting detachment from all current fabulations and the desires that fuelled and generated them. This 'mystical' move should also include detachment from the images and fabulations that make up the self. Only then, Bergson states, will it become possible for real potential to be accessed and for real newness to be created and enter the world.

Phenomenology and existentialism

Critique of Bergson

Sartre's first full length philosophical work was on the image and imagination. The book, *L'Imagination* (Sartre 1965), was originally published in 1936. There is no coincidence, as we shall see, in the fact that one of the world's foremost voices in phenomenology and one of the founding existentialists cut his philosophical teeth on the topic of images and imagination. There is also no coincidence in the fact that Sartre used quite some space in the book to provide a critique of Bergson's work which, at the time, was quite dominant both in French academia and beyond. As is by now well known, Bergsonism would later, after the demise of existentialism in the 1960s, resurface in the work of Deleuze and Guattari. But let us here have a look at Sartre's critique of Bergson's writings on the image and on imagination. Sartre focuses on Bergson's work up until *Creative Evolution* (he makes no reference to *Les Deux Sources de la Morale et de la Religion* which had been published only a few years before his own *L'Imagination*).

There is a lot in Bergson that Sartre actually admires and subscribes to. The former's insistence on constant change and flux, and on creative capacity, for example, all resonate very well with what Sartre, in his mature work (i.e. already in his *Les Carnets de la Drôle de Guerre (Novembre 1939 – Mars 1940), 1939–40* (1983), and also, of course, in his *Being and Nothingness*, 1943 (2003)) would call 'negation'. The world evolves in processes of negation whereby that which is, is constantly negated by that which is becoming, with 'negation' itself emerging from instances of nothingness. Sartre's 'negation', however, also includes elements that are quite irreconcilable with a Bergsonian view (and we shall come back to those later) but Sartre certainly agrees with what he deems a successful attempt, by Bergson, to 'make the notion of consciousness supple by giving it fluidity, spontaneity, life' (Sartre 1965: 57; all translations from *L'Imagination* by the author). Indeed, Sartre's existentialism does not have a problem with vitalism *per se*. In another of his early works, *Esquisse d'une Théorie des Émotions* for example (1960, published originally in 1939), Sartre goes a long way to read emotions, in a Bergsonian vein, one might add, as 'brusque fall of conscience into *magic*' (Sartre 1960: 62), as a 'spontaneous and lived degradation of a conscience facing the world' but unable to grasp it reflectively (Sartre 1960: 54). But that is where the agreement ends: emotion, in Sartre's view, is a 'fall', lived by a conscience that is first and foremost reflective.

One of the problems, according to Sartre, resides in Bergson's materialism: 'Rather than conceive of consciousness as a light that flows from the subject to the thing, [Bergson's is] a luminosity that goes from the thing to the subject' (Sartre 1965: 44). To Sartre, it remains an enigma, and a problem, to see how non-conscious images, emerging from the very depths of intensive potential and the virtual (as imagined by Bergson), could ever become actual in the sphere of the extensive, in actually conscious consciousness. In other words, 'how can a sub-conscious and impersonal consciousness become conscious consciousness of an individual subject?' (Sartre 1965: 45).

The other problem with Bergson's view is that despite his insistence that 'there are no things, there are only actions' (Bergson, 1911: 192; already quoted above) Bergson ultimately accepts a conception of images as 'inert' objects that remain, in duration, as objects, that can be disassembled and re-assembled, in consciousness, like 'mosaics' (Sartre 1965: 61), and that remain available in the depths of duration like 'tiles at the bottom of the lake' (Sartre 1965: 57). This conception of images as 'things', Sartre surmises, is one of the reasons why Bergson had to invent (or imagine) the *schemas* ('abstract machines', or 'diagrams', say Deleuze and Guattari; see above) in the sphere of the virtual. As 'inert objects' they had to be produced, made, or indeed *created* somewhere, at least by something, in the impersonal current of duration where an infinite reservoir of available images are supposed to be flowing, readily available for decomposition and recomposition.

And so Sartre concludes: 'There are no, and there could never be any images *in* consciousness. The image though is *a certain type of consciousness*. The image is an act. It is not a thing. The image is consciousness *of* something' (Sartre 1965: 162). In other words: there are actually no images (if by that that we mean 'things'). There is only the *act* of imagination. The act of imagination is done by consciousness. Consciousness itself has *nothing* in it. It is a void and *precisely because it is a void* it is able to imagine. Precisely because of its nothingness (or in other words: precisely because it is sheer indeterminacy), surrounded as it is by that which it is not (i.e. determinacy), it has an inclination towards that surrounding world. The result of this intentionality is imagination. Precisely for those reasons, consciousness is an 'image-producing intention' (Sartre 1965: 146). Sartre's conclusion is indeed quite heavily inspired by his reading of Edmund Husserl's phenomenological work. There is in Husserl, he writes, a 'radical distinction between consciousness and that which it is conscious about' (Sartre 1965: 144). Consciousness imagines by producing 'active syntheses', fuelled only by its own 'free spontaneity' (Sartre 1965: 157). It is to Husserl's phenomenology that we now turn, to his *Cartesian Meditations* (1977, published originally in 1929) in particular. Then we shall explore how, in Sartre's second philosophical work, *The Transcendence of the Ego* (2004, published originally in 1937), he made a serious attempt to move even beyond Husserl. That particular attempt formed the plinth on which his mature existentialist philosophy (which, alas, falls outside the scope of this chapter) was built during the war years.

The constitution of the world, ex-Nihilo

Whereas vitalists such as Bergson began from life itself, phenomenologists such as Husserl take the conscious Ego (the *cogito*) as the starting point of their philosophical endeavours. In his *Cartesian Mediations*, Husserl is clear: 'The world is for me absolutely nothing else but the world existing for me and accepted by me in such a conscious cogito' (Husserl 1977: 21). The question then immediately arises as to the nature of this Ego. All philosophy, according to Husserl, should begin with this question. A philosophy that discards this question could never say anything worthwhile (i.e. universal) at all since it would not realise that it itself, i.e. all that it posits (e.g. statements about life, or about the 'élan vital'), is nothing but the constituted effect of its own cogito. The first task of philosophy, then, is to delineate the boundaries of that which thus constitutes the world. That entity can only be intimated through a process of 'reduction' whereby the thus 'reduced Ego' is, so to speak, purged from the world that is not it. Indeed:

> just as the reduced Ego is not a piece of this world, so, conversely, neither the world nor any worldly object is a piece of my Ego, to be found in my conscious life as a really inherent part of it, as a complex of data of sensation or as a complex of acts
>
> (Husserl 1977: 26)

The boundary between the cogito and the world that is not it is absolute. The line that divides both is clear. The 'reduced Ego' can only be intimated by what Husserl calls 'epoché', i.e. the constant, intentional *bracketing off* of the cognitive constitutions in the 'natural attitude'. The aim here is to 'reduce' the 'sphere of [constituted] meanings to an unalloyed freedom from prejudice – striving for a universal description [...] free from all interpretations that read into [objects] more than is genuinely *seen*' (Husserl 1977: 36; emphasis added). In and through this effort the transcendental, reflective Ego emerges.

The boundary between the conscious Ego and the world that is not it may be clear, but that does not mean that the cogito is completely empty. It is, at the very least, and quite paradoxically so, intentionality. Husserl defines: 'the word intentionality signifies nothing else than this universal property of consciousness: to be consciousness *of* something; as a cogito, to bear within itself its *cogitatum*' (Husserl 1977: 33). Consciousness as such could never be. It only appears as consciousness *of something*. If there were no objects, there would be no consciousness. Whatever else consciousness may be, it is, first and foremost intentionality, i.e. an inclination towards the world. In Husserl's view, however, the cogito is not just pure intentionality. It also includes the results of its intentional encounters with the world, its *cogitatum*. The cogito is also able to encounter and reflect upon itself. It has the capacity to take itself as an intentional object. The results of such reflections also become part of the intentional cogito, where they will help build and constantly modify a 'horizon' of potential (but also of restriction) for further intentional action.

There is one more notion that, for our purposes, we need to introduce here. Intentional consciousness, or the cogito, has as its most fundamental *modus operandi* the operation of 'synthesis'. The objects constituted by the cogito enter it 'as *intentional effect*[s] produced by the synthesis of consciousness' (Husserl 1977: 42). In other words, the most fundamental operation that intentional consciousness performs, constantly, and unrelentingly, is the production of syntheses, and indeed the synthesis of syntheses. This implies the constant drawing of lines, and the constitution 'as one', so to speak, of objects, and, ultimately, of its own *world*. This fundamental operation of synthetic production, it should be noted in passing, not only underpins the constitution of the own synthetic Ego, it also allows, as Husserl is at pains to stress, for the synthetic constitution of collectives. All are constituted in and by the cogito and all, as synthetically constituted 'objects' (that are constantly reflected upon, modified, and synthetically re-constituted), add to the former's incessantly modulating 'horizon'.

Here, however, is where we should return to Sartre. In *The Transcendence of the Ego* (2004, published originally in 1937), Sartre engages thoroughly with Husserl's conception of the cogito. Consciousness has, in particular locations, the capacity to reflect upon itself. The total of those locations one could perhaps call the human condition. Whenever consciousness reflects upon itself, we have a location called the Ego. The main problem with Husserl's view, Sartre claims, is that the constituted effects of consciousness reflecting upon itself at the location of the Ego (these effects form what Sartre calls the 'psychical and psychophysical *me*') are unnecessarily included within consciousness (Sartre 2004: 5). Those effects of self-reflection, in Sartre's view, are part of the world, and fall outside the boundaries of the reflecting consciousness. The 'me', i.e. the reflected part of consciousness (as a collection of worldly effects) is no longer part of consciousness itself. It is an 'object'. Consciousness itself is 'clean and lucid: the object lies opposite it, in its characteristic opacity, but consciousness, for its part, is purely and simply consciousness of being conscious of this object' (Sartre 2004: 7–8). Indeed, as Husserl himself posited: consciousness can only be consciousness *of something*.

Consciousness, then, is just consciousness. There is no difference between the reflecting consciousness and the reflected consciousness. The products, however, of the process whereby consciousness reflects (and that includes reflections upon itself) are no longer consciousness. They are products. They are objects. They are world. The 'me' is part of the world of reflected objects. That does not mean, however, that the 'I' would then be found in the unreflected part of consciousness. There, one only finds consciousness. This consciousness is just intentionality, 'clear and lucid' intentionality, reflecting. If an 'I' there must be, then it is the dynamic element in the cogito or Ego: 'The *I* is the Ego as the unity of its actions', whereas 'the *me* is the Ego as the unity of states and qualities' (Sartre 2004: 21). However, those 'actions', 'states' and 'qualities' are not 'emanations' of a deeper, underlying core that one should then call 'Ego'; nor are they 'actualizations' of potential. They are the result of what Sartre calls 'poetic production', indeed of 'creation'. The Ego is the result of creation. But who, or what, or where is it created? Sartre is superbly clear: it is 'a creation *ex nihilo*' (Sartre 2004: 32). The Ego is created out of the void of nothingness that is pure intentionality, pure reflecting consciousness, 'clear and lucid', an 'impersonal spontaneity' (Sartre 2004: 46).

Here, Sartre touches upon what would later become one of the core tenets of existentialism, i.e. the primacy of consciousness. Consciousness is itself not a product. It is primordial. It is 'really first' (Sartre 2004: 34). As a void, it is first, it is the plinth on which the world rests. It is the well out of which the world flows. As pure intentionality, pure reflection, it constitutes states, and those may later form the Ego, but at the heart of the Ego there will be this void. 'The transcendental field', Sartre recapitulates, 'is a *nothing*, since all physical, psycho-physical and psychical objects, all truths, and all values are outside it since the *me* has, for its part, ceased to be part of it' (Sartre 2004: 43).

However, one could ask whether this void, this nothingness, this sea of intentional waves constantly probing, shaping and reshaping the shores of the world is really empty. Are those 'lakes of non-being' in the 'flesh of the world' (cited in Merleau-Ponty 1968: 66) that one would be inclined to call consciousnesses utterly void? Are we talking about a total vacuum? This question is of course unanswerable. 'Clear and lucid' it may be, the void of consciousness is also pure reflectivity, pure intentionality. And this nothing is also '*everything* because it is the *consciousness* of all [the] objects [that it constitutes]' (Sartre 2004: 43). The void of consciousness, then, is *radically impenetrable* (Sartre 2004: 45). The question as to the nature of the void is simply unanswerable. Another way of putting this is by saying that the void stands for total, radical *indeterminacy*, i.e. that it is the radical and radically creative origin from which all the determinacy in the world of objects is both generated and intentionally reflected upon. Sartre concludes: 'The world did not create the *me*, the *me* did not create the world, they are two objects for the absolute, impersonal consciousness, and it is through that consciousness that they are linked back together' (Sartre 2004: 51).

It should come as no surprise that Sartre would later go on, in the path-breaking existentialist work which he undertook during the Second World War, to explore notions such as *radical freedom* and *choice* in order to get to grips with the human condition and human existence. As said, this is not the place to expand on this. What we can stress here, however, is that from an existentialist perspective the world originates at the location of a radically deep dividing line, i.e. the strict boundary between the pure reflective intentionality of consciousness on the one hand, and the world that it constitutes on the other hand. This line of division is radical, absolute even. This means that none of the products of creative negation that emerge in the world *ex nihilo* could ever cross this radical boundary back again and completely fill up the void of indeterminacy whence it came. This is particularly the case when human existence is concerned, but it also means that all objects constituted by consciousness, and that includes the objects that are constituted by a consciousness that is reflecting upon itself (i.e. the 'me'), as reflections, as inevitably local and localised reflections, are *bound* to be finite, limited, enclosed by boundaries. In a way all objects constituted by consciousness carry, with them, or better, *around* them, the trace of their origin, i.e. the act of intentional reflection that occurred on the far side of the deepest line of division, the line that separates the void of consciousness from the world it creates. All consciousness is consciousness of 'objects' that are constituted in the process of intentional reflection, and all thus constituted 'objects' are necessarily local and localized. Even 'objects' such as 'the absolute All', 'the Sublime' or 'the Universal', and so on, are all mere constituted 'objects'. 'Synthetic' products, Husserl would have said. They have boundaries. As mere 'objects' they could never cover, or fill up the primordial open infinity of consciousness. We know from Sartre's earlier work that the 'objects' thus constituted by reflective consciousness are not 'things'; they are 'acts', i.e. the ever-moving results of conscious acts of *imagination*.

Concluding remarks

It looks like two opposing and largely irreconcilable philosophical perspectives, i.e. Spinozism on the one hand, and phenomenology-existentialism on the other hand, agree on one thing at least. The world (the human world in particular) cannot but generate dividing lines. Those tend to carry, within them, the potential for opposition and conflict. These lines, and this potential, are ineradicable. There is no escape here. In the introduction we surmised that this message is unlikely to be one that will be welcomed enthusiastically by the segment in the criminological community that is still hoping (hoping against hope perhaps, one would be inclined to add) for what some might assume would be a blissful world of total, complete, division-less inclusion.

It should be noted, albeit in passing perhaps, that later authors such as Merleau-Ponty made very serious attempts to combine vitalism (Bergson's in particular) and existentialism (Sartre's). In his final but unfinished book, *The Visible and the Invisible*, for example (the book was published posthumously in 1964), Merleau-Ponty argued for a philosophy that would acknowledge 'wild' or 'brute being' of the sensible 'flesh of the world' as the ground of Being. In this ground there are no divisions. There is no 'I' there, there is no 'other'. There are, in those very depths, no lines or boundaries between concepts, images, outsides and insides, and so on. The ground, however, does produce, in processes of 'dehiscence', variety and separation (e.g. in human bodies through language, etc) but the task of the philosopher is, says Merleau-Ponty, to realise that and to explore how all variation and separation all result from, and are rooted in the ground of intertwined and interconnected bodies that, being part of undivided 'wild being', constantly 'encroach' upon and into each other, and indeed, are not even 'other' to each other. Merleau-Ponty's philosophy gave rise to a whole new strand in phenomenology in which the focus came to rest on descriptions of expressions of embodied, sensory experience.

However, the ramifications of the philosophical explorations undertaken above (however superficial those may have been, and we readily admit that they were) go beyond hopes of total inclusion (even a Merleau-Ponty has to make distinctions) and have a bearing on themes that are directly relevant to criminological theory and research. Let us just consider one illustration of this relevance. The theme that could be used by way of an illustration is sovereignty (not state sovereignty, but personal or individual sovereignty). One might be able to discern the emergence of a particular trend, or indeed perhaps only an attitude, in the wake of the Second World War. This attitude, one could argue, formed the kernel of a gradually crystallizing *form of life*, fuelled, at its very heart, by a desire for (if you are a *vitalist*, you would probably prefer this term), or a will (an existentialist would rather go for this one) to absolute, radical sovereignty. This is not the place to expand on this. It is perhaps permitted here to refer to work that has been done elsewhere by this author on exactly this point. However, let us focus here on just one element in this debate.

There are of course many forms of 'radical' or 'absolute' sovereignty imaginable. The word 'imaginable' is used here on purpose since radical or absolute sovereignty, however much aspired to, could never be anything else but imaginary (some would say, illusory). In one such imaginary form of radical, absolute sovereignty, the aspiring sovereign desires, or *wills* to live in a zone that is completely and utterly before or beyond all law, all code. Unhindered and unfettered by even the least of strictures, and floating utterly freely on pure and inexhaustible potential (that is the zone where the aspiring radical sovereign wants to dwell in) this imaginary form of life has something mystical, something godly about it. Any choice made or decision taken in this utterly code-less zone will not diminish in any way this infinite reservoir of pure potential, not even to the slightest extent. In this imaginary form of life, there are no dividing lines, since there is no code, no law whatsoever. To use Deleuze's and Guattari's (1972, 1980) words, this is a pure 'smooth space' (as opposed to 'striated space'). Here, however, is the inevitable tragedy: life in this imaginary zone – or better: imagining living in this zone – will prompt the aspiring radical sovereign to instantaneously imagine and suspect potential hindrances, blocks, strictures, codes and laws (etc) everywhere. One could add: the more code-less the zone of imagined radical sovereignty, the more numerous and unbearable the hindrances and strictures that the aspiring sovereign will imagine to be lurking behind even the tiniest of specks in his or her world of utter sovereign omnipotence. Lines of division will tend to crystallize in the aspiring radical sovereign's imagination, everywhere. However, there is more to this. Aspiring sovereigns are no longer prepared to accept, and much less live, with even the most insignificant of strictures or codes. This in turn leads them to imagine and subsequently put in place all kinds of measures in order to block off anything that even remotely resembles a hindrance on their road to an absolutely sovereign form of life. There is no coincidence in the fact that late modernity is the era when something like a 'precautionary culture' emerged and developed to the extent that it did (on this, see e.g. Pieterman 2009). However, all these 'precautionary' measures will, of course, instantaneously, and again very paradoxically, undermine any attempt at achieving radical sovereignty. The aspiring sovereigns are thus bound to find themselves both utterly *dependent* on and annoyingly hindered by their very precaution, but *dependency* for example could itself, of course, never be part of a radically sovereign form of life, and so the 'precautionary' measures themselves will ultimately also be included in further bouts of precautionary purification. The life of an aspiring radical, absolute sovereign is shot through with sheer and utter, unbearable agony.

This precautionary culture, as it is sometimes called, has, one might add, also fuelled (and here again, very paradoxically so) a considerable element of the victim movement which emerged from the late 1970s onwards. The desire for, or will to absolute sovereignty, that is, the desire for and will to dwell in the absolutely pure, smooth zone of inexhaustible potential, before and beyond all dividing law and code, tends to simultaneously generate an almost infinite succession of imaginary lines that separate 'victims' from 'victimizers'. The aspiring radical sovereign feels constantly threatened or actually 'victimized' by all kinds of victimizing forces. To fight those forces or to make constant efforts to keep them at bay in a bid to keep the imaginary zone of absolute sovereignty pure, then becomes the aspiring sovereign's main preoccupation. Lines of division will be generated.

Epilogue: no boundary?

At this point one could, of course, object and point in the direction of Buddhism. In his popular classic *No Boundary* (1979), Ken Wilber argued that the point is to achieve a state where all boundaries around particularities (including the boundaries around the self) have dissolved into the boundless Whole. Either one dissolves the self by means of a plunge into the undifferentiated energy of the earth, or through transcendence into the void of pure reflection, but even there, I suspect, there will be lines. In the earthy Whole or in the pure Void the issue becomes to keep at bay – that is: to draw a line around – anything that threatens to resemble a line, or a boundary, but that includes anything imaginable.

Acknowledgement

I would like to thank James Hardie-Bick for the many discussions on existentialism. During one, the image of consciousness as sea waves touching and shaping the shores of the world came to me.

Bibliography

Andrieu, B. (2006) 'Brains in the Flesh: Prospects for a Neurophenomenology', *Janus Head*, 9 (3): 135–55.
Bergson, H. (1911) [1907] *Creative Evolution*, New York, NY: Henry Holt & Co.
Bergson, H. (1967) [1932] *Les Deux Sources de la Morale et de la Religion*, Paris: Presses Universitaires de France.
Damasio, A. (2003) *Looking for Spinoza. Joy, Sorrow, and the Feeling Brain*, New York, NY: Harcourt.
Deleuze, G. (1988) [1984] *Foucault*, London: Athlone.
Deleuze, G. (1995) [1990] *Negotiations*, New York, NY: Columbia University Press.
Deleuze, G. and F. Guattari (1972) *Anti-Oedipe*, Paris: Minuit.
Deleuze, G. and F. Guattari (1980) *Mille Plateaux*, Paris: Minuit.
Husserl, E. (1977) [1929] *Cartesian Meditations: An Introduction to Phenomenology*, The Hague: Martinus Nijhoff.
Lippens, R. (2003) 'Imagining Lines, Assembling Criminologies. Speculations towards Negotiation' in K-L. Kunz and C. Besozzi (eds) *Soziale Reflexivität und Qualitative Methodik. Zum Selbstverständnis der Kriminologie in der Spätmoderne*, Bern: Haupt Verlag, pp. 167–88.
Merleau-Ponty, M. (1968) [1964] *The Visible and the Invisible*, Evanston, IL: Northwestern University Press.
Moore, N. (2013) 'Image and Affect: Between Neo-Baroque Sadism and Masochism', *New York LS Law Review*, 57 (1): 97–114.
Murrow, G.B. and R.W. Murrow (2013) 'A Biosemiotic Body of Law: The Neurobiology of Justice', *International Journal for the Semiotics of Law*, 26 (2): 275–314.

Pieterman, R. (ed.) (2009) *The Many Facets of Precautionary Logic*, Special Issue *Erasmus Law Review*, 2 (2): 97–286.
Sartre, J-P. (1960) [1939] *Esquisse d'une Théorie des Émotions*, Paris: Hermann.
Sartre, J-P. (1965) [1936] *L'Imagination*, Paris: Presses Universitaires de France.
Sartre, J-P. (1983) [1939–40] *Les Carnets de la Drôle de Guerre (Novembre 1939 – Mars 1940)*, Paris: Gallimard.
Sartre, J-P. (2003) [1943] *Being and Nothingness*, London: Routledge.
Sartre, J-P. (2004) [1937] *The Transcendence of the Ego*, London: Routledge.
Spinoza, B. de (1996) [1977] *Ethics*, London: Penguin.
Wilber, K. (1979) *No Boundary*, Boston, MA: Shambhala Publications.

Chapter 2

To criminology and beyond!
A polemic

Don Crewe

Introduction and method

Taking our lead from the doubting of the Sceptics and the *epoché* of the phenomenologists, it is evident that it is important that we know whether or not we are duped by the products of criminology and by the ordering horizons of thought that give it its meaning. If criminology were not important, then this question would be of no importance; however, if criminology is important – and Western governments seem to think that it is important – then we need to know whether its output can be trusted, and, hence, whether it can be of use in making sense of the world. A significant hurdle becomes evident when considering this question – should we start from anywhere within criminology itself, this would involve us taking for granted certain ideas the origins of which criminology has itself covered, and by which very covering, by which mystification, it may dupe us. It is necessary, therefore, to start from some position beyond criminology that we might strip away any illusions that there might be by which criminology supports itself: any *ideology* by which criminological *discourse* generates and maintains its *hegemony*. We must first dissociate ourselves from the hegemon. We must step outside the criminological *eco-nomy*. We immediately find, however, that there then stands before us a philosophical problem of great antiquity; the problem of the *ek*-static, the transcendent, the 'Beyond'. Before we can ask what the world would look like *from* such a 'Beyond', we must ask what such a 'Beyond', such an *ek*-static (*out*-standing) position would look like. To answer this question we must enter into considerations of exteriority.

What *is* criminology about? Consider, for a moment that we never attribute criminality to animals (let us leave plants out of this). What this tells us is that criminology is always (though not only) about humans.[1] If we are to know whether or not we are duped by the product of criminology, we must examine it from beyond: we must find some foundation beyond criminology

---

1 I do not mean to get into a discussion about reduction and methodological individualism here or about group agency (see Amatrudo, Chapter 6 in this collection).

as a body of thought. The classical Greek (Neo-Platonist) word for foundation is *hypokeimenon*, that which lies under, or the underlying. Figuratively, this equates to that which will not change accidentally, that is, the *essence* of an entity. The essence of an entity, since it is immutable, is not taken prisoner by processes of objectification. This quality of essentiality in Latin belongs to the *subjectum*, the 'thrown under', or, in (philosophical) English, the subject, and this is the foundation from which I intend to start. The suggestion that I wish to sketch out in this chapter is that criminology is an inherently modern enterprise. Its roots lie in the enlightenment view of the self-of-rationality or the ordering-subject-of-modernity. I will sketch the way in which the subject of modernity justifies itself towards itself and hence awards itself ontological and epistemological privilege, and I will suggest that much criminology thrives on this heritage: that modernity and violence may be seen to be co-constituting of the object of criminology. I further wish to sketch out a suggestion that engagement with the 'subject of Levinas', which is drawn from a position beyond metaphysics where ethics is first philosophy, helps us to move beyond the criminology-violence nexus towards a post-criminological age. To do this, I will illustrate one train of argument that suggests that we should support Levinas' claim that ethics is first philosophy[2] and that we should govern all our enterprises, criminology included, by the principles that such a conception brings to light.

Criminology

Foundations, and the subject of modernity

What lies at the very core of all kinds of humanity is its finitude. This is set over against the infinitude of the 'there is'. Through the Middle Ages the idea of the infinite 'there is' was encompassed by the idea of 'One God' – 'One God' is taken to be infinite: paradoxically $1 = \infty$. Despite the views of later pantheists like Spinoza, Schelling or James, for example, the observations of the Early Renaissance natural philosophers such as Galileo or Copernicus weakened the capacity of the idea of 'One God' to sustain faith in an 'all knowing'. The 'there is', in this circumstance, becomes not a single whole, but a totality, a sum of parts. In an infinite 'there is' (universe) that sum must have an infinite number of parts each infinitesimally different from the other: an infinite universe of infinitesimal differences. We may subscribe to a view (Berman 2010 [1982]) which has come to carry some authority, that the attempts to make sense of this situation constitute the birth of the Modern

---

2 The process through which Levinas' ethics is revealed to us by him is also the process through which this ethic is *revealed* as 'truth'. Levinas is not saying 'look at what I have made – I have made truth', he is saying 'in attempting to reveal something about the nature of our "being with", I appear to have uncovered something that seems to be universal and indefeasible, *sub specie æternitatis*'.

episteme. Modernity is its product; the One is fractured, '*All that is Solid Melts into Air*' (Berman 2010 [1982]).

In a universe of an infinite quantity of infinitesimal differences, the scale of difference between entities that assemble the totality that is taken to be material is arbitrary. This is in part because the nature of infinity is such that it renders all differences in scale or proportion *simultaneously* infinite *and* infinitesimal. In an infinite universe there can be no scale; scale must be *created*. We assume, for example, that the scale of difference that separates humans from other animals is far greater than the scale of difference that separates human individuals. Which of these scales of difference is taken to be material depends upon the problem of which we are trying to make sense. Hence, the classificatory boundary that we use in making sense of a problem is *constructed* in order to make sense of that problem: do we need to speak of humankind, or of this or that ethnic group? Do we need to speak of tall people or thin people, of beggars or of criminals? Or, do we make criminals *of* beggars? Do we need to speak of the number of stamens on a flower, or do we create an order *of* the numbers of stamens? This relationship also operates in reverse particularly where empty signifiers (Levi-Straus 1987) are concerned. This means that some may *wish* to speak of healthy, fit unemployed people, for example, and contrast them to unhealthy, unfit, unemployed people. This kind of distinction is brought to bear in the mobilisation of public opinion concerning the 'deserving and undeserving poor'. In this case, the judgement about materiality *defines* the problem as having a particular character. It permits certain problems to *become* material to other problems. Should we take power to equate merely to 'can' as I have suggested elsewhere (Crewe 2010), then we may make a claim something like this: the powerful *can* define which problems *they would like us* to take to be important by defining the classificatory boundaries in line with their definition of the problem at hand, and they can do this, in part, because the range of kinds of difference is infinite and judgements concerning the materiality of this or that difference are in the gift of power. What this means, further, is that the supposed mode of *solution* to, or making sense of, a problem is informed by the success of the definition of (the power – capacity – to define) the materiality of the boundaries used to *specify* the problem: the problem is constituted *of* the divisions thus created. The modern constitutes the problem from his sphere of ownness. He, like God, assembles the world in his own image.

It is apposite, at this juncture, that I unpack the preceding sentence somewhat. This situation is not merely a feature of the modern episteme, it is a feature, claims Levinas, of Western philosophy as a whole (Levinas 1969). Western philosophy and modern science (criminology included) have conspired to present a world dominated by the concept of totality.[3] This whole, as we have seen above, used to belong to God, but in the modern episteme this

---

3 See also, of course, Deleuze, *passim*.

totality has been assembled by the arbitrary definition of its constituent parts. We might suggest that this is not surprising in a philosophy that, concurring with Spinoza, cannot know about how we should act until we know what we are. The concomitant of this state of affairs is that it gives privilege to ontology and epistemology, and by these methods moderns have misappropriated the knowledge of the 'available to all' and re-formed it in *their* own image. That is, the constructions, categories, concepts and divisions of modernity (and, hence, criminology) are the product of moderns-as-subjects involved in objectifying the world from *their* subjectivity: from *their* sphere of ownness. For sure, the idea of the self is as old, if not older than Heraclitus. The notion of the psyche was important to Plato, Socrates, Aristotle, Pythagoras, and others. The Copernican revolution, however, brought a shift from the situation where the object impacts upon the viewer-as-object, to one where the viewer-as-subject constitutes his object or goes in search of it. The seventeenth and eighteenth centuries, however, may be seen as a most important time in the development of this concept of the self. Cartesian scepticism concerning what the *res cogitans* could *know* of the 'available to all' beyond the subject's ownness, encouraged the search for firmer grounds on which to base claims concerning the 'reality' of the world: 'How can I *show* that I am not a monad?'. The answer to this question is: 'I will give evidence'. The Cartesian thinking individual apprehends his own content securely as it is 'ready to hand'. Knowledge of the content of the 'available to all' must be striven for. This striving, and its foundation, radical self-knowledge, are the ground for the claims of epistemological privilege evident in enlightenment and post-enlightenment modernity. In Hobbes, the rational self and its desire is the foundation of social organisation and of sovereignty. Then, in Locke, the identification of liberty, right and power is fractured, permitting rights to become the central feature of justice. In Adam Smith, the subject-of-rationality[4] is the motivator of the '*Wealth of Nations*' (and, incidentally, of relatively contemporary resistance to progressive taxation in writers such as Nozick (1974) for example). These rights, however, are to be determined by the 'rational' free-thinking, 'enlightened' man. However, the principle of apperception shows us that a view thus achieved is merely partial, the result is a very limited view: it is a view from the self. It is a view that permits the error of mistaking 'this is how I perceive it' for 'this is how it is', and the incorrigibility of this modern arrogance appears to know few bounds. Justice is appropriated by 'knowledge'[5] and 'knowledge', because its constitution consists of its divisions, which are arbitrary, is surrendered to the throw of the dice. The Other,[6] the object of investigation, or of justice, is constructed

---

4 The definition of what constitutes rationality is, of course, tautological.
5 See Foucault 1970 [1966], 1989 [1969], *et pasim*.
6 The Other is not an other one, an object of my subjectivity, but is a conceptualisation of otherness *beyond* my subjectivity: the Other is an idea.

merely from the subjectivity of the modern, working within an episteme whose rigidity and inhumanity has been well documented.[7] Humanism, it turns out, is inhuman.

When the modern, of which class the criminologist is a species, does this to human objects and ideas, he constructs these entities from knowledge solely of his *own* subjectivity. We know this is so because the subject can never stand outside itself, let alone take a view 'from there', that is, from the view of the object: the Other. Imposing this subject's-view discounts the Other's experience (this, of course, is a particularly heinous limitation when all we are is what we experience). When this results in increased capacities of the powerful (particularly capacities of governance; and this is taken to be one of the things that criminology is for: to govern crime) it does violence to the other: real violence. Indeed, this situation, this mechanism, is analogous to the idea of conducting a trial without the defendant being present, since all sociality is normative and all normativity involves giving account. When the object of governance is absent or cannot be heard, when they are unable to give account, the powerful (the subject of governance) is able to construct the governed (the object of governance) in his own image: in his own interests. Hence modernity and violence are ineluctably joined. They are tyrannical forces, each co-constituting the other's hegemony.

Criminology is modern

It is appropriate now, in the context of the theme of this book that we explore a little more how these two malignly-conjoined forces operate together in criminology. The theme of this portion of this chapter is that criminology operates as a facilitator of the modernity/violence nexus. It does this, I shall claim, amongst other things, by partaking in classificatory practices that ignore the subjective experience of the criminological object. I will readily concede – at least to avoid accusations that I have made of criminology a straw man – that this produces a methodological critique that we receive from Schütz (1967) or Gadamer (2004 [1960]), for example, and that this is a critique that guides much valuable ethnographic criminological research. However, much criminological theory or research is not this way. We might suggest that the modernist criminology *par excellence* is that body of theory known as control theory. An examination of this body of theory in these terms is worthy at least of one whole chapter on its own. Suffice it to say, therefore, that I will merely touch on some of the stronger illustrative points. As Schinkel (2002) points out, such literature separates the delinquent (*sic*) from society *a-priori* and as a consequence ends up saying that the delinquent is not of society, *therefore* he does not behave as a part of society and this is *because* he is not part of society: the deviant deviates! The theory is tautologous. Is this

---

7 See Kuhn 2012; Feyerabend 2010; Lakatos and Feyerabend 1999; Peterson 2003, *inter alia*.

a modern problem, we may ask. Well, yes, it is. As we have seen above, the modern's project is to reconstruct the whole making use of categories and distinctions that are constructed from knowledge solely of the hive-subjectivity of himself and his colleagues. The object, delinquent, which is subject to the modern's *caesura* of her from society taken as a whole, is constructed without reference to her subjectivity: she is absent from the court that objectifies her. To paraphrase Hulsman (1986), the category of the delinquent is not the object, but the product of control theories.

A further modern problem with control theories lies simply with the modern's need to create categories and distinctions: to draw lines (see Lippens, Chapter 1 in this collection). Such theories set freedom of will, or freedom to express libidinal desires over against controls: self-control, parental control and the like. However, these categories of 'the free' (bad) and the 'controlled' (good) are, again, categories *created* by the modern criminologist solely from knowledge of criminology's hive-subjectivity. It is evident, with a little thought, to see that these two categories do not stand over against one another, they are inextricably intertwined: the dichotomy is a false one. This is made clear when we realise that no human behaviour is free from some kind of constraint or control (Crewe 2013). The control to whose absence the modern criminologist wishes to attribute delinquency, or to whose presence he wishes to attribute prevention, is determined by the criminologist's own specification of the problem from *his* subjectivity. Sometimes, this is the lack of guards; sometimes, the lack of good parenting. Sometimes, this is the lack of money; sometimes, the lack of self-control. It will be evident that not all of these absences are bound to what are conventionally called control theories. Explanations of criminality associated with the constraints of financial hardship are often referred to as strain theories. The point I wish to make strongly here is that all human behaviour is the product of adaptation to strain or change and hence subject to some kind of constraint (control). All criminological theory, therefore, is control theory *and* strain theory of one stripe or another. Contemporary modern criminological theory is a product of the sense-making practices of the subject-of-rationality that reassembles the world solely in the image of the modern criminologist's hive-subjectivity. The modern, just like God, constructs the world in his own image.

A further modern criminological classification apposite to the subject of this book is that which gives rise to the concept 'gang' (see Amatrudo, Chapter 6 in this collection). It is evident from many sources that the term 'gang' is an empty signifier (Richardson and Kennedy 2012, *inter alia*). The existence of empty signifiers is readily associated with the subject of modernity. Faced with an infinite quantity of infinitesimal differences, the modern, wishing to make sense of his world identifies his problem (problems having to do with substantial associations of 'outsiders') by *specifying* that problem in terms of substantial associations of 'outsiders': which he labels 'gangs'. He makes a box, writes the word 'gangs' on it, and then goes in search of entities to put in the box. What is signified by the term 'gangs' is more or less arbitrary. Moreover, essentialism in any form is more or less arbitrary and particularly in this case because the definitions available posit a degree of stability in the associations deemed to be problematic. The word degree is important. The 'gang' is recognised as being *more or less* stable, therefore it *must* be recognised as being more or less fluid. The degree to which either the fluidity or stability the taken-to-be-problematic association is awarded 'reeks of arbitrariness'. In this circumstance, the modern criminologist creates gangs and gang members in the image of modern criminology's hive-subjectivity. Males of colour, merely associating, are *cast as* gangs and *hence* problematic. Associations of economically disenfranchised Caucasian people are cast as gangs and *hence* as problematic. Violence is done to those thus cast.

We come now to the most significant concept in criminology, crime. Crime is, by definition, that behaviour that involves infraction of the law. Harm is harm; crime is law-breaking (see Crewe 2011). Criminals are those who indulge in law-breaking behaviour. It is not new to suggest that the law is modern or that it is a product of the Enlightenment. The law is a product of the radical self-knowledge-belief of the Enlightenment (which is itself a species of modernity, and in particular, one conceived by powerful modern, *enlightened* men – WASPs[8]). This radical self-knowledge-belief is also the ground for the *claims* of epistemological privilege evident in law. Thus the product of the law and the *claims* to authority of the law justify each other on the same grounds: an incorrigible modern arrogance that appears to know few bounds. As Schinkel would have it, '[t]he nature of its self-deceit, or of its conceptual self-referentiality ... lies in an abstraction that is due to a misrecognition of itself' (Schinkel 2002: 135). The object of the law is subject to the violence of the law in these terms, because the object of the law is *absent* from the law. And here we come to the nub of the matter to be addressed in this book, 'What is criminology about?'. Criminology as a species of modernity is that study that constructs the criminal Other as the possible object of governance by constituting that Other in her absence. The categories thus created (prostitutes, beggars, gangs, fraud, terrorism, burglary, etc.) are empty signifiers. They are the very *sub*-stance (*hypokeimenon*) of criminology. *They are what criminology is about*. The emperor has no clothes.

Beyond

The 'post-modern' subject and a post-criminological world

Above, I have sketched some suggestions concerning the symbiosis between criminology and modernity and its resultant, violence. We might, quite simplistically, say that this is not a satisfactory state of affairs, after all, is

---

8 White Anglo-Saxon Protestants (males).

not criminology associated with justice, not merely governance? We may, of course be right, however, this would merely be an intuition. If we are to fight for change in the world, as I believe we should, we need more than intuition to rely upon. I propose now to step beyond modern criminology and that we reconsider the role of criminology in the light of a 'phenomenological' (for want of a better term) subject. We begin again with the subject as foundation.

We may posit two ways of being: being *simpliciter*, and being-with. Understood this way, the being *simpliciter* is a monad: we might reasonably ask whether existence as a monad is possible. Descartes encourages us to 'doubt' the existence or the reality of the world around us, that we should entertain the idea that the world is an illusion: that I might have been duped about the existence of the 'available-to-all'. This is a fruitful exercise, though we should not be too keen to reach Descartes' conclusion that we *could* doubt the existence of the world. All experiences are experiences *of* some phenomenon *as* some phenomenon. This is the phenomenologist's core mantra, and, to be sure, Descartes could be experiencing the phenomenon *of* an illusion. However, if this were the case, then there would be no need for language (and he would not have us to write for!), since all language is communicative of meaning and all meaning presupposes the existence of another with whom that meaning is shared or negotiated. We take this to be a powerful claim following what has come to be known as Wittgenstein's private language argument (Wittgenstein 1967). Examination of our doubt concerning the facticity of the 'available-to-all' reveals that it cannot be an illusion. Our experience is experience *of* it, and we experience features of it (language) that would be unnecessary or even impossible if that of which we were having an experience *were* an illusion. This means that of the two modes of being postulated above (being *simpliciter*, and being-with) only the latter is possible. There *are* other subjects in the world, and in consequence we find ourselves in the realm of the basic problem of social ontology: that of the Other, of inter-*subject*-ivity. That is, that Other with whom I AM[9] in the world. That other whom, we will discover, since she is necessary to my being, *constitutes* me. It is to this question we must address ourselves next.

We have seen above that, drawing on Wittgenstein (and many others), the presence of language most strongly suggests that co-present beings share meanings through language. This issue was very much of interest to Husserl. In his *Cartesian Meditations* (1969), Husserl transformed the ontological question, 'Are there other minds?' and the epistemological question, 'How, or what can we know (of other minds)?' to the question, 'How is it that meanings can be shared?'. This is not the solipsistic sceptic's question, 'Am I a monad?', but the question concerning our being-in-the-world-with-others, 'How is the intentional content of our experience of other minds constituted?', or 'How is meaning constituted?'. These questions 'bracket' meaning

---

9 I AM as process and entity.

from the physical composition of the elements of an entity and concentrate on the uncanny capacity of humans to comprehend, more or less, each other's meanings: to make compossible (Husserl explains this in terms of what he calls 'transcendental subjectivity'). This painting is 'a Rothko' not simply because it was painted by someone called Mark Rothko but because its meaning for me *as* 'a Rothko' recognises that being 'a Rothko' involves being part of a cultural tradition, indeed it recognises that my experience of this painting *as* 'a Rothko' includes the viewing experience of every one who has looked at it, even the person who defaced it, and even people I have never heard of. Hence, the Other (as any and all others) is implicated in the construction of *my* meanings. Others, therefore, are other-constituting subjects: meanings are not just shared with or by others, they are *co-constituted* by them. That is, the heterogeneous intentional content of each mind is synthetically unified by the normative judgement of meaning.

If we are to address this Other-centred constitution of meaning, it becomes necessary to establish the elemental facticity of that *Other-as-she-is-for-herself*. That is, not mere difference from me (that would not do, since it would require my presence, involving my ownership of that difference) but absolute alterity: the way in which she is for herself before any kind of communality or co-presence with me, or intellection of mine. The products of this inquiry in the hands of Levinas stand in stark contrast to the solipsism of Husserl's reasoning. For Husserl, *'the intrinsically first other* (the first non-Ego) *is the Other ego'* (Husserl 1969: 107; original emphasis). That is, only after an-Other is constituted by *my* intellection can the differences between she and I be grasped. However, for Levinas this will not do since, in such a circumstance, that Other has already been constituted by me, from my sphere of ownness: she is already existent as a part of my subjectivity. Hence, this cannot constitute the structure of the Other since she absolutely must exist for herself before I have any intellection of her and hence objectify her – do violence to her. It is helpful at this point to rehearse a product of Sartre's enquiry into the nature of the Other. Sartre comes to the conclusion that our first encounter with the other is in the form of shame (Sartre 1967: 302). Sartre recognises that Husserl's account is solipsistic in that it fails to take into account the subjectivity of the Other and his solution is to suggest that questions concerning our experience of the Other's subjectivity cannot begin with *our* apprehension of something in the world (*our* sphere of 'ownness') it must begin with the way we experience ourselves as an *Object*. Sartre encourages us to consider ourselves in a world absent the other. In this circumstance we would be able to experience the world's hæcceity (i.e. to consume its mere isness) but we would not be able to thematise it because there would be no other with whom to share or negotiate meanings. Moreover, it is because it is not possible to experience oneself as an object in the world. It is not possible to stand entirely outside of oneself, which such an experience would require. So, if it is not possible for me to stand outside myself and experience myself as an object, my experience of myself as object must begin elsewhere. Sartre suggests that my experience of myself begins when an Other approaches. As he would have it, I now have an 'outside'. '[B]ehold, now I am somebody!' (Sartre 1967: 353). I can be cast as the *pure consumer* of the mere isness of the world, by the other who has entered my presence: I am cast as 'voyeur' (Sartre 1967: 353). And the use of the word 'voyeur' reveals that the normative content of our experience of the other is, for Sartre, primordially invested with shame. However, it is not the investiture of the experience of the other with shame that is important here, indeed our experience with young children and their utter lack of shame (sometimes) reveals to us that shame is learned. Moreover, it is difficult to see how investiture of the primary experience with the quality of shame can take us beyond the solipsism evident in Husserl. The important revelation here is that the inter-*subject*-ive experience is normative. A further revelation is that to experience the Other as a subject in the world cannot be the same as experiencing an entity merely *composed* of properties. I cannot experience myself as an object, and neither is it the case that my objectification is something I merely *imagine* is part of the experience of the other. For Sartre, it is something I experience affectively as an element of my freedom: the degree to which the for-itself is *merely present to* the in-itself – is *not* the in-itself. This, however, leaves us needing to answer how freedom and normativity can live alongside one another. Surely normativity is constraint, and freedom is the total absence of constraint. The answer to this conundrum is to be found in Levinas.

For Levinas, the equation of freedom merely with absence of constraint is an inadequate conception. We must recognise that our quotidian liberal conception of freedom means freedom equally to do ill or good. This would mean that freedom had no ethical content. Why does this matter, you may ask. You might say, 'I am not interested in ethics – particularly as a criminologist – I am interested in knowing how: how to reduce crime, how to explain crime, etc. If I were to take these questions philosophically, they might be questions of epistemology, not ethics'. Well, we might suggest that it matters because we agree with Levinas when he says 'ethics is an optics' (Levinas 1969: 29). Ethics is 'first philosophy': ethics stands *beyond* all other branches of philosophy. This means that the nature of the ethical relationship precedes all other intersubjective inquiry: the ethical relation with the other constitutes the very *possibility* of inter-*subject*-ive relations at all. Crime is a species of social relation and so, the subject-matter of criminology is about communal – inter-*subject*-ive – relations. This means that for criminology to have any contact with a 'real' world, it must start with an understanding of the ethical relationship in which I, the subject, stand *vis-a-vis* the Other.

So, how does Levinas get to this point? The conventional view of the relationship between freedom and normativity rests on the convention that there exists a dichotomy between these two concepts, a dichotomy that places normative constraint over against freedom. It is readily observed that this dichotomy is a false one. Try to imagine, for example, just one thing that you did today by your own *free* will: something you chose to do without *any kind of influence whatsoever*. You should find there is nothing. Levinas' revelation is rather more startling than this. For Sartre, there is an ethical component to the intersubjective relation that manifests itself in the normative constraint found in shame. The Other of this Sartrean relationship exists as the bringer of a law that defines my freedom by showing its limits. This contestation, between two freedoms, however, can only take place if I have already recognised the Other as the source of the other freedom with which my freedom is in conflict: that is, the normative assessment which defines the limits of my own freedom. This leads Sartre to say, 'my making an object of the Other [therefore] must be the *second* movement in my relation to him' (Sartre 1967: 382; emphasis added). However, since Sartre conceives of this relationship ontologically, that is, as conflict between two entities (two consciousnesses) he cannot identify the root that establishes the relationship *as* a normative one that produces shame in him. Levinas suggests that it is not merely that I experience the presence of another consciousness like my own that I am objectified by this Other-as-subject: that I am judged by him normatively in the form of feeling shame. Rather, what the Other brings to this relationship, as she appears from her existence even before my intellection of her, is not a law but a command. A command does not merely come into conflict with my freedom as a law, but creates an obligation from which I cannot resile. The command revealed by (the face[10] of) the Other is 'thou shalt not commit murder' (Levinas 1969: 199). The response, claims Levinas is, 'here am I' (*me voici* – here see me). We should also note, as would Levinas, that this is the Hebraic *hinneni*, Abraham's response to the command of God as he attempts to sacrifice Isaac. Levinas further has it that this conception is 'the end of powers' (Levinas 1969: 87) the end of my freedom – my 'I can'. That is, not that this shows that my freedom can be done away with but that it shows the fullest possibility of extending my freedom. Anything that was beyond this would be beyond freedom, rather like Buzz Lightyear's beyond infinity. This conception of Levinas shows us 'the end of freedom' because the command is utterly irrecusable. It is not the case that we are not able to kill the other ontologically speaking, of course we can, however, what we cannot do is fail to be obligated by the other's command. Should we kill her, we should simply have chosen not to obey that command: neither the command, nor the obligation goes away. In killing, I have failed in my obligation, not eradicated it. Hence the command (the obligation) discloses the normative nature of the intersubjective relationship, that is, the way in which I can experience entities *as* something at all. The normative basis of the structure of meanings, of commonplaces, is revealed: meaning is exposed as a species of normativity.

10 There is not room in this chapter to examine Levinas' concept 'The Face'. For a discussion of this concept, see Peperzak 1997; Morgan 2011; Perpich 2008.

This irrevocable asymmetry is a phenomenologically necessary quality of my relationship with the Other since she constitutes me in *my* experience by my response to my obligation to her and her command, prior to her in any way entering my experience: my subjectivity. My first experience of myself is formed in my subjective experience of my obligation to her even before I have any intellection of her: before any kind of communality.[11] Ethicality and the very foundation of the *possibility* of meaning are one and the same. Intersubjective relationships are only made possible by this ethical relationship. Ethics *is* 'beyond': ethics *is* first philosophy. This command gives rise to obligation. This obligation is characterised by Levinas in terms of responsibility. This is the foundation of the Levinasian subject, and the subject that I wish to use to project a foundation for a 'beyond' for criminology.

From obligation to responsibility

Thus far, Levinas has made a strong case for replacing Sartre's shame in the ethical relation with the Other, with command and obligation. For Levinas, the question, 'Who am I?' cannot be answered by experience merely of myself, but only through distinguishing myself from the Other by responding to her. We have not yet seen, however, how that response, that obligation, manifests itself, as Levinas claims it does, as absolute responsibility. We might suggest that there are several ways of characterising responsibility: responsibility to myself, responsibility for myself, responsibility for myself to others, and responsibility for others. Conventionally, this latter is exemplified by the relationship between parent and child, where the former is responsible for the latter. The parent's responsibility stands *in substitution* for that of the child. This kind of responsibility, however, arises from the *doxa* that children are in some way deficient: the parent is first and the child second in this relationship. The content of the parent's responsibility has nothing to do with the subjectivity of the child, it arises entirely from the parent's subjectivity – it is hence a species of violence. Moreover, it is a kind of responsibility that arises from a conception of freedom that is absent any conception of constraint: the responsible is guilty of any infraction *in virtue* of their possession of free rationality and we know that the definition of rationality is tautologous. In the light of this we might suggest, as I have done elsewhere (Crewe 2011) that this constitutes *mere* responsibility. Levinas, however argues for a far more radical conception – an *absolute* responsibility – that has nothing to do with first and second, or with guilt conventionally conceived, and certainly nothing to do with any solipsistic conception of responsibility that arises solely

---

11 Whilst this description of mine is temporal in appearance and the temporal relation *is*, ontically speaking, we should be aware that Levinas' distinction is ontological: absolute responsibility is *conceptually and essentially* prior. What Levinas is talking about is an ethics *of* ethics: a kind of metaphysics of quotidian experience.

from my subjectivity. Levinas' responsibility is not an 'answering for' (another or oneself), as in the parent/child relationship, or a giving account, but a substitution where the responsible acts 'instead of' (the Other). Paradoxically, I am an irreplaceable substitute. Or as Critchley (1992) paraphrasing Husserl has said, my 'intentionality reaches into that of the other and vice versa' (Critchley 1992: 7) thus prohibiting any kind of subjective telos (Waldenfels 1995). This sublimation of my responsibility for myself into responsibility for the other results in erasure of the ego. The ego here is the self-replicating bunker from whence modernity launches its violence: that violence that constrains the freedom of the other solely from my sphere of ownness – my subjectivity. This is the violence that modern criminology does.

We have established from Levinas that the Other pierces my horizon in a way that has nothing to do with my subjectivity, her demand is irrecusable. Hence, I am not only primordially responsible for the Other emblematised in this manner but I am responsible to her for myself under her gaze. Because I am placed under this demanding gaze, I am not an autonomous free agent. Moreover, if this responsibility is not chosen freely, I cannot be free to pass it on to anyone else. No one else can be substituted for *my* obligation to the Other. Hence not only am I:

> responsible *to* the other for [myself], but [I am] responsible *for* the other. We may readily say when thinking of the horrors of Auschwitz for example 'we must not let this happen again'. So to say reveals our own responsibility for the atrocity, and indeed, radically, since one can say this even if one's parents or grandparents were murdered at Auschwitz, it becomes clear that I am responsible *even for the actions, against me, of my persecutors*
> (Crewe 2011: 169; original emphasis)

Conclusion: toward a post-criminological world

Should we accept this call of Levinas' to invert the conventional ethical relation with the Other, then, in the context of this book, we do well to consider what this means for criminology. One of the most significant features of modern scientism and hence of criminology, as I have suggested above, is its attempt to *re*-assemble the totality of the 'there is' by co-proximating entities that its practitioners constitute from their own subjectivity. This process I have characterised as violence. Violence is done to the object of our subjectivity in that her 'otherness-that-counts-as-such' is eradicated in her objectification. The realisation that no action or thought is without some kind of determination shows us that constructions that rely upon guilt as a mode of responsibility have arbitrary borders (on immediacy and judgements of cause, see Crewe 2013). In criminological theory, we might ask whether a burglary was caused by poor parenting, economic strains or simple wickedness. Which of these explanations we adopt has to do with our adjudication concerning the materiality or otherwise of causes and effects based on their relative immediacy, and that view arises solely from the criminologist's subjectivity: it is imposed, tyrannically on the criminological object. This means that we not only take the law to be *sub specie æternitatis* and hence, also, the nature of criminality, but we assume that the categories of criminology, gangs, prostitutes, burglars, drug addiction, terrorist, etc. to be possessed of the quality 'truth' rather than normativity. These empty signifiers, because they serve a purpose in objectifying the Other in the process of governance, are *beyond* emptiness. They have a surfeit of emptiness that overflows into, and penetrates the Other thus objectified. This is not merely passively to ignore the Other, this is a rapacious abduction of the other and a colonisation of her sphere of ownness parasitically[12] by the subjectivity of the modern criminologist.[13] Hence, we can never know the content of the other's subjectivity. We can never fully empathise with the problems faced by the object of modern criminology.

In this circumstance, criminology needs to erase its *doxa*. Since the imposition of its categories constitutes violence, those categorisations must be dissolved. More radically, since criminology is itself *constituted by* its categories, *it* must be dissolved and we must move towards a post criminological society. Such a dissolution would inevitably usher in a more just world since the subjective experiences of people whose behaviour was problematic would have to be given *absolute* privilege. Not only that, but *I/we* would have to take on responsibility for that person's actions or thoughts. *I/we* would be responsible for the racism of the racially motivated offender. *I/we* would have to take on responsibility for the economic strains that face the burglar. *I/we* would be responsible for the difficulties faced by the struggling parent. *I/we* would be accountable for school's failure to engage students. *I/we* would be responsible for the dreariness of the quotidian lives of those who drink to excess and then cause problems in our cities. *I/we* would be responsible for the global inequalities that fuel terrorism. *I/we* would be responsible for the political and economic disenfranchisement that gives rise to problematic street cultures. *I/we* would be responsible for the culture of greed and license that brought about the banking crisis. *I/we* would be responsible for the school shootings in the United States. '*We are all guilty of all and for all men before all, and I more than the others*' (Dostoevsky 1880).[14] It is absolutely crucial, however, that this does not mean the same thing as being responsible to ourselves and

---

12 I say parasitic because this is not mere colonisation but the means by which the modern criminological imagination survives and multiplies hegemonically.
13 I insert here the mandatory caveat that I concede that there are manifold problematic behaviours that cause great harm to others about which we should be concerned.
14 Guilt is not used here in its common usage but in the sense used by Dostoevsky in *The Brothers Karamazov*, about which Levinas has this to say:

> I am responsible for the Other without waiting for his reciprocity ... Reciprocity is his affair ... It is I who support all, [... as in] that sentence in Dostoevsky: 'We are all guilty of all and for all men before all, and I more than the others.' This is not owing to such or such a guilt which is really mine, or to offences that I would have committed;

others for prevention, neither can this responsibility be used to justify punitiveness. Either would require the prior and tyrannical objectification of the problematic individual from our subjectivity alone. What it means is that we must accept our irrecusable responsibility *for* the thoughts and actions of the Other before we have any kind of communality with her or intellection of her whatsoever, reminding ourselves that to say, 'not my problem mate' does not recuse us, but merely indicates a failure on our part to satisfy our obligations. If we are to improve the lives of those who experience the problematic adaptations of others, or the lives of those who in some way have to do with 'criminal justice systems', then we must recognise our failure adequately to know the Other and we must act in a way that is compatible with that recognition. This can only happen if we move *beyond* the stultifying tyranny and violence of criminology.

Bibliography

Berman, M. (2010) [1982] *All That Is Solid Melts into Air: The Experience of Modernity*, London: Verso.
Crewe, D.J. (2010) 'Power: the supposed definitions revisited', *Journal of Theoretical and Philosophical Criminology*, 2 (2): 22–68.
Crewe, D.J. (2011) 'Crime, Harm, and Responsibility', in R. Lippens and J. Hardie-Bick, *Crime Governance and Existential Predicaments*, Basingstoke: Palgrave, pp. 156–74.
Crewe, D.J. (2013) *Becoming Criminal: The Socio-cultural origins of Law Deviance and Transgression*, Basingstoke: Palgrave.
Critchley, S. (1992) *The Ethics of Deconstruction*, Oxford: Blackwell.
Dostoevsky, F. (1880) *The Brothers Karamazov*, Moscow: The Russian Messenger.
Feyerabend, P. (2010) *Against Method*, 4th edn, New York, NY: Verso Books.
Foucault, M. (1970) [1966] *The Order of Things: An Archaeology of the Human Sciences*, London: Tavistock.
Foucault, M. (1989) [1969] *The Archaeology of Knowledge*, translation by A. Sheridan, London: Tavistock.
Gadamer, G. (2004) [1960] *Truth and Method*, 2nd rev. edn, translation by J. Weinsheimer and D.G. Marshall, New York, NY: Crossroad.
Hulsman, L. (1986) 'Critical criminology and the concept of crime', *Contemporary Crises*, 10 (1): 63–80.
Husserl, E. (1969) *Cartesian Meditations*, translation by D. Cairns, The Hague: Martinus Nijhoff.
Kuhn, T.S. (2012) *The Structure of Scientific Revolutions*, 4th edn, Chicago, IL: University of Chicago Press.
Lakatos, I. and Feyerabend, P. (1999) *For and Against Method: Including Lakatos's Lectures on Scientific Method and the Lakatos-Feyerabend Correspondence*, edited by Matteo Motterlini, Chicago, IL: Chicago University Press.

> but because I am responsible for a total responsibility, which answers for all the others and for all in the others, even for their responsibility. I always have one responsibility more than the others.
> (Levinas 1998: 98–99; see also Vinokurov 2003)

Levinas (1969) *Totality and Infinity*, translation by A. Lingis, Pittsburgh, PA: Duquesne.
Levinas, E. (1998) [1981] *Otherwise than Being*, translation by A. Lingis, Pittsburgh, PA: Duquesne.
Levi-Straus, C. (1987) *Introduction to Marcel Mauss*, London: Routledge.
Morgan, M.L. (2011) *The Cambridge Introduction to Emanuel Levinas*, Cambridge: Cambridge University Press.
Nozick, R. (1974) *Anarchy, State and Utopia*, New York, NY: Basic Books.
Peperzak, A. (1997) *Beyond: The Philosophy of Emanuel Levinas*, Evanston, IL: Northwestern University Press.
Perpich, D. (2008) *The Ethics of Emanuel Levinas*, Stanford, CA: Stanford University Press.
Peterson, G.R. (2003) 'Demarcation and the Scientific Fallacy' *Zygon: Journal of Religion and Science*, 38 (4): 751–61.
Richardson, C. and Kennedy, L. (2012) '"Gang" as Empty Signifier in Contemporary Canadian Newspapers', *Canadian Journal of Criminology and Criminal Justice/La Revue canadienne de criminologie et de justice pénale*, 54(4): 443–79.
Sartre, J.P. (1967) [1957] *Being and Nothingness*, translation by H.E. Barnes, London: Methuen.
Schütz, A. (1967) *The Phenomenology of the Social World*, Evanston, IL: Northwestern University Press.
Schinkel, W. (2002) 'Modernist Myth in Criminology', *Theoretical Criminology*, 6 (2): 123–44.
Waldenfels, B. (1995) 'Response and Respnsibility', in A. Peperzak, *Ethics as First Philosophy*, New York, NY: Routledge.
Vinokurov, V. (2003) 'Levinas's Dostoevsky: A response to "Dostoevsky's Derrida"', *Common knowledge*, 9 (2): 318–40.
Wittgenstein, L. (1967) *Philosophical Investigations*, translation by G.E.M. Anscombe, Oxford: Blackwell.

Chapter 3

Criminology as 'chaosmic' art: a jazz perspective

Claudius Messner

Introduction

The problem with criminology seems to be that it is still a wicked problem for criminologists. A recent anthology aiming at the definition of the 'nature of criminology' ends up anew with observing divisions, disagreements, and fragmentation (Bosworth and Hoyle 2011). It is hard to resist the conclusion that criminology is whatever criminologists say it is: there is evidently no particular 'something', the one thing that would subject to truth the consensus that is sought. What eventually unites criminologists is the endeavour to make sense of crime, i.e. to tell the difference between 'crime' and 'not-crime' or, more specifically, to distinguish between 'legal' and 'illegal' and between 'just' and 'unjust'. In its attempt to draw the line between these paired sets, criminology or what I prefer to call 'ordinary crime discourse' (Messner 2010: 138) evokes a sense of 'law' and 'justice' respectively which functions as unspoken premise of the attempts to make sense of crime. Criminology is about imagining the boundaries of 'crime': it is a representation practice next to other sciences, politics and the arts.

Terming something 'crime' implies judging. In the real world, judging is a social practice with a wide range of conception, acceptance and historical shapes, from 'natural' everyday life forms to elaborated institutional forms. In a highly abstract manner, judging may be explained as a 'normative abstraction of something, founded upon the social practices of deciding' (Messner 2014: 364), such as precomprehension, perception, taste, imagination or experience (Douzinas 2008). The formation of judgements about 'crime' constitutes the main problem for criminology's claim to rationality. Ordinary crime discourse readily connects this claim with certain types of methodical inquiry as the form of production of criminological truth, taking for granted that science is the general form of the knowledge to be gained.

As we know, this has not always been the received view. Law and justice once were considered issues of politics and ethics. In Plato's *Republic* and in Aristotle's *Politics*, judgements of lawful/unlawful or just/unjust are political-ethical judgements; in Aeschylus' *Eumenides* the tragedy of law is seen in the fact that the law-making decision of a court, its 'law-saying' (*iudicium, iurisdiction*), is at once a coercive suppressing of the law. However, modernity has tried to replace the allegedly speculative *multiversum* of premodern philosophical and poetic discourses by the *universe* of a 'system of positive philosophy' governed by scientific method. Ever since its establishment as a 'discipline', criminology – a bastard born of the liaison between political ideas, legal principles, moral values, and 'practical' governmental requirements – has taken part in the scientistic game where judgements of the (un-)lawful and the (un-)just are assumed to be founded on true propositions. Consider, for example, Edwin H. Sutherland's famous definition of criminology starting with the insight that 'crime' is defined by 'political society', i.e. inevitably relative to social practices. The definition embraces in a complex way politics, science, law, justice, ethics and aesthetics. However, the modernist hope was kept that true or 'truth-oriented' judgement would, some day, take the place of the ancients 'subjective' responses. So-called post-modern thinking has shown that ordinary crime discourse, rather than eschewing 'external' foundations, has lost the faculty of judgement. Moreover, post-modernism has raised questions about judgement as the only or, at least, adequate form of knowledge.

Ordinary crime discourse, however, ignores this loss of judgement and continues to construct a link between 'truth' and 'justice'. But what if crime discourse was subjected to 'laws' of form other than scientific ones? Have not the arts and judgement a common source in what Aristotle called 'aisthesis', in senses and perception? Can we imagine aesthetic experiences and procedures as a more fruitful ground for understanding criminology's 'aboutness' (Danto 2000: 133)? To my eyes, an attempt to juxtapose the prevalent scientific sense of criminology with an aesthetic sense is worth the effort. I will argue, first, that the modernist figuration of ordinary crime discourse, which entails disregard for the aesthetic dimensions of law and justice, creates certain pitfalls that cause criminology's perennial identity crisis and irresponsiveness. The following section, drawing upon reflections on art and aesthetics, explores jazz, the contrapuntal form of today's world music, as an 'aesthetics of imperfection'. Using a model of what I call, borrowing from Deleuze, a 'chaosmic' ethics, jazz is then presented as a pioneering practice for the development of a different sense of criminology.

Crime discourse: theme and variations

A short overview of certain rules which determine the form of ordinary crime discourse shows that criminology is in an important way conditioned by both the classical tradition of theorising the criminal law and the positivistic understanding of social science. The dependency on this canon causes the major part of criminology's unresolved problems and its continuing incapacity to imagine what the ancient world called a 'good society' and what today bears the name of a democratic world society. 'Democratic society': this translation does not imply the normative continuation of present-day regimes or constitutional forms. Rather, it indicates the problem of contemporary political society as well as the scope of tasks waiting for a specific criminological answer: how to imagine forms of living together of people, without regulation, amidst such diversity.

Time signatures 1: 'rogues'

The line of thinking that brings together politics, law and justice under the heading of 'democracy' has been recalled in Jacques Derrida's vivid essay on *rogues*. Since the age of restoration, Derrida (2005) explains, 'roués' or, with slightly changing accent, 'voyous' are called those who are without principles and morals, rogues, solitary men living in a state of indifference and worklessness, playful partners only in dissolute life:

> In the idea of the roué there is thus an allusion to debauchery and perversity, to the subversive disrespect for principles, norms, and good manners, for the rules and laws that govern the circle of decent, self-respecting people, of respectable, right-thinking society
> (Derrida 2005: 20)

It is obvious for criminologists that Derrida is speaking here about what they know as the 'dangerous classes', a term popularised in 1840 through Fregier's study on *Des classes dangereuses de la population dans les grandes villes, et des moyens de les rendre meilleurs*, which later became the manifesto of a criminology focussing on social defence.

To be sure, that which attracts Derrida's attention is not class struggle, instruments of power, or processes of stigmatisation and marginalisation at the dawn of modern society. Rather, he is interested in the democratic question of any society. If democracy has to do with the direction of life through choices taken by the individuals rather than through enforced laws, then democracy is whichever ways people choose to live together. Hence all the variables and variations, hence the great variety, 'the multicolored beauty' offered by democracy, according to Plato (Derrida 2005: 26). The sheer abundance of ways of living makes democracy resemble a rich bazaar and makes up its fascination and its threat. For, what is the right choice to make in this unlimited market? At the very heart of democracy lies inevitably the problem of distinguishing and marking the perennial *crisis* of how to differentiate with regard to the power to do as one pleases 'between the good of democratic freedom or liberty and the evil of democratic license' (Derrida 2005: 21). This is why democracy, 'every passage to democracy, democratisation', will always be suspect, associated 'with taking too many liberties, with the dissoluteness of the libertine, ... with malfeasance, with failing to live according to the law, with the notion that "everything is allowed", that "anything goes"' (Derrida 2005: 21). Can one imagine a good society to be born out of this breeding ground? Is freedom to be understood simply as the 'I can' of a free will? If not, 'how far is democracy to be extended, the people of democracy, and the "each one" of democracy' (Derrida 2005: 54)? Democracy's fundamental problem is the need to separate what cannot be separated democratically. This is the question the roué stands for. Since, if:

> democracy does not exist and if it is true that … it never will exist, is it not necessary to continue, and with all one's heart, to force oneself to achieve it? Well, yes, it is necessary; one must, one ought, one cannot not strive toward it with all one's force
>
> (Derrida 2005: 74)

Modernity: law, crime, and science

As is well known, the understanding of any social practice demands that the story one produces concerning it embraces both the point of view of the participants and the contexts (social, economic, historical, political) in which it takes place. The classical tradition of theorising about criminal law eschews contextual analysis, preferring to tell the insider's story. It attempts to explicate doctrinal rules in terms of underlying moral values and/or social interests, thereby presenting itself as coherent, systematic and principled. This is all the more the case when criminal law is announced, in the wake of the nineteenth century German science of criminal law (*Strafrechtswissenschaft*), as a system which results from the collective pursuit of truth (Baratta 1982; Dubber 2005). The commitment to truth has two central consequences. First, criminal law is not about given (national) legal orders, rather it is the necessary universal form of any science of crime and punishment. Second, it does not allow for foundations external to criminal law science itself. Taxonomic ambitions and characteristics make it resemble biological sciences, 'most notably botany and zoology' (Dubber 2005: 1051). As a consequence, theoretical work, which tends to focus on issues supposedly common to all crimes, results in the double construction of criminal codes as comprising, besides the 'general part', also a so-called 'special part' that contains the statutory definition of single crimes. In other words, criminal law disposes only of decontextualised notions of right and wrong. The result is to deflect attention away from social and other injustices. The contradictions and inconsistencies between the social practice of criminal law and the story told about it offered an open flank to criticisms of every type – from Comte to German Sociology of Law; from American Legal Realism to 'Critical Legal Studies' and other movements; from Lombroso's and Ferri's 'positive school' of criminal sociology to the large number of radically different late modern criminological 'approaches'. All of these criticisms borrowed from the unquestioned (or less questioned) scientific status of the social sciences, and one might safely say that almost all of present day criminologies are variations of the social science theme. Its principal traits are the anti-philosophical ('anti-metaphysical') turn, epistemological realism, the positivistic paradigm of explanation (Messner 2002, 2010), methodological individualism, and the myth of control as emphatically expressed in Comte's triplet *savoir prévoir pouvoir*. Since this is not the place to expand on these issues, I shall restrict myself to explore what I find particularly surprising in today's ordinary crime discourse by making three points: ordinary crime discourse is conditioned by the idea of the legal actor, it has a false idea of the law, and it holds on to the myth of control.

First, the 'offender' of the criminal law is not a real world person or social actor, but a 'legal person' whose description is not based on direct or indirect observation of his or her body and mind, but on the attribution of fictitious capacities. Legal personality is a status, an artifact of legal rules serving to construct the logical point of reference for the imputation of legal 'acts'.

Criminology, in referring to crimes as ('real' or 'socially attributed') acts, tends to confuse the legal and the humanistic form of reasoning and fails to acknowledge the law as a conventional system of interpretation that operates logically and socially at once (Messner 2012). As a consequence, criminology does not feel any need to propose its own idea of the 'actor'. This flaw is all the more serious as the fundamental question of how to grasp the subject quality of the 'offender' remains simply unanswered by criminal law. To be sure, this is not a problem of offender rights nor is it a problem to be resolved at the level of the law alone. Rather, it implies the question of the liberal constitution of society as such.

Second, law constructs facts from fiction. The prerequisite for the attribution of causalities is a supposed imaginative activity of the (accused) actor. But legal imagination does not 'refer' to a reality outside the law. Moreover, the examination of the world 'out there' is knowingly excluded (Messner 2012: 546). Fiction in law does not raise the question of the relationship between legal representation and reality. Therefore, there is no question of truth. Rather, fiction is to be understood and explained as a narrative mode.

From this point of view, law appears as juridical communication, i.e. as a system of meaning (Messner 2010, 2012, 2014). Inasmuch as this system is built 'upon speech that claims meaning for experience' (White 2006: 204), it can be marked as a *rhetorical* system and can be understood as a social practice.

Certainly, one does not begin then with the imagined individual in imagined isolation, but, rather, from where Wittgenstein tells us to begin, i.e. from forms of life, language, gesture, and radical uncertainty. By applying a more open logic exploration rather than the model of explanation which follows the logic of subsumption (Messner 2012: 546), one is able to 'see' that the:

idea of the legal actor as one who is either making policy choices himself (or herself) or obeying the choices made by others is inadequate, for he is a participant in the perpetual remaking of the language and culture that determines who he is and who we are

(White 1985: 35)

Contrary to what many tend to believe, rhetoric is not a 'second-rate way of dealing with facts' (White 1985: 32) or failed science. Rather, it is an art. Both rhetoric and law start in a particular place among particular people. Both use different approaches at different times and for different purposes. Both are *specific*. Rhetoric and art are united by their being 'inventive': both try to find in an expression the possibilities for development that are there to be found. They acknowledge limits of functioning and uncertainty of results; they are modes of apprehension and expression. As a way of 'seeing', rhetoric addresses questions in an organised and coherent, but not rule-bound way. Rather than seeing rules as instructions or commands, they are questioned insofar as they are considered places (*loci*, *topoi*) from which to start inquiring. Since a speaker can not but recognise him or herself as a speaker amongst speakers, rhetoric is genuinely self-reflexive. Hence the questions that determine rhetoric's political-ethical character: 'What kind of community shall it be? How will it work? In what language shall it be formed?' (White 1985: 39).

However, while the law's mode of representation is narrative and rhetorical in the aforementioned sense, law is not reducible to a way of talking, to discourse. Operative law is performance of law. Performance does not mean that something is done with words, but that a 'doing' is staged (Krämer 1998). In this sense, law is demonstration, production, *mise en scène*. In its functioning, legal order is not simply repeated, but actualised as new and as newly situated event (Messner 2012: 547). The rendering of the 'facts' so that judges can hear them is a rendering that propounds the 'world' in which its descriptions make sense.

Third, ordinary crime discourse is incapable of understanding law as both an order constituted by social communication and an operational mode that artfully constructs the 'worlds' into which it wishes to intervene. Rather, adhering to early modern mechanistic models, it envisions the law as a trivial machine transforming, on the basis of static operative rules and fixed functions, certain inputs in predictable outputs. The law is *seen as if* it were a unique big apparatus executing programmes. Thus, the standard analysis of the criminal law is oriented to 'functions'. The assumption – underlying repressive as well as reformist perspectives – is that the 'system' can best be explained and regulated by a proper understanding of the functions it is ('declared') to serve. The idea is that, once a consensus upon purposes has been found, the system can be designed accordingly and actions within it controlled. This kind of talking about social institutions is, as famously shown by Foucault, the basis for modern talk about 'social policy', i.e. the nexus of politics, law and justice. To be sure, the governmental myth of 'control' sounds still rational to the ears of many (Latour 2007).

From exactly this perspective of the criminal justice system's capacity to control society, Douglas Husak states that, nowadays 'criminal law itself is not important' simply because 'it fails to implement the rule of law' (Husak 2003: 262). 'Criminal theory' in particular is concerned by Husak's verdict because it seems 'important only if the criminal law that we have is important' (Husak 2003: 268–69). This is an all too evident restatement of the positivistic triad of knowing – foreseeing – being able to act. Good theory – 'best practices', as the current short-circuit goes. Theory *must* guide practice; if it fails to do so, theory has no title to speak. This is not the place to argue with this position (see Messner 2010: 150). More important in the present context seems the fact that one can hardly elude Husak's conclusion: 'there is good reason to have a criminal law that is important. Imaginative responses to the problem present a formidable challenge for criminal theorists' (Husak 2003: 270), criminologists included. Imaginative responses are needed here, but perhaps not in Husak's sense.

I rather think that the challenge for criminology consists in imagining differently the link between the criminal justice system and society and, in general, the 'rule of law' in contemporary society. A first step in this direction is to stop reproducing the control myth and to give up the idea of law as a system of 'rules' to be stated, applied and enforced. This ideology prevents us from connecting normativity to and within our experience as 'composed' (Deleuze and Guattari 2000: 228) by the multiple traces that imagination produces of reality when narrating it. However, critique alone is not enough. It must be followed by a second step which requires imaginative proposals of forms of social life organised by a communal normativity different from religion, morality, and science. For, the control myth presents only half the normative universe we live in:

> We inhabit a *nomos* ... We constantly create and maintain a world of right and wrong, of lawful and unlawful, of valid and void. The student of law may come to identify the normative world with the professional paraphernalia of social control. The rules and principles of justice, the formal institutions of the law, and the conventions of a social order are, indeed, important to that world; they are, however, but a small part of the normative universe ... Once understood in the context of the narratives that give it meaning, law becomes not merely a system of rules to be observed, but a world in which we live
>
> (Cover 1983: 4–5)

The world in which we live is social communication to 'create and maintain' always anew our normative universe (Messner 2012). From this point of view, the control myth turns out to be what one might call with Cover the 'imperial' pattern of world maintenance: 'In this model, norms are universal and enforced by institutions. They need not be taught at all, as long as they are effective' (Cover 1983: 13). Since discourse is premised on objectivity, not upon subjectivity and sociality, precepts of law 'are marked off by social control over their provenance, their mode of articulation, and their effects' (Cover 1983: 17). But, what is excluded by sharp discursive boundaries is not eliminated, only moved beyond the lines drawn: 'the other' of the included remains present and efficient, but is radically uncontrolled.

The other way of world maintenance indicated by Cover can be explained as the 'communal' mode. Premised on the fact that there is no private normative life, it is founded on narratives as a form of communication about events. Its primary concern is not theoretical, but pragmatic. It is an exercise in unity. As Walter Benjamin (1977) argued, the value of narratives does not depend on informational content. On the contrary, half of the art of narration consists in presenting a story, in creating and revealing patterns of commitment, resistance and understanding, without any explanation. Narration in this way allows the listener to draw conclusions from his or her own understanding of the narrated events. This, Benjamin says, bestows on narration a 'scope of oscillation' that information fails to have (Benjamin 1977: 445). For this reason, the 'good story' is a form that resists time and force, whereas information 'lives' only once, in the moment of its first apprehension when it makes a difference.

To summarise, ordinary crime discourse is fascinated by the insider story which modern law narrates about itself and about its functions. Always busy defending or refuting this story, criminology has neglected to develop ideas of its own about the normative universe of contemporary society. Since the central difficulty indicated by discourses on 'crime' is the significance of rules and our relationship to rules, the various aspects which put together define criminology's task, converge in one fundamental question: 'Can one imagine a good society – "good" being a measure not reducible to a set of features or a taxonomy – in which regulation is not a condition?'. If the answer is negative, criminology's specific dilemma consists in both continuing to work on the demystification of 'crime' and insisting on 'rules'.

In what follows, I will argue that criminology could do worse than expand its analysis in a way that accounts for the whole normative universe, the *kosmos*, of democratic society. Rules are not simply regularities to be discovered or norms of thinking and acting to be observed and enforced. Rules can be conceived of as the 'laws of form' which guide our ways of world constitution and maintenance. Rules are our expectations towards a 'good form' of our world.

Thus criminology could do worse than become a theory of reflection. But to be fully responsive, criminology also needs to be perceptive. It needs a specific empirical ethics which I call chaosmic ethics, i.e. a way of assessing what we do in terms of ways of existing. Michel Foucault envisaged it as a philosophy of 'curiosity'. It is not contented with reclaiming praxis as a term. It is about exploring different forms of existing. It is about an 'aesthetics of existence'. This means, first, that it is not about what is true or false, but about our relationship to truth. It is not about reality and possibility, but about our 'sense of reality' and our 'sense of possibility' (Messner 2010). It is about the strange and the familiar. It is a *critique* aiming:

> à faire exister une œuvre, un livre, une phrase, une idée; elle allumerait des feux, regarderait l'herbe pousser, écouterait le vent et saisirait l'écume au vol pour l'éparpiller. Elle multiplierait non les jugements, mais les signes d'existence; elle les appellerait, les tirerait de leur sommeil. Elle les inventerait parfois? Tant mieux, tant mieux
>
> (Foucault 1980)

No jurisdiction is claimed here, no 'veridiction'. Differences of existence are explored in order to enable us to think and to act differently – 'pour devenir autre que ce qu'on est'. This is about maximising connections, powers, possibilities of life. But how to practise the *art* to 'make play the differences', how to create the principal *œuvre* of one's own becoming 'different'? Art is so much more than a medium of expression. Elaborating on the triad art, science, and philosophy, Gilles Deleuze has explained the art world as a 'chaosmos' produced by various plots of 'composition' (Deleuze and Guattari 2000: 228–42). 'Devenir', becoming itself is critical, for if identity is what defines a world of representation (re-presenting the same world), then becoming means presenting a world of presentation anew. Here as elsewhere (see Messner 2011: 57), Foucault trusts the mentor-model of joint experience. This is a personal relationship which, centred on the common performance of the 'aesthetics of imperfection', aims at increasing a person's power to act, whilst at the same time not diminishing the other's similar powers: the common exploration of possibilities emphasises the best of each one. In the next section, I will present jazz as a model of this art.

Jazz: aesthetics of imperfection

Aesthetics and art

A major difficulty in reclaiming the aesthetic in this section is that modernist aesthetics leave us with a reduced notion of art and, in general, aesthetics (Levine 1994) and a tendency to identify the artistic with the aesthetic. Ever since the invention of 'experience' and the development of the idea of the aesthetic in the eighteenth century, we are used to think of art as the 'fine arts' and of aesthetics as limited to (comment on) the 'originality' and 'beauty' of these forms (Manderson 2000; Andina 2012). Driven by a desire for order and coherence, modernist aesthetic discourse is guided by the fiction of unity and aims at synthesising the diverse. Preference is given to the visible and to eye 'evidence', not to the ear and listening. Much as is the case in science, the 'system' does not admit fields of indeterminacy or even 'chaotics'. But, 'what makes something art is not something that meets the eye' (Danto 2000: 138). Ironically, this view can not conceive of aesthetics as reflexive thinking concerned with the conditions of constructing and judging the world. It fails to consider aesthetics as a kind of 'perceptology' (Ferraris 1997) which is independent from art, and it fails to grasp both aesthetics and art as modes of our 'seeing as' of objects in Wittgenstein's sense, i.e. as 'worldmaking' responses to events (Nancy 2014). We will use the term 'aesthetics' here in order to indicate, on the one hand, perceptions which rest on the senses, and, on the other, interpretations of art which rest on 'thinking trough perceptions' rather than through 'concepts' or 'functions' (Deleuze and Guattari 2000: 235).

Wittgenstein's late philosophy provides the *practical* instruction (not to think but) to 'look' (Wittgenstein 1977: para 66) at the many uses we make of 'languages' as different modes of playing open ended 'games' and to describe the distinct 'life forms' we are living in 'naturally'. It is by their description as particular activities that we are led to notice new 'aspects' of things, to 'see' them 'suddenly anew and differently'. This approach embraces ordinary language, discourse and art as practices. On this common ground we will explore in what follows the analogy between discourse and music. For the moment it may suffice to say that we consider music a non-referential 'parallel practice'. As the musical 'game' is organised by time, the paradigm it follows is rhythm, not theme (Kaduri 2006). So, it seems especially true for music what Lyotard once said about art: it says that it cannot say. But then, one must promptly add that what music has to tell us does not depend on any 'saying'. For it is also true that the schism between the eye and the ear, and the mind and the body (Nancy 2008), is constantly evaded by music (Le Guin 2006). As performative utterance in a specific situation or, if one prefers, as a staging, music is essentially characterised by its visuality, sheer physicality and material effects. Polymorphic as it is, music seems to disavow even the tale of the 'fine arts' by combining 'the temporal aspects of film and dance with the spatial aspects of painting and sculpture, where pitch space (or frequency space) takes the place of three-dimensional physical space in the visual arts (Levitin 2008: 17).

Aesthetic terms, after all, are to be considered a peculiar genre, but they are as little esoteric as any other. Following Wittgenstein, Frank Sibley proposed to speak of aesthetic concepts 'when a word or expression is such that taste or perceptiveness is required in order to apply it' and characterised 'taste' just as the ability 'to notice or discern things' (Sibley 1959: 421, 423). Examples span from most common terms (lovely, dainty, graceful, elegant) to others such as unified, balanced, lifeless, serene, somber, dynamic, powerful, vivid, delicate, moving, trite, sentimental, tragic, and others still. What all such expressions have in common is that we are required to exercise judgement to apply them. This means, as Sibley observes, 'that there are no non-aesthetic features which serve as conditions for applying aesthetic terms' (Sibley 1959: 424). Nor are they 'rule-governed' (Sibley 1959: 435). Neither legal nor aesthetic concepts admit of a 'mechanical' employment of rules and procedures. Within the law, to respond to new 'cases' we are required to exercise reflective judgement (Messner 2012: 546) guided by a complex set of examples and precedents. What is true for the law is also true for aesthetics. We learn from samples, examples and precedents and they 'play a crucial role in giving us a grasp of aspects; but it's impossible to derive from these examples conditions and principles ... which will guide us consistently and intelligibly in applying the terms to new cases' (Sibley 1959: 431). How, then, do we support our judgements, and how do we bring others to 'see' what we 'see'? We have already given the answer: by rhetorically 'drawing' attention to the relevant 'aspects' and relations. It is pointless to say that non-verbal bodily communication is no less important here than words and sentences.

However, all that said, it seems that the notion of art remains as amorphous and disputable as those of law and justice. But if this fact constitutes a problem, it cannot be resolved by relating the relative claims to 'art' to given models or paradigms in an attempt to determine correspondence. Rosch and Mervis (1975) showed that categories do not always have clear boundaries, they have fuzzy boundaries. Thus, we cannot hope to define 'art' in the sense of giving individually necessary and jointly sufficient conditions for it.

Yet it is possible to characterise art. Wittgenstein (1977: paras 66–77) proposed that category membership is determined not by a definition, but by 'family resemblance'. Following Wittgenstein, Berys Gaut indeed rendered a 'cluster account' of art plausible (Gaut 2000). We call something art if it resembles other things we have previously called art (Mandelbaum 1965). We may be able to indicate sufficient conditions for the application of the concept, but none of them will be individually necessary and no record of items will display all sufficient criteria. Rather than using a static list of definitions, family resemblance relies on a list of features that may or may not be present. It is a matter of properties being possessed in common, and is consequently vacuous without further specification. By specifying what the relevant properties are, a cluster account makes substantial claims and holds properties as criteria, but it does not hold them as exhaustive for considering something as art. Undoubtedly, this allows a great deal of indeterminacy. But what would appear a difficulty within a resemblance-to-paradigm approach, is not problematic here: since no appeal is made to paradigms, there is no incompleteness. So, the cluster account may elude the pitfalls of formalist, functional, institutional, and historical accounts (Levinson and Galbusera 2012). It gains its very importance as a heuristic tool for philosophical ethics and aesthetics. What is more, it 'fits naturally with a view of the value of art as consisting in a set of diverse values, rather than one single kind of excellence' (Gaut 2000: 41).

Time signatures 2: jazz roots

Ted Gioia writes:

> An elderly black man sits astride a large cylindrical drum. Using his fingers and the edge of his hand, he jabs repeatedly at the drumhead – which is around a foot in diameter and probably made from an animal skin – evoking a throbbing pulsation with rapid, sharp strokes. A second drummer, holding his instrument between his knees, joins in, playing with the same staccato attack. A third black man, seated on the ground, plucks at a stringed instrument, the body of which is roughly fashioned from a calabash. Another calabash has been made into a drum, and a woman beats at it with two short sticks. One voice, then other voices join in. A dance of seeming contradictions accompanies this musical give-and-take, a moving hieroglyph that appears, on the one hand, informal and spontaneous yet, on closer inspection, ritualised and precise
> (Gioia 2006: 3)

This is the primal scene in which Gioia epitomises the origin of jazz. It is New Orleans in 1819, when on Sunday mornings slave dances take place in Congo Square. 'New Orleans jazz' historians are used to link the rise of 'hot' music to sin and licentiousness in a city 'named after a debauched noble' – the Duke of Orléans – a city that was 'populated with prisoners and prostitutes ... and came of age as the Big Easy, a place where the rest of world flocks for a fast and loose time' (Gioia 2006: 29). Such stories aside, it is no coincidence, Gioia argues, that the birth of jazz happened in this city because the mixture of Spanish, French and African elements with Latin-Catholic culture had produced there a multi-ethnic milieu far more tolerant in accepting social hybrids than the English-Protestant ethos.

African music may be cautiously characterised by the predominance of call-and-response-forms, the cross-fertilisation between music and dance, and the integration of the musical performance in social practices. Playing music does not mean the production or reproduction of 'works' or models of form, but participation in social action. What qualifies the musician as a group member or as a soloist is not the correspondence to the requirements of a score, but rather the individuality of his voice within a community, an idea totally alien to Western efforts to standardisation (Kunzler 2005). In contrast to modern Western music, there is no separation between audience and artist, and 'personal' sounds of human or instrumental 'voices' are focused on in instances where Western composers would rely on notes. In general, the musical qualities shared and communicated are improvisation, spontaneity and, most distinctively, rhythm:

> In African music, in both its original and its various Americanised forms, different pulses are frequently superimposed, creating powerful polyrhythms that are perhaps the most striking and characteristic aspect of these traditions. In the same way that Bach might intermingle different but interrelated melodies in creating a fugue, an African ensemble would construct layer upon layer of rhythmic patterns, forging a counterpoint of implied time signatures, a polyphony of percussion
> (Gioia 2006: 11)

So it seems that the only history of jazz one can tell is the story of its continuous transformation, describing the fast evolution of the jazz idiom from popular music to art music, and narrating how, since the dawn of the twentieth century, such gentle 'wild' figures like Louis Armstrong became 'musicians' and how they won over American and, only one generation later, European audiences as well. But this story would be incomplete if it would not report at once how jazz assimilated elements of the European tradition of composition, thereby contributing to the advancement of modern music (Gioia 2006: 8). Being the widely understood art music of our time, jazz might justly be called 'world music', namely a universal musical language that allows different idioms to co-exist. In this sense, jazz is at home everywhere but probably will never have a definite residence. It is the nomadic reason of contemporary music, a music of becoming, fusion, and opening towards the possible.

Counterpoint

From the above discussion of the concept of art, it should be clear that we will not try to define jazz. However, armed with the knowledge of Wittgenstein, one may decide that some music can be more or less a member of the jazz family. The following characteristics can describe jazz as modern art music (Gioia 2007). To begin with, jazz is not, in any sense, a so-called primitive art. On the contrary, jazz 'more than any other form of modern art ... holds the standards of technical capability' (Gioia 2007: 62). To be sure, jazz – as every form of art deriving from oral/aural traditions (think of Benjamin's illustration of narration) – shows its severity and precision in ways that differ from annotated or written forms of art. If music is always 'organisation of time' and 'ordering of sounds' (Kunzler 2005: 11; de Groot 2010: 133), jazz is to be considered as a 'thick' management of time and sounds, as 'jazz' always means a specific, situated performance. Jazz 'lives and dies in the instance of performance' (Gioia 2007: 111). Pleasure, inclusiveness, discipline, and invention are the key notions.

Let me make two points here. *First*, all this relates to the polyphonic or contrapuntal structure of jazz mentioned in the long passage cited above. Polyphony or, in classical composition, the counterpoint is a musical texture characterised by two or more melodic lines of equal importance being sung (or played instrumentally) simultaneously (de la Motte 1991). Usually, polyphony rests upon the conception of equality between voices. There is typically no domination of one voice over the others, and if there is, it is temporary, the role of prominence switching from one voice to another (de Groot 2010: 130). Let us look briefly at the use of polyphony in jazz and baroque music, following Ted Gioia's reference to the fugues of Johann Sebastian Bach (Wolff 2000). The fugue is one of the most significant types of compositions in the baroque era and is polyphonic by definition. It is a composition characterised by one main theme, called the subject, and the imitation of that theme by different voices. The imitation of the subject starts at equally spaced intervals of time in each of the other voices. First the subject, then the second voice, then the third, and then the fourth. Polyphony in jazz however does not originate from a compositional master plan, but, as we will see in a moment, from the improvisational nature of jazz. 'New Orleans jazz', for example, is known for its polyphonic texture of many different melodies being played together by different instruments in a small group of performers. Out of the performers, 'front-line players' (trumpet, trombone and clarinet) all improvise melodies at once (think of Louis Armstrong's 'When the saints go marching in').

In both examples polyphony, the ensemble of the different independent voices playing distinct melodies at once, is used to create more expressive sounds. Polyphony indeed makes music more complex and enjoyable. With a multitude of different melodic lines playing at once, one can create many different combinations which, to be appreciated, require more than one listening session, and every listening could be very different from any other. This of course is true not only for the audience, but for the group of performers as well. Polyphonic performance needs polyphonic listening. From this point of view, one may consider polyphonic listening as a 'practice of mutual respect' (de Groot 2010: 131). At any rate, polyphony requires considerable discipline of composing, performing and listening.

Second, by working with deliberated rhythmical 'irregularities', jazz proves to be serious about the ordering of perceptions in a particular way. Since the metrical rule is not contained in the melodic organisation, the melodic construction can be opened for further rhythmical influences. In order to do so, the metre – or more precisely, the principle of measure called 'beat' – is played as *a conditio sine qua non*, or is varied, or is even merely imagined. The fundamental respect for the beat – even when its dissociation is under way – allows for always new and surprising caprice: the beat is then perceptible as the in-between of irregularities. Thus, musicians have to practise the particular discipline of allowing an idea to be expressed which is still being elaborated in the performance. As Elliott Carter once said, the musical score, if there is any, 'serves fundamentally to avoid that the musician plays what he already knows and to guide him while exploring new ideas and technics' (cited in Gioia 2007: 73). What the performance requires, then, is improvisation and spontaneity, but both will increase rather than reduce the commitment of artists. The performance shows how one assumes risks and draws the appropriate consequences. Jazz tries to practise contrapuntal necessity and inventive freedom at once.

Jazz is not a static theme. Rather than communicating a 'what', jazz is oscillating about the un-notational 'how', about events. This 'how' is always determined by the artists constant commitment to persons, time, and situation of the performance. As the relative stance assumed by the artist: his *ethos*, the 'how' has its own story and tradition.

'Chaosmic' ethics

In concluding this section, let us consider the field work in aesthetics and ethics that jazz is from the participants' point of view. Herbie Hancock, in the *Norton Lectures* (Hancock 2014), has presented jazz as a common endeavour where 'high value' is placed 'on collaboration, on openness to new ways of seeing and a generosity of spirit' (Hancock 2014). It is an exercise in curiosity built on exploration, courage and co-operation. There was a time, Hancock recalls, when being a member of the Miles Davis Quintet he felt musically stuck. 'Everything I played sounded the same', he reports. Davis saw his frustration and offered some enigmatic advice:

> 'Don't play the butter notes', he said. 'Butter notes?', I thought. 'What is that?' Does 'butter' mean 'fat'? Or does it mean 'obvious'? I had to think about it, and finally realised that if I left out the notes that most clearly define the chords it would allow the harmonies to open up to various views
>
> (Hancock 2014)

Collaboration is explained here as an ethics of common learning fostered by the kind of personal relation that is the mentor-disciple relation with its alternation of reciprocal speaking and listening. What you hear, Hancock explains, is not jazz or a trumpet, 'you hear Miles'. Commitment, then, means to live fully up that relation, at the edge of the moment, without a 'plan B'.

Jazz is the moment. Possibilities, no judgement here. Hancock remembers one extraordinary moment in Stockholm in 1967, during a performance by the quintet. 'This night was magical', he recounts. 'We were communicating almost telepathically', playing one of the group's signature pieces, 'So What':

> Wayne [Shorter] had taken his solo. Miles was playing and building and building, and then I played the wrong chord. It was so, so wrong. In an

instant, time stood still and I felt totally shattered. Miles took a breath. And then he played this phrase that made my chord right. It didn't seem possible. I still don't know how he did it. But Miles hadn't heard it as a wrong chord – he took it as an unexpected chord. He didn't judge what I played

(Hancock 2014)

The line between 'right' and 'wrong' depends upon our expectations. Why would we not dare to expect differently and to be surprised by unknown possibilities? There is no wrong playing, only better choices. This is why one *must* follow the beat. There is always the possibility to transgress. But only those who know the rules will be able to break them. Rules do not cut off, rules *support possibilities*. 'Rule-breaking' is a key notion here. The interaction of 'voices' enables one, as Edward Said put it, to develop an attitude of 'moving from one domain to another, the testing and challenging of limits, the mixing and intermingling of heterogeneities, cutting across expectations' (Said 1991: 55).

If in this sense jazz means 'making oneself understood by anyone', would it be too much to recommend it as critical model for speaking democratically of democracy, namely speaking 'on the subject of democracy in an intelligible, univocal, and sensible fashion' (Derrida 2005: 71)?

A different sense of criminology

Edward Said, as is well known, considered polyphony an antidote against totalising schemes of thought (Said 1991, 1994). Using polyphony and counterpoint as a metaphor, he emphasised music as an elaboration of civic society (Said 1991: xiv). In music, the coercive form is sonata, the 'classical' form of European compositional music (Said 1991: 100). By comparison, one would have 'being' on the side of the counterpoint, 'knowing' on the side of the sonata, a living figuration here, a static scheme there. Sonata is characterised by forced homogeneity of themes. Since its beginning with the often conflicting themes of the 'exposition', the progressive development of themes is the dynamic factor that, in the course of time, unifies the diverse elements of the composition. The principle of progress tends, through its consequential realisation, to incorporation and synthesis. Pretending to be a universal form, sonata asserts the oneness of reason and claims jurisdiction on diversity. Without any doubt, the alternative offered between democratic polyphony and the 'monophony' of classical European reason is very suggestive. Sonata seems to be an expression of the 'imperial mode' of world-making.

However, this is not the line of thinking we followed throughout this chapter. I did not recommend jazz or music in general as a metaphor, but tried to show analogies between different 'languages', considering music, the least denotative of the arts, as a 'parallel practice'. The general question has been what (scientific) 'thinking through concepts' eventually could learn from aesthetical 'thinking through perceptions'. In conclusion I will return to this question and will delineate some points concerning crime discourse.

For criminology as a scientific discipline it is more important to resist opinion, dogma (Messner 2010) and 'governmental' forces (Latour 2007) than to defend itself from whatever is seen as chaos. If, therefore, it follows art in constructing 'a chaosmos ... a composed chaos' (Deleuze and Guattari 2000: 242), it cannot decline to elaborate a view of the *kosmos* wherein 'crime' happens. This leads to a perspective on *nomos* which, focussing on the *ensemble* (think jazz music here) of politics, law and justice rather than on the opposition of actor and society, constitutes a definitive disclaimer of the nineteenth century defence-of-society cliché. Reorienting the perspective from social control to *nomos* entails some consequences regarding the envisioned alternatives to state-centred thinking, beginning with the communal (not: communitarian) assumption that there is no private normative life. Rejecting the obsolete notion of language as a system of signs in favour of an idea of language as a communicative practice (Messner 2012), 'law' itself is to be considered as a sign to be explored by means of aesthetics. Structurally open to diversity and difference, this view does not offer a cosmic closed 'world', but, in fact, an art world of chaosmic composition. Within this composition, criminology will have to elaborate on its own idea of (liberty and) rule breaking as expression of diversity. Furthermore, criminology could do worse than take the step from a hermeneutics of jurisdictions to a hermeneutics of the good life. Lastly, if needs be, it may wish to reflect on a cluster theory of crime.

From a methodological point of view, criminology has to become specific and, again, chaosmic. Becoming specific means doing the kind of 'field work' that, as John Austin more than half a century ago predicted, would 'soon be undertaken in, say, aesthetics; if only we could forget for a while about the beautiful and get down instead to the dainty and the dumpy' (Austin 1956–57: 9). What counts then is research and exploration, not knowledge. Becoming chaosmic means to accept that field work as an empirical, experimental ethics is to be developed, by means of perceptology and on the ground of our being *touché* (Derrida 1998).

Bibliography

Andina, T. (2012) 'Realismo in ontologia, idealismo in arte. Una tensione mortale', *Methode* 1 (1): 29–45 (online http://www.methode.unito.it/methOJS/index.php/meth/index, accessed 9 June 2014)
Austin, J.L. (1956–57) 'A Plea for Excuses', *Proceedings of the Aristotelian Society*, New Series, 57: 1–30.
Baratta, A. (1982) *Criminologia critica e critica del diritto penale*, Bologna: Il Mulino.
Benjamin, W. (1977) 'Der Erzähler. Betrachtungen zum Werk Nikolai Lesskows', in W. Benjamin, *Gesammelte Schriften*, vol. II, 2, Frankfurt: Suhrkamp, pp. 438–65.

Bosworth, M. and C. Hoyle (eds) (2011) *What is Criminology?*, New York, NY: Oxford University Press.
Cover, R.M. (1983) 'Nomos and Narrative', *Harvard Law Review*, 97 (4); 4–68.
Danto, A.C. (2000) 'Art and Meaning', in N. Carroll (ed.) *Theories of Art Today*, Madison, WI: University of Wisconsin Press, pp. 130–40.
De la Motte, D. (1991) *Il contrappunto*, Milano: Ricordi.
Deleuze, G. and Guattari, F. (2000) *Was ist Philosophie?*, Frankfurt: Suhrkamp (original publication: (1991) *Qu'est-ce que la philosophie?*, Paris: Minuit).
Derrida, J. (2005) *Rogues. Two essays on reason*, translation by P.-A. Brault and M. Naas, Stanford, CA: Stanford University Press.
Derrida, J. (1998) *le Toucher. Jean-Luc Nancy*, Paris: Galilée.
Douzinas, C. (2008) 'Sublime Law: On Legal and Aesthetic Judgements', *parallax*, 14 (4): 18–29.
Dubber, M. (2005) 'The Promise of German Criminal Law: A Science of Crime and Punishment', *German Law Journal*, VI (7): 1049–71.
Ferraris, M. (1997) *Estetica razionale*, Milano: Cortina.
Foucault, M. (1980) 'Le philosophe masqué', *Dits et Écrits*, vol. IV, text n. 285.
Gaut, B. (2000) "Art' as a Cluster Concept', in N. Carroll (ed.) *Theories of Art Today*, Madison, WI: University of Wisconsin Press, pp. 25–44.
Gioia, T. (2006) *The History of Jazz*, 2nd edn, Oxford: Oxford University Press.
Gioia, T. (2007) *L'arte imperfetta. Il Jazz e la cultura moderna*, Milano: excelsior1881 (original publication: (1988) *The Imperfect Art*, New York: Oxford University Press).
de Groot, R. (2010) 'Music at the limits: Edward Said's musical elaborations', in W. Otten, A. Vanderjagt and H. de Vries (eds) *How the West Was Won: Essays on Literary Imagination, the Canon, and the Christian Middle Ages for Burcht Pranger*, Leiden: Brill, pp. 127–45.
Hancock, H. (2014) *The Ethics of Jazz*, Set 1 – The Wisdom of Miles Davis, Set 2 – Breaking the Rules, *The 2014 Norton Lectures*, Cambridge, MA: The Mahindra Humanities Center at Harvard University (online http://mahindrahumanities.fas.harvard.edu/content/norton-lectures, accessed 9 June 2014).
Husak, D. (2003) 'Is the criminal law important?', *Ohio State Journal of Criminal Law*, 1: 261–71.
Kaduri, Y. (2006) 'Wittgenstein and Haydn on Understanding Music', *Contemporary Aesthetics*, 4 (online http://www.contempaesthetics.org, accessed 10 May 2014).
Krämer, S. (1998) 'Sprache – Stimme – Schrift: Sieben Thesen über Performativität als Medialität', *Paragrana*, 7 (1): 33–57.
Kunzler, M. (2005) *Jazz Lexikon*, Berlin: Directmedia.
Latour, B. (2007) 'How to Think like a State', in W. van de Donk (ed.) *The Thinking State*, The Hague: Scientific Council for Government Policy, pp. 19–32.
Le Guin, E. (2006) *Boccherini's Body. An Essay in Carnal Musicology*, Berkeley and Los Angeles, CA: University of California Press.
Levine, G. (ed.) (1994) *Aesthetics and Ideology*, New Brunswick: Rudgers University Press.
Levinson, J. and A. Galbusera (2012), 'Defining Art', *methode*, I (1): 80–6 (online http://www.methode.unito.it/methOJS/index.php/meth/index, accessed 9 June 2014).

Levitin, D. (2008) *The World in Six Songs: How the Musical Brain Created Human Nature*, New York, NY: Dutton/Penguin.
Manderson, D. (2000) *Songs Without Music: Aesthetic Dimensions of Law and Justice*, Berkeley, CA: University of California Press.
Mandelbaum, M. (1965) 'Family Resemblances and Generalizations Concerning the Arts', *American Philosophical Quarterly*, 2: 219–28.
Messner, C. (2002) 'Die kriminologische Beobachtung der Kriminalität', in P. Rusterholz and R. Moser (eds) *Wege zu wissenschaftlichen Wahrheiten*, Bern Berlin Wien: Lang, pp. 109–35.
Messner, C. (2010) 'Crime, Crisis, Critique. On Dogmatic and Creative Use of Foundations', in R. Lippens and P. Van Calster (eds) *New Directions for Criminology. Notes from Outside the Field*, Antwerpen: Maklu, pp. 135–53.
Messner, C. (2011) 'Subjectivation as Problem and Project. Is there an Existentialist Motif in Foucault?', in J. Hardie-Bick and R. Lippens (eds) *Crime, Governance and Existential Predicaments*, Basingstoke: Palgrave Macmillan, pp. 36–60.
Messner, C. (2012) "'Living' Law: Performative, Not Discursive', *International Journal for the Semiotics of Law*, 25 (4): 537–52.
Messner, C. (2014) 'Luhmann's judgment', *International Journal for the Semiotics of Law*, 27 (2): 359–87.
Nancy, J.-L. (2008) *Noli me tangere: on the raising of the body*, translation by S. Clift, P.-A. Brault and M. Naas, New York, NY: Fordham University Press.
Nancy, J.-L. (2014) 'Quand le sens ne fait plus monde', *Esprit*: 3–4.
Rosch, E. and C. Mervis (1975) 'Family resemblances: Studies in the internal structure of categories', *Cognitive Psychology*, 7: 573–605.
Said, E.W. (1991) *Musical Elaborations*, New York, NY: Columbia University Press.
Said, E.W. (1994) *Culture and Imperialism*, New York, NY: Vintage Books.
Sibley, F. (1959) 'Aesthetic concepts', *Philosophical Review*, 68 (4): 421–50.
White, J.B. (1985) *Heracles' Bow: Essays on the Rhetoric and Poetics of the Law*, Madison, WI: University of Wisconsin Press.
White, J.B. (2006) *Living Speech: Resisting the Empire of Force*, Princeton, NJ: Princeton University Press.
Wittgenstein, L. (1977) *Philosophische Untersuchungen*, Frankfurt: Suhrkamp.
Wolff, Chr. (2000) *Johann Sebastian Bach*, Frankfurt: Fischer.

Chapter 4

The quantum holographic turn
"Normal science" versus quantized, holographic affirmative nomadology

Dragan Milovanovic

Introduction

In responding to the question, "What is criminology about?", we find that our answers are limited by the ontological assumptions on which the question is constructed. Contemporary criminology is rooted in an outdated Newtonian-based, classical-materialist ontology, vacuous as to any credible statement on agency, and fundamentally rooted in an axiomatic, normal science. Elsewhere (Milovanovic 2011, 2013a, 2013b, 2014), we have made a call for a paradigm shift to a more quantum holographic orientation, and to a process-informational paradigm. Here we want to address the methodological restrictions within a contemporary criminology that is associated with normal science, and suggest an alternative, expanding on an "affirmative nomadology." We shall then extend on this orientation and advocate a quantized, holographic affirmative nomadology. It is a call for reintegrating political philosophy and the findings of quantum and holographic theory into criminological "sciences."

Newtonian physics ushered in a comprehensive model by which disorder was brought within an empirically verifiable universe of experimentation and truth construction. Our concepts of objects, space, time, causation, and knowledge itself were now situated within a bounded scientific discursive framework within which reality could be understood. This classical-materialist paradigm was to be incorporated in the social sciences as core assumptions. However, more recent developments in quantum mechanics and holographic theory suggest a re-orientation toward a process-informational paradigm. The former, too, has been challenged as to a convincing statement about agency.[1]

---

1 We have offered an inter- and intra-subjective, de-oedipalized version of Jacques Lacan's (1977) schema R. In our revised view, schema QD is the source of a modulated signature wave that engages a holographic field, accessing, producing, and in turn constitutively being produced by the interactions. Lacan's schema R was a significant advance in studies on agency, even Deleuze having co-authored a major polemic, *Anti-Oedipus*, against dominant psychoanalytic approaches based on the *oedipus* function and a "lacking" subject, still ultimately paid homage to the considerable insights Lacan advanced. We are in this direction. Our schema QD acknowledges Lacan's topological structure of agency, but

Given these differences, we want to explore the associative methodological orientations in the social sciences, particularly in criminology.

The orientation we want to explicate builds on the comparative analysis of Deleuze and Guattari, particularly in *A Thousand Plateaus* (1987) and *What is Philosophy?* (1991), Delanda's (2002) *Intensive Science and Virtual Philosophy*, and Holland's (2011) *Nomad Citizenship*. Deleuze and Gattari (1987) developed the direction in "Treatise on Nomadology." They conceptualized dominant orientations as "royal" or "state science" and compared them to an alternative "problematic approach." Delanda (2002) has re-conceptualized this effort in terms of a "deductive-nomological approach," or normal science, as compared to a "problematic approach." More recently, Holland (2011) has compared a "scientific" orientation to a philosophically-based affirmative nomadology. All three draw considerably from complexity theory and nonlinear dynamics and particularly from the Nobel Prize winning work by Ilya Prigogine (1977).[2] These authors agree that philosophy is about creating concepts that respond to contemporary conditions and problems. Whereas Delanda's approach is predominantly analytical, Deleuze, Guattari and Holland argue for a political philosophy. It is toward Holland's recent position that we now move.

The developed affirmative nomadology certainly advances studies in the social sciences, and, in particular, has considerable potential for reviving contemporary criminology. We, however, want to re-orient their approach by incorporating the insightful studies in quantum and holography theory just beginning to make inroads in the social sciences (see Bradley 1998, 2011; Robbins 2006, 2011, 2014; Wendt 2010, 2015).[3] Affirmative nomadology's incorporation of dynamic systems theory in itself is a re-orientation, which, regrettably, contemporary criminology has yet to address seriously. Be that as it may, quantum and holography theory are yet further areas which can be

---

    introduces how an agent is both internally constituted and subject to interactional social processes. This is a quantized constitutive process. From Robbins' (2006, 2011) work, we incorporate and revise his idea of the brain as a modulated signature wave, meaning, the brain is a source of quantum waves that interact with information always already embedded in a holographic in-formation field within which we are immersed. Contrary to dominant neurological studies that situate information in our brains in distinct neural clusters, a holographic approach argues in one approach (Laszlo 2007) that it is encoded in holographic form (interference patterns) non-locally in the spaces within which we are immersed. Our revised statement argues that the "modulated" component is so because of the outcome of schema QD, represented now as a four-cornered matrix (four interrelated corners being ego, ego-ideal, Other, community generalized other, each varying in intensity, magnitude, frequency, and priority), which, in encounters, produces a distinctive signature wave that engages the in-formation field, and in process is in turn constituted.

2 A number of influential works by Massumi, Delanda, and Protevi and Bonta have emphasized this aspect of Deleuze and Guattari's work. For some basics, see my *Critical Criminology at the Edge* (Milovanovic 2003).

3 See also applications of quantum theory to cognition in Busemeyer and Bruza (2014); for applications to the social sciences, see Haven and Khrennikov (2013); for more interdisciplinary applications, see Atmanspacher *et al* (2013).

usefully integrated. Indeed, one could argue that quantum theory is already suggestive in affirmative nomadology (see Massumi 1992).[4] We want to make it more explicit on the one hand and, on the other hand, further this direction of inquiry in criminology.

Orientations of thought: normal science versus quantum, holographic affirmative nomadology

Introduction

"Normal science" in contemporary social sciences, and in particular, criminology, we have argued, has been deeply rooted in Newtonian physics. Methodologies, too, are grounded on the derived ontology. The first wave of disruption was complexity theory, particularly the work in chaos theory. The second wave upon us is rooted in the findings of quantum and holography theory. Let us first look briefly at "normal science" and then move to a quantized, holographic version of affirmative nomadology. We want to focus on the works of Deleuze, Guattari, Delanda and Holland, particularly in so much as their work appears most accommodative to our developing notion of a process-informational paradigm rooted in quantum and holography theory. Accordingly, we will first summarize the key differences between "normal science" and an "affirmative nomadology" or "problematic approach." We will then show how quantum and holography theory builds on affirmative nomadology, but also argue that the reliance on complexity theory does not go far enough. In responding to the question, "What is criminology about?", we argue that situating the question within "normal science" will reify dismal contemporary orientations in criminological investigation. As Einstein has said, "We can't solve problems by using the same kind of thinking we used when we created them."

Normal science

Contemporary, dominant social sciences, and in particular, criminology have been conceptualized by the aforementioned critics as a "deductive-nomological," axiomatic, "royal," "state," or major science. The key components of this approach include (see especially Deleuze and Guattari 1987: 351–423; 1991; Delanda 2002: 117–56; Holland 2011: 1–26): reliance on particle-like essences located in an absolute space and time; wholehearted acceptance of

---

4 Henri Bergson's *Matter and Memory* (2002), originally published in 1896, has been shown to have anticipated the key thrusts of holography theory (Robbins 2013, 2014). Holography theory was more formally developed by Nobel Prize winner Dennis Gabor's work in the 1940s. Bergson's work had a continuous major influence on Deleuze throughout his writing career. We can trace the present article's maturation through this history.

a metric, striated (Euclidean) space within which mapping and empirical examination transpires; extracting non-dynamic invariants or constants from everyday flow of social interactions; reduction ("de-potentiation") of complex phenomena (variables) to limited, static expressive forms (operationalization of variables); factoring out possible multiple, interacting perturbations by holding constant a set of variables (reducing complexity to sterile simplicity); locating functions, limits, and derivatives on an idealized, metric representation of reality ("plane of reference"); predominant use of linear equations; use of classical logic, probability and causality; valorizing linguistic statements of patterned regularities, and deductions from them as causal explanations; a goal of discovering fundamental laws which lead to a completely understood picture of reality (determinism), i.e. a "clockwork universe"; establishing representative snapshots, photographs, "freeze-frames" of reality (static blocs of space-time); reliance on establishing axioms (postulates and theorems) which crystallize in fundamental "truths" from which, deductively, everyday derivative truths are manufactured; subsumption of problems to established solutions; and a reliance on a passive, disembodied, objectified subject.

Contemporary criminology is imbedded in normal science. In asking the question, "What is criminology about?", the entering graduate student in the top-ranked criminal justice departments realizes very quickly that abstract empiricism is the answer. Rankings of university departments are based heavily on empirical studies. Grant procurement has high emphasis on data collection and analyses. Hiring, promotions, and tenure decisions often look to quantifying a faculty member's scholarly work. Top rated journals such as *Criminology* are replete with quantitatively-based articles. The newly entering graduate student finds that required courses in methodology and statistics are predominantly about doing normal science. Very little, if anything, is provided on the philosophy of science, of alternative methodologies, of competing ontologies, of "minor science." The former student, now with PhD in hand, well-versed in normal science, ventures forth into the employment world and finds positions demanding empirical examination abundant. S/he finds a faculty position and now transmits normal science to her/his student. Repetition, reification, hegemony; how can s/he respond to the question, "What is criminology about?" differently than the circumscribed methodologies suggest?

When confronted with the question that only up to 40 per cent variance is explained in the empirical criminological literature (Weisburd and Piquero 2008), our practitioner quickly tells us better operationalizations, better data collection, overcoming internal and external validity with the use of true experimental research designs, with better control and experimental groups, etc. will lead to greater validity and larger variance explained. Consider that over 60 per cent is unexplained variance and the conclusions nevertheless surge forward. Consider the many "minor" determinants, or "rounding up" that eliminates sensitivity to initial conditions, iterative and disproportional affects, that chaos theory suggests.[5] No matter, normal science continues its parade. Perhaps Jock Young (2011) is compelling, with agreeing Nietzsche waving his finger up and down in the background: late modernity has ushered in more instability, insecurity, and uncertainty suggesting new adaptations from the very form of "othering" that distances, categorizes and limits.[6] This extends to scholarly researchers who find normal science comforting in their confrontation with the dilemmas of their trade and understanding problems of living of their subjects. Enter, what Jock Young sarcastically calls the "datasaur":

> a creature with a very small head, a long neck, a huge belly and a little tail. His head has only a smattering of theory, he knows that he must move constantly but is not sure where he is going, he rarely looks at any detail of the actual terrain on which he travels, his neck peers upwards as he moves from grant to grant, from database to database, his belly is huge and distended with the intricate intestine of regression analysis, he eats ravenously but rarely thinks about the actual process of statistical digestion, his tail is small, slight and inconclusive.
>
> (Young 2011: 15)

We are not opposed to including mathematical schemas, but question the use of abstract empirical analysis that focuses exclusively on regularities and patterns without sufficient examination and analysis of causal mechanisms that are at play. We are also, with Deleuze, Guattari and Holland, suggesting that in the social sciences, and criminology in particular, we need to bring philosophy and philosophy of science back in. Moreover, we need to re-visit developments in other disciplines, particularly mathematics and physics, for

---

5 Consider a practice of normal science, for example, that rounds independent variables to the tenth place, or hundredth place. Inconsequential? Chaos theory shows clearly that through iteration, disproportional effects result. Add to this Heisenberg's uncertainty principle concerning how we artificially capture a phenomenon in our operationalization of the variable at the very first instant, and we must conclude that we do not do justice to the complex, dynamic state of the phenomena under consideration. We are at best doing snapshot criminology.

6 Young (2011) has shown how perceiving the other can change in historically-based political economies. Conservative othering projects onto the other values of negativity which are contrasted with the virtues of the attributer. Liberal othering is where the other is seen as deficient; if s/he would only ascribe to the values of the dominant group all would be better. Both essentialize, reducing the other to an objective status, and in the process maintains the virtuous status of the attributer. Elsewhere (Milovanovic and Henry 2001), we have referred to derivatives as harms of reduction and harms of repression. Yet another outcome is what Deleuze (1989: 126–45), inspired by Nietzsche, referred to as the "man of truth." This person makes claim to a higher truth, judges life according to prophesied transcendental, universal values, and often seeks revenge against perceived transgressors. Alternatively, with Levinas (1998), we could acknowledge in our everyday encounters an infinite duty of care, understanding, and compassion for the other; with Deleuze (1989: 126–45), there is compatibility with the "power of the false" whereby things can always be otherwise, where reality is an ongoing creation not a discovery.

new developments. After all, Albert Einstein was eagerly reading philosophy, particularly Hume and Kant; Bohr was reading Kant, Kierkegaard, and some Eastern Philosophy; Heisenberg wrote a book entitled *Physics and Philosophy*. Indeed, many of the founding figures of quantum theory in the mid-1920s were familiar with Eastern Philosophy (see Marin 2009; Eddington and Jeans 1984).

Quantum, holographic affirmative nomadology

Affirmative nomadology or, alternatively, a problematic approach, or nomad or minor science, has been provided much impetus by the recent work of Eugene Holland (2011), who builds on Deleuze and Guattari's "Treatise on Nomadology" and on Manual Delanda's *Intensive Science and Virtual Philosophy*. It is in fundamental disagreement with "normal science." It problematizes what normal science takes for granted and through repetition has reified.

Deleuze and Guattari's use of "nomad" suggests an alternative to a polis, logos and law (Holland 2011: 14–15). "Nomad" implies an outside, a space within which being otherwise exists in virtual form. And "affirmative," according to Holland (2011: xxi), is employed because this approach not only critiques what is, but stresses the creation of concepts that provide creative responses to our current societal situation. In other words, this goes beyond a Hegelian, even a Marxian master-slave dialectic where value creation by the "slave" (read proletariat) can only take place by a double negation in creating a positive. It is, rather, a *transpraxis* by which reaction and negation is inseparably linked with active creation of alternatives.

We integrate quantum and holography theory in resituating affirmative nomadology in a more holistic noology, or image of thought.[7] Quantum theory having its key thoughts formulated in the 1920s, and one form of holography theory developed by Dennis Gabor in the 1940s, is often found implicit in Deleuze and Guattari's work. For the latter, this "line of flight" in thought in turn can be traced to Henri Bergson's *Matter and Memory* (1896), which anticipated many of the key ideas of holographic theory. Massumi (1992) has made quantum theory more explicit in their work. Capek (1971) has argued that quantum theory is implicit in much of the work of Bergson. Thus both Holland and Delanda's understandings of Deleuze and Guattari's can be traced to these footprints. We combine these ideas in suggesting a quantum, holographic affirmative nomadology.

Let us provide some of the key salient points of quantum, holographic affirmative nomadology. These are not meant to be definitive or conclusive.

---

7 Deleuze (1989) introduced the notion of an image of thought to refer to how each society thinks itself through a particular stabilized set of images. Noology can be seen as a study of these images: How have they been given the form within which they appear? What and whose values are they upholding? What other potential images of thought can be developed that offer visions of what is and what could be?

They highlight some of the differences with normal science. The key components include: reliance on a wave-like notion of "reality" located in complex, dynamic space-time. In this view any entity can be conceptualized in terms of a quantum wave function (mathematically symbolized as Ψ) that indicates the multiple possibilities that it harbours. In quantum language it is symbolized as a basis, i.e. $|V_i\rangle$. This suggests a variable possessing many virtual possibilities of expression, or subscript "i."[8] In this view with a collapse of the wave function (which is a "cloud of possibilities") one instantiation materializes that now appears particle-like.[9] These waves are located in space-time or in complex space-time such as in complex Minkowski space-time, topological space, or in a holographic field sometimes referred to as the zero point field, holofield, or in-formation field. Holography theory also suggests that all entities are vibratory in nature. All emit and absorb vibratory energy encoded with information.[10] The cosmos, in this view, is a sea of interference patterns that encode information. Extracting invariants from the everyday flow, or conventionally understood operationalizing variables, "de-potentiates" the possibilities inherent in the virtual forms. Complexity or multiplicity is then reduced to static expressive forms. By holding variables constant – which is a conventional normal science pre-occupation – interacting effects are

8   A signifier, for example, has in the abstract (virtual), many possible meanings. It is context that collapses the wave function to one amongst many. Of course, we more accurately argue that context + agency collapses the wave function.
9   The classic, definitive study that indicates the wave- and particle-like nature of all entities has been represented by the "double-slit" experiments. Schrödinger's cat, a thought experiment, has also indicated how an otherwise unmeasured/unobserved state will collapse into a particle-like state with measurement or observation. In one version (Copenhagen) of quantum theory, it is measurement or observation that collapses the wave function producing the instantitations ("real") which become the basis of our everyday reality constructions and actions. A tree falling in the forest does not make "noise" absent an observer.
10 See Bergson's *Matter and Memory* (1896). More recently, see Laszlo (2007). Space, in this view, is not "empty," but a fluctuating field of energy (Puthoff 1989), a zero point field. Information is stored holographically in this field, according to one version. Another version (Pribram 1971) has it that information is stored non-locally in the brain. Yet another version developed by cosmologists ('t Hooft 1993; Susskind 1995; Bekenstein 2003) studying black holes suggest that the cosmos is composed of bounded regions and an internal "bulk." All information within the bulk composed of the everyday space-time encounters is encoded in one less dimension on this boundary surface. One extrapolation argues that we are all ultimately projected holograms from this boundary region. Elsewhere in application, we (Milovanovic 2014) argue that sociologists and criminologists who often use the term social or group boundaries are already suggesting an enclosed space or niche. Quantum holography provides a physicality to these terms. We can therefore see how Sutherland's differential association theory is about how information is embedded not only in particular spaces (bulk) which is accessed by its residence, but in the more radical view, this information is further encoded on the "boundary" to this niche. The more radical view, with well-based mathematical support by physicists would therefore suggest that information on the boundary is projected into the bulk producing holographic projections that all is. Certainly we resist this possibility, after all, we quickly say, we can feel, see, smell and engage other objects in our environment. But consider for a moment the dreams you had last night. They seemed very real, even as the dream was not consciously controlled by us.

substantially reduced, and results are mere sterile abstractions of complexities that are ever in the process of becoming. Rather than locating interactions on a static, one-dimensional, striated "plane of reference," an alternative approach is to locate them on a "plane of immanence," a flowing field of interacting vectors and intensities, on which we can make various "mobile cuts of space-time," always indeterminate, as Heisenberg's uncertainty principle informs us (we cannot simultaneously pinpoint momentum and location with 100 per cent accuracy). Gabor's (1946) notion of "logons," or space-time constrained holograms, embedded with information, suggests that information is always incomplete in its momentary construction (mobile cuts of space-time). This is due to Heisenberg's uncertainty principle that limits precision in simultaneously defining space *and* time. Thus information construction is always in-process, a becoming. From chaos theory, too, given the central idea of sensitivity to initial conditions and interactive effects, even the very smallest differences with iteration produce disproportional effects.

Linear equations do not suffice. Consider Stewart's (1989; cited in Delanda 2002: 153) classic critique, "if you decide that only linear equations are worth thinking about, self-censorship sets in. Your textbooks fill with triumphs of linear analysis." As Delanda (2002: 153) explains, the call for solvability ushers in linearizing otherwise nonlinear events. This takes place by focusing on, or constructing, low intensity states, and/or by subsuming problems to given solutions. We witness a similar logic at play in judges' decision-making. In the more often appearing "easy cases" subsumption, subsuming the "facts" of the case, either as they are, or constructed, under a particular rule in law, expedites applying deductive logic to a conclusion in law (Lefebvre 2008). If we acknowledge variability in intensity too, such as a more attentive compared to inattentive recognition orientation of consciousness (Bergson 2002), then linear equations, at best, may tell us something about low intensity states (e.g. Matza's pacified agent, 1969). Attentive recognition, however, problematizes otherwise linear "eventing," indeed, can be the basis of creativity, mutation, change, metamorphosis and transformation, a "creative evolution" (Bergson 1996).

Classical logic and probability theory make use of Boolean logic (see Pitowksy 1989; Busemeyer and Bruza 2014). In other words, variables (or in Deleuze's language, "multiplicities") are given static form (de-potentiation), or reduced to particle-like entities. Once reduced to Boolean logic, deductive logic and syllogistic reasoning can discover truth which always already remains embedded in the axiom or postulate. In other words, distinct trajectories (e.g. path analysis) can be created that delineate a clear pathway of development. Quantum logic and probability differs (see von Neumann 1996). Before a decision is made a person can be in a superposition state (more than one possibility of actualization exists at an instance). No fixed trajectories exist, since all that follows begins in wave-like form (recall the "cloud of possibilities"). However, once an initial collapse takes place, the next is affected. Busemeyer and Bruza (2014: 4) provide an example of a questionnaire. They suggest an "order effect" whereby the way a question is asked, and the response to it, will then order the subsequent answer. In other words, it contextualizes it, and contributes to the collapse of the wave function. However, this is, following Deleuze and Guattari (1987), always in "continuous variation"; meaning, that rather than a distinct line we have a moving "cloud of possibilities". A collapse leads to the next instantiation, but that, in turn, creates a new starting point for the next collapse.[11] This contrasts with normal science that assumes linearity through the whole series.

Quantum probability theory, too, suggests that we must look to implicated "subspaces" that are vector spaces (Busemeyer and Bruza 2014: 5).[12] Delanda (2002: 129–34, drawing from the work of Alan Garfinkel (1981), has provided further analysis in discussing "contrast space."[13] In answering the "why" question, we must be sensitive to the contrast space within which a person operates (see also Salmon 1984). Each contrast space is also a holographically constituted semantic space populated with relatively stable discursive invariants, master signifiers, or what Bergson referred to as "shining points." This is a holographic lexicon structure (Jones and Mewhort 2007; Cox *et al* 2011) accessible by an agent's modulated signature wave (more below; see also note 1, and Milovanovic 2014: chapter 4). As Garfinkel (1981: 21; see also Delanda 2002) tells it, if a priest asks a thief why he robs banks, the thief's answer would not be situated in the contrast space of the priest (say, for example, why rob a bank rather than getting a legitimate job?); rather, the thief's contrast space concerns the choice of what to rob. Questions of validity, therefore, must entail an understanding of the contrast space of different subjects of experimentation, interviews, and questionnaires.

Deleuze, in *The Logic of Sense* (1990; see also Delanda's explication, 2002), has also offered the notion of quasi-causality which recognizes singularities that appear on an otherwise linear appearing trajectory.[14] The robust, and

---

11 See also the notion of the Markov chain.
12 A vector space suggests a field (subspace) of forces in which variations in magnitudes, speeds, locations, directions, intensities, and potential affects exists. Each field, then, varies with each person; it is a background space, a form of a diagram of virtual possibilities from which instantiations produce the real. Kurt Lewin's (1997) idea of a "life space," or a hodological space (Deleuze 1989: 127–13) suggesting a striated field of forces in Euclidean space has compatibilities. However, a virtual space, a non-Euclidean space exists below this level, a "pre-hodological (Deleuze 1989: 127–13) which is yet to be captured within the grids, categories and typologies of normal science. Criminal conceptions, for example, are localized in the hodological space; becoming otherwise, in a pre-hodological space.
13 Garfinkel (1981: 40; cited in Delanda 2002: 130) defines contrast space as being "similar to what physicists call state space. A state space is a geometric representation of the possibilities of a system; a parametrization of its states, a display of its repertoire."
14 See also his discussion (Deleuze 1990: 58–66) of a non-classic view of chance and probability. Unlike, he tells us, a roulette wheel or a throw of dice in which the rules of chance are fixed at these points, when considering virtual states and quasi-causal mechanisms, "we must allow the rules to change with every throw and inject chance at every point, to yield a truly non-metric (or nomadic) distribution."

as of yet, little explored Deleuzian notion of quasi-causality includes how "quanta of information" (Delanda 2002: 103) are transmitted between agents which represent "centers of vibrations" (Deleuze and Guattari 1991: 23, 35). It is through coupling, entrainment and resonance, Deleuze informs us (1990: 239–40; 1994: 118–19; Delanda 2002: 160–61, 219), that transmission of information and "flashes" take place.[15]

As a corrective to the sterile approach of normal science, Deleuze and Guattari (1991; see also Delanda 2002; Holland 2011) suggest a problematic approach. The key, given a problematic situation, is asking or constructing the right question. Thus a well-posed problem and question is fundamental[16] particularly being sensitive to the contrast spaces at play. This is in accord with Busemeyer's and Bruza's (2014: 5) discussion of subspaces as vector spaces representing a superposition state, but with not necessarily Boolean possibilities. In other words, we are not limited to yes-no possibilities. The latter is imposed by the continued idealization, valuation and prioritizing deductive logic and axiomatic systems. This valuation is at play in the "criminal justice model," even as it is belied by everyday Weberian substantive rational principles. This valuation extends to political economy whereby the attendant axiomatic system produces the subjects it needs by way of disciplinary mechanisms and a system of capture (see Patton 2000, 2010), as well as by providing "points of subjectification" (Deleuze and Guattari 1987) in which subjects of speech are suggested. Creating well-posed questions, therefore, is a problematic endeavor.

We must go beyond a two-logic approach, an image of thought sustained by our understandings of the classically constituted computer. Rauscher and Targ (2001), for example, argue for a four-logic. Thus, rather than a Boolean two-logic of yes-no conceptualizing light, for example, as either a particle or wave, a four-logic would see the possibilities as a wave, not a wave, both

---

He continues: information is, however, being transmitted amongst the series cast by ongoing resonance (Deleuze 1990: 60).

15 A reasonable direction of further inquiry is to see how this notion of resonance, coupling, and frequency entrainment can be productively integrated with the quantum holographic notions of phase conjugation by Schempp, Marcer and Mitchell, as well as with Cramer's transactional interpretation. All imply quanta of information are transmitted during the harmonic resonance phase. In other words, when two entities establish a common interference pattern – the electromagnetic waves from two interacting entities are congruent – we have resonance. It is during this phase that information is established and exchanged. Beginning from the early influential work of Bergson (2002), all entities emit and absorb electromagnetic waves. Studies have shown that living beings emit bio-photons and these are encoded with information about the entity.

16 A number of years ago I was fortunate to meet Mark Kennedy at a conference. Invited up to his hotel room to play chess and have a drink, I asked him how he came to developing his insightful conclusion in "Beyond Incrimination" (Kennedy 1969) where he reduced the differentia of crime to politicality and definitions attached. The only thing, in other words, to distinguish crime (say a mugging and death) from punishment (say a state execution) were these two. He said a student asked a "stupid" question in class: is crime and punishment the same thing?

a wave and not a wave, neither a wave nor not a wave (the latter being more aligned with quantum theory, Rauscher and Targ 2001). A Greimasian square (Greimas 1987) could also be useful in discovering these possibilities beyond a two-logic.[17] Perhaps with the final development of a quantum computer, acknowledging the existence and functionality of superpositioned states, a state of quantum coherence in the form of "qubits," classical-materialist orientations and normal science will be sufficiently shaken to consider seriously quantum and holography theory.

The notion of linear causality is further replaced by such conceptualizations as "catalysis" (Delanda 2006), retro-causal effects, and backward time referral of quantum information (Libet *et al* 1979; Sheehan 2006; Radin 2013). Delanda (2006), for example, in his notion of catalysis, argues that all entities have their own internal threshold levels that trigger action. Thus, the same external "determinants" (consider the many criminogenic forces suggested in conventional criminology) can have different effects because of the differential internal capacity to affect and be affected of entities. Research also suggests that information can go backward in time to influence the present. As strange as this may sound, quantum theory is on firm footing in its ongoing research findings that indicate that the unidirectional time implied by normal science does a disservice to understanding how instantiations take place.[18]

Further, as Delanda (2002) has explained, unexamined linguistic statements concerning patterned regularities often lock us into deductive logic which now becomes presented as causal explanations. These sedimented linguistic statements, with repetition, coalesce into a core set of axioms and postulates from which derivative theorems can be engendered. This functioning by normal science then produces the basis of "truth" construction in syllogistic-deductive reasoning.

Alternatively, in a quantum, holographic affirmative nomadology, truth is ongoingly *created* (see especially, Deleuze and Guattari 1987, 1991; Deleuze 1989).[19] Gabor's (1946) notion of the logon is in this direction, suggesting a fundamental uncertainty in any creation of information. Thus snapshots, freeze-frames, and photographs of "reality" are obfuscations. Media effects, as has been cogently demonstrated by cultural criminologists (see Ferrell *et*

17 A Greimasian square is a four-cornered structure whereby we situate contraries on each corner and then look at the implications. It is a vehicle of discovery beyond mere thinking in "yes" and "no" possibilities.
18 In doing normal science in criminology, for example, we are still limited in understanding the extent and scope of *ex post facto* constructions at various intervention levels, from confrontation, arrest, charge, prosecution, defense including prison experience and exposure to scripts supplied in inmate cultures redefining the charge. In other words, facts do not speak for themselves. They are constructions as labelling theory has earlier suggested. We go further in arguing that this also entails how the wave function collapses. From the many possibilities, one dominant reality is constructed, with real effects.
19 Deleuze (1989) counters the man of truth with the "power of the false," the always inherent possibility of being otherwise, of mutation, change, transformation, becoming. Truth is created in process; it is not discovered.

al 2008: 123–57), through "loops" and "spirals" tend to spin this already abstracted reality into new form, providing viewers a static, cleansed version of what happened, or is happening in the everyday world.[20]

Normal criminological science is vacuous in its offering of an active agent. Rendered either as a product of her/his environment (positivism) or a creature of rational choice (rational choice theory), the person is stripped of her/his complexities and potentialities. Only recently has the work on edgework (Katz 1988, 1999; Lyng 2005), and more recent statements by cultural criminologists integrating edgework, ushered in some recognition of an active agent, not necessarily dictated by the logic of positivism, nor of rational choice. Elsewhere (Milovanovic 2014), we have provided a possible corrective in our inter- and intra-subjectively constituted Schema QD inextricably immersed in a holographic field (see note 1). It draws from a de-oedipalized Schema R (Lacan 1977), a notion of the brain as a modulated frequency wave traversing the holographic field (Robbins 2006, 2011), a "transactional interpretation" of the collapse of the wave function (Cramer 1986, 2006), and phase conjugation[21] (Schempp 1992; Marcer and Schempp 1997, 1998; Mitchell 2008; Mitchell and Staretz 2011). Our view is that our four-cornered agent diagramed on a Möbius band (ego, Other, ego-ideal, community generalized other), ontologically based on production not lack, immersed in interpersonally constructed and sustained emotionality, generates a particular matrix in action in particular encounters from which is generated a unique QD matrix signature[22] wave that both interacts with the informational-encoded holographic field and is constituted in this very activity by this field. Time flow is both forward and backward. The importance, here, for our quantum, holographic affirmative nomadology is to stress that perceptions or gestalts are created at the quantum level and become, in the classic world, the basis of reality construction. In a more attentive form of orientation, creativity is always in a virtual potential state; in more inattentive, or where "pacified" (Matza 1969), repetition and reification are more apparent. Action is mobilized based on the perception-images created. Our orientation, therefore, provides a physicality to how images are created. Cultural criminology's current work, as well as Quinney's early work on the notion of the social reality of crime, can be rethought along quantum holographic lines in order to suggest the mechanism by which "realities" are construction, the basis of action in the actual world.

Criminology needs a subject. In answering the question, "What is criminology about?," we already assume a potential knowing subject. But this

---

20 Richard Quinney's classic and still persuasive book *The Social Reality of Crime* (Quinney 1970), has already established how the social reality of crime can be explained in a constitutive, holistic manner.
21 Phase conjugation is defined as two waves in resonance, the basis of information exchange (see note 15).
22 See note 1.

subject needs to be rescued from the sterile positivism and rigid rational choice approaches that have gained increased popularity even as variance explained belies its efficacy.

One could, for example, revisit and reinvigorate the 1960s and early 1970s version of the societal reaction approach (labelling) by showing how the interaction between an audience and a person engaged in problematic behavior follows the model suggested by Cramer,[23] Marcer, Schempp and Mitchell, and already suggested by Bergson's *Matter and Memory*, but with the addition of an active agent which actively constructs images. It is resonance with interference patterns embedded in the holographic field ("in-formation" field) that a normative image is instantiated and through repetition, reified. In other words, in inattentive modes, the quantum wave function ("cloud of possibilities") that each person is, collapses in a systematic fashion giving static instantiations from the many virtual possibilities. Following labeling theory, it is this instantiation which undergoes further resonance with various social control audiences (criminal justice practitioners) that becomes the "real," now circulating in our societal body of knowledge (noosphere), as a set of core axioms. The notion of secondary deviance indicates how this singular instantiation now becomes the core identity trait for self and others.

Quantum, holographic affirmative nomadology strives to bring philosophy back in. Contrary to Deleuze's and Guattari's (1991) separation of science, art and philosophy, we argue that in doing critical criminology, all three need to be integrated. For them, science strives for clarification in the representation of existing objects; art for expression, percepts and affects; and philosophy for producing concepts responding to problems in being and becoming. An affirmative, ethical approach links the three forms in transformative practices (transpraxis). Paraphrasing Marx, the purpose is not to just theorize, but to change the world. Only by incorporating all three forms in an integrative,

---

23 Cramer's (1986) transactional interpretation, cited as a source by Schempp, Marcer and Mitchell in their model of phase conjugation, has four stages. It assumes all entities are both emitters and absorbers of quantum waves: in the first stage, all entities are the source of quantum waves (Ψ) that spread outward in a forward time in all directions ("offer wave"): the second stage is where some "absorber" takes action on this wave, re-emitting a time reversal "confirmation wave," a "complex conjugate" of Ψ, or $\Psi*$, which "travels in the reverse time direction and arrives back to the source at precisely the instance of emission with an amplitude of $\Psi\Psi*$" (Cramer 1986: 22); the third stage is a "stochastic choice" made by the source of the initial emitting wave which selects one from the many possible actualizations based on the strength of the $\Psi\Psi*$ wave; and the fourth stage is "repetition to completion" – "reinforcing the select transaction repeatedly until the conserved quantities are transferred and the potential quantum event becomes real." The actual instantiation, he informs us, takes place at the emitter. The completed instantiation is his version of the collapse of the wave function. He discounts the play of consciousness. We, on the other hand, suggest a pivotal role of consciousness collapsing the wave function in our model of schema QD (Milovanovic 2014: chapter 4; see also note 1 above). This is in line with the Copenhagen interpretation of quantum mechanics whereby measurement or observation collapses the wave function producing the real from the virtual possibilities that the wave function (as a "cloud of possibilities") reflects. A person in constant process of becoming has many potentials: How is it that we find ourselves in political economy disciplined within a narrow range?

holistic approach, guided but not dictated by a political normativity of becoming can we hope to achieve this aim. Doing philosophy without an understanding of scientific discoveries, such as quantum and holography theory, can only lead us to build edifices on faulty foundations. Doing philosophy and science without art is to devalue the emotionally constituted subject as is suggested in the work of Lyng (2005), Katz (1988, 1999), Denzin (2007), and more recently in the work of cultural criminology (Ferrell *et al* 2008). A normative philosophy, statements on ethics, and guidelines are certainly possible and desirable (Patton 2000, 2010; Milovanovic 2011, 2014). More abstractly, Holland (2011) has suggested a form of "nomad music," a form that is improvisational jazz, as a potential guideline (Deleuze's "image of thought").[24] Other alternative images of thought have been offered: Deleuze has suggested a "jurisprudence"[25] rather than formal rational law; Hardt's (1993) view of Deleuze's work on Nietzsche and Spinoza, is that is suggests an ethic that centers on increasing the capacities in beings affected and having affects by way of active affections and joyful encounters; and Hardt's and Negri's (2009) recent trilogy suggests a striving for a "commonwealth." There are other clear suggestions in the literature incorporating a Deleuze-Guattari driven ontology. A revisionist constitutive criminology (Milovanovic 2014) and cultural criminology that incorporate quantum holographic ontological orientations provide a substantive direction in critical criminology to save us from the despairs of the classical-materialist paradigm and normal science. From a quantum holographically invigorated constitutive theory[26] we are sensitized to nonlinearity and degrees of uncertainty in the co-construction of reality; from cultural criminology (Ferrell *et al* 2008), the dynamic, fluid, reflexive, transgressive, boundary crossing, and visceral nature of everyday problems in becoming; from both, we "re-potentiate" images of thought that are the basis of alternatives.

Conclusion

Doing normal science is at an impasse. We need to rejuvenate, we have argued, or replace it with key findings from quantum and holography theory. Quantum, holographic affirmative nomadology suggests an orientation which

---

24 Improve jazz is, Holland (2011) instructs us, much more like soccer and the game of "Go," than orchestral music, American style football, and chess.
25 Jurisprudence is opposed to formal, universal rights since they attain static form, whereas for the former they are always a subject of invention, such as in case law.
26 Delanda (2006) has well critiqued many constitutive approaches for their statement on social change. A quantum holographic approach, unlike a classic version, offers greater possibilities due the inherent uncertainty in the construction of quanta of information (Gabor's logons), the effects of catalysis, nonlinearity dynamics, and retro-causation, particularly, we argue, due to the shifting matrix values of schema QD which produce modulated frequency waves accessing the holographic field (see note 1).

brings philosophy of science back in, as a key component of reflexively confronting its own emergent principles. This is not an axiomatic approach, for principles are always in process responding to the complexities of life. We are ever in search of asking well-posed questions to well-posed problems. Subsumption practices are reductive of the potentials that we are. We must strive toward the affirmative, transformative forms.

Bibliography

Atmanspacher, H., E. Haven, K. Kitto and D. Raine (eds) (2013) *Quantum Interaction*, New York, NY: Springer.

Bekenstein, J. (2003) 'Information in the Holographic Universe', *Scientific American*, 289 (2): 58–66.

Bergson, H. (2002) [1896] *Matter and Memory*, New York, NY: Zone Books.

Bergson, H. (1996) *Creative Evolution*, London: MacMillan Co.

Bradley, R. (1998) 'Quantum Vacuum Interaction and Psychosocial Organization', in D. Loyle (ed.) *The Evolutionary Outrider*, Westport, CT: Praeger, pp. 117–49.

Bradley, R. (2011) 'Communication of Collective Identity in Secret Social Groups', *Behavioural Sciences of Terrorism and Political Aggression*, 3 (3): 198–224.

Busemeyer, J. and P. Bruza (2014) *Quantum Models of Cognition and Decision*, Cambridge: Cambridge University Press.

Capek, M. (1971) *Bergson and Modern Physics*, New York, NY: Humanities Press.

Cox, G.E., G. Kachergis, G. Recchia and M. Jones (2011) 'Toward a Scalable Holographic Word-Form Representation', *Behaviour Research Methods*, 43 (3): 602–15.

Cramer, J. (1986) 'The Transactional Interpretation of Quantum Mechanics', *Review of Modern Science*, 58: 647–88.

Cramer, J. (2006) 'Reverse Causation and the Transactional Interpretation of Quantum Mechanics', in D. Sheehand (ed.) *Frontiers of Time: Retrocausation-Experiment and Theory*, Melville, NY: AIP Conference Proceedings, vol. 863, pp. 20–26.

Delanda, M. (2002) *Intensive Science and Virtual Philosophy*, New York, NY: Continuum.

Delanda, M. (2006) *A New Philosophy of Society*, London: Continuum.

Deleuze, G. (1989) *Cinema 2: The Time-Image*, Minneapolis, MN: University of Minnesota Press.

Deleuze, G. (1990) *The Logic of Sense*, New York, NY: Columbia University Press.

Deleuze, G. (1994) *Difference and Repetition*, New York, NY: Columbia University Press.

Deleuze, G. and F. Guattari (1987) *A Thousand Plateaus*, Minneapolis, MN: University of Minnesota Press.

Deleuze, G. and F. Guattari (1991) *What is Philosophy?*, New York, NY: Columbia University Press.

Denzin, N. (2007) *On Understanding Emotion*, New Brunswick, NJ: Transaction Publishers.

Eddington, A.S. and J. Jeans (1984) *Quantum Questions: Mystical Writing of the World's Greatest Physicists*, New York, NY: Random House.

Ferrell, J., K. Hayward and J. Young (2008) *Cultural Criminology*, London: Sage.
Gabor, D. (1946) 'Theory of Communication', *Journal of the Institute of Electrical Engineers*, 93: 429–41.
Garfinkel, A. (1981) *Forms of Explanation*, New Haven, CT: Yale University Press.
Greimas, A. (1987) *On Meaning*, Minneapolis, MN: University of Minnesota Press.
Hardt, M. (1993) *Gilles Deleuze*, Minneapolis, MN: University of Minnesota Press
Hardt, M. and A. Negri (2009) *Commonwealth*, Cambridge, MA: Harvard University Press.
Haven, E. and A. Khrennikov (2013) *Quantum Social Science*, Cambridge: Cambridge University Press.
Holland, E. (2011) *Nomad Citizenship*, Minneapolis, MN: University of Minnesota Press.
Jones, M. and D. Mewhort (2007) 'Representing Word Meaning and Order Information in a Composite Holographic Lexicon', *Psychological Review*, 114 (1): 1–37.
Katz, J. (1988) *Seductions of Crime*, New York, NY: Basic Books.
Katz, J. (1999) *How Emotions Work*, Chicago, IL: University of Chicago Press.
Kennedy, M. (1969) 'Beyond Incrimination', *Catalyst*, 5: 1–37.
Lacan, J. (1977) *Écrits*, New York, NY: Norton.
Laszlo, E. (2007) *Science and the Akashic Field*, Rochester, VT: Inner Traditions.
Lefebvre, A. (2008) *Images of Law*, Stanford, CA: Stanford University Press.
Levinas, E. (1998) *Entre Nous: Thinking of the Other*, New York, NY: Columbia University Press.
Lewin, K. (1997) *Resolving Social Conflicts and Field Theory in the Social Sciences*, Washington, DC: American Psychological Association.
Libet, B., E. Wright, B. Feinstein and D. Pearl (1979) 'Subjective Referral of the Timing for a Conscious Sensory Experience', *Brain*, 102: 193–224.
Lyng, S. (ed.) (2005) *Edgework: The Sociology of Risk-Taking*, New York, NY: Routledge.
Marcer, P. and W. Schempp (1997) 'Model of the Neuron Working by Quantum Holography', *Informatica*, 21: 519–34.
Marcer, P. and W. Schempp (1998) 'The Brain as a Conscious System', *International Journal of General Systems*, 27 (1): 231–48.
Marin, J.M. (2009) '"Mysticism" in Quantum Mechanics', *European Journal of Physics*, 30: 807–22.
Massumi, B. (1992) *A User's Guide to Capitalism and Schizophrenia*, Cambridge, MA: MIT Press.
Matza, D. (1969) *Becoming Deviant*, Englewood Cliffs, NJ: Prentice-Hall.
Milovanovic, D. (2003) *Critical Criminology at the Edge*, Monsey, NY: Criminal Justice Press.
Milovanovic, D. (2011) 'Justice Rendering Schemas', *Journal of Theoretical and Philosophical Criminology*, 3 (1): 1–56.
Milovanovic, D. (2013a) 'Quantum Holographic Critical Criminology', *Journal of Theoretical and Philosophical Criminology*, 5 (2): 1–29.
Milovanovic, D. (2013b) 'Postmodernism and Thinking Quantum Holographically', *Journal of Critical Criminology*, 21 (3): 341–57.

Milovanovic, D. (2014) *Quantum Holographic Criminology*, Durham, NC: Carolina Academic Press.

Milovanovic, D. and S. Henry (2001) 'Constitutive Definition of Harm', in S. Henry and M. Lanier (eds) *What is Crime?*, Boulder, CO: Rowman and Littlefield, pp. 165–78.

Mitchell, E. (2008) *Nature's Mind: The Quantum Hologram*, Lake Worth, FL: Institute of Noetic Sciences.

Mitchell, E. and R. Staretz (2011) 'The Quantum Hologram and the Nature of Consciousness', *Journal of Cosmology*, 14: 1–19.

Patton, P. (2000) *Deleuze and the Political*, New York, NY: Routledge.

Patton, P. (2010) *Deleuzian Concepts*, Stanford, CA: Stanford University Press.

Pitowsky, I. (1989) *Quantum Probability-Quantum Logic*, Berlin: Springer-Verlag.

Pribram, K. (1971) *Languages of the Brain*, Monterey, CA: Wadsworth.

Prigogine, I. (1977) *From Being to Becoming*, San Francisco, CA: W.H. Freeman.

Protevi, J. and M. Bonta (2004) *Deleuze and Geophilosophy*, Edinburgh: Edinburgh University Press.

Puthoff, H. (1989) 'Source of Vacuum Electromagnetic Zero-Point Energy', *Physical Review*, 40: 4857–62.

Quinney, R. (1970) *The Social Reality of Crime*, London: Little Brown and Company.

Radin, D. (2013) *Supernormal: Science, Yoga, and the Evidence for Extraordinary Psychic Realities*, New York, NY: Deepak Chopra Books.

Rauscher, E. and R. Targ (2001) 'The Speed of Thought: Investigation of a Complex Space-Time Metric to Describe Psychic Phenomena', *Journal of Scientific Exploration*, 15 (3): 331–54.

Robbins, S. (2006) 'Bergson and the Holographic Theory of Mind', *Phenomenological Cognitive Science*, 5: 365–95.

Robbins, S. (2011) *Time and Memory*, North Charleston, SC: CreatSpace Independent Publishing Platform.

Robbins, S. (2013) *The Mists of Special Relativity: Time; Consciousness and a Deep Illusion in Physics*, North Charleston, SC: CreateSpace Independent Publishing Company.

Robbins, S. (2014) *Collapsing the Singularity*, North Charleston, SC: CreatSpace Independent Publishing Platform.

Salmon, W. (1984) *Scientific Explanation and the Causal Structure of the World*, Princeton, NJ: Princeton University Press.

Schempp, W. (1992) 'Quantum Holography and Neurocomputer Architecture', *Journal of Mathematical Imaging and Vision*, 2: 279–326.

Sheehan, D. (ed.) (2006) *Frontiers of Science: Retrocausation-Experiment and Theory*, AIP Conference Proceedings, vol. 863, Melville, New York, NY.

Steward, I. (2002) *Does God Play Dice?*, Malden, MA: Wiley-Blackwell.

Susskind, L. (1995) 'The World as a Hologram', *Journal of Mathematical Physics*, 36: arxiv:hep-th/9409089.

't Hooft, G. (1993) 'Dimensional Reduction in Quantum Gravity', arxiv:gr-qc/9310026.

von Neumann, J. (1996) [1932] *The Mathematical Foundations of Quantum Mechanics*, Princeton, NJ: Princeton University Press.

Weisburd, D. and A. Piquero (2008) 'How Well do Criminologists Explain Crime?', in M. Tonry (ed.) *Crime and Justice*, Chicago, IL: Chicago University Press, pp. 153–202.

Wendt, A. (2010) 'Flatland: Quantum Mind and the International System of Hologram', in M. Albert, L. Cederman and A. Wendt (eds) *New Systems Theories of World Politics*, London: Palgrave, pp. 279–310.

Wendt, A. (forthcoming, 2015) *Quantum Mind and Social Science*, Cambridge: Cambridge University Press.

Young, J. (2011) *The Criminological Imagination*, Malden, MA: Polity Press.

Chapter 5

Criminology: What is it about?

Raffaele De Giorgi and Luciano Nuzzo

Object: What is it about?[1]

Theories, even those which are apparently more modern and complex, are generally designed, organised and constructed using conceptual architecture which corresponds to a typical construction technique. Let us look at the procedure.

First of all, the object of the theory needs to be determined. *What is it about* exactly? The object justifies the structure of the theory. It requires its own theory. A theory, in fact, is always the theory of an object. Just as an object is always the object of a theory. Law, state, but also more specifically, contracts, property, crime, are all objects of theories. The first step, then, is to determine the object, define its limits, indicate the qualities of its autonomy, the nature of its constituents, its origins, just as we find outlined in the first chapters of all theories. In other words, the *object* must be presented as something which is *objective*. Since an object can be considered as something objective – something for which we can suppose others share the difference – the object must be isolated, differentiated. If it is not different from something else, an object cannot be identified. When it is identified, an object has an identity, that is to say, it is different from everything else. Identity, in fact, is the result of difference. Identity is that which makes the preservation of difference evident regardless of time. So, we can say, without doubt, that the foremost and perhaps only objective characteristic of an object is its identity, which is to say, its difference. An object, though, is not a given of nature. Its identity is not something natural. On the other hand, even something given by nature, for the reason that it may be considered or dealt with as an object of knowledge, must be able to be differentiated. It is not something which bears its own name, and, even if it did, the name would need to be interpreted, deciphered, presented, exposed, pointed out as the name of something that is different from everything else. That which makes an object an object, its identity, is

---

1 The paragraph headings – except for the paragraph entitled '"Was ist der Fall?" und "Was ist steckt dahinter?"' – must be understood as answers to the question, 'What is criminology about?'.

a difference which has to be stated and because it has to be stated it must be constructed. It is impossible to confuse the *what is it about* of one theory with the *what is it about* of another theory. Once construction of identity has begun (Luhmann 1981: 198–227; 1990: 14–30), that is to say, the difference between the object and everything else has been established (Spencer-Brown 1969), the characteristics of the theory which can be best applied to the object can be delimited.

This is the second step. Considering the properties that make up the difference that constitutes the object, or that have been attributed to the object, different theoretical constructions can be considered and the nature of the construction which is most apt for the object can be determined. Thus, the characteristics that allow us to best comprehend the difference which, in turn, identifies the object as an object of knowledge are determined. The theoretical construction is appropriate because it is different from all other theoretical constructions which would not contain the epistemological potential that is suitable for describing the same object for which we intend to construct a theory. In other words, it is the object that requires a theory to be determined and it is the object that makes a theory appropriate for it. Like objects, theories are not a given of nature either. Whether or not knowledge of a particular theory can explain and objectify the object of that theory determines its adequacy, making it so that it can be dealt with legitimately, elaborated upon, presented, shown as knowledge *of the object*. So, the subject of the question of the theory is the object. That which 'What is it about?' refers to is the object. The original question, thus, should be reformulated in this way, 'Object: What is it about?'. The theory reflects its object, in the sense that it is a reflection of the object on itself: the theory gathers within itself and is the result of the activity of reflection that *comes from* the object. This is the only meaning that the expression *adequate theory* can have. It is an obvious question. What is called object is an object from the point of view of the theory, which, from the point of view of the object is the result of the operations of reflection through which the object differentiates its difference. The Pagans were Pagans from the Christians' point of view, who were infidels in the eyes of the Pagans and without whom they could never have represented the prerogative of their faith. Naturally, it is not necessary to start from the beginning each time; that which happens for creation does not occur for theories. Theories are not originated by *ex nihilo sui et subjecti*. Once created, objects already exist. We can, therefore, without doubt consider an object of a theory one which other theories have already determined and we can proceed with its redefinition. It is then delimited in new ways: its boundaries are extended or the very same delimitation is criticised. This creates the conditions for considering other theories inadequate and useless. At the end of the process we arrive at the formulation of a theoretical framework that justifies itself because it is the fruit of the criticism of what has been proved inadequate. In this way the theoretical construction avoids becoming hostage of its object. It is justified through the criticism of other theories. What really occurs, however, is that the new theoretical construction deals with the object – for which it is theory – as a prerequisite, as an outward appearance, as a metaphysical object or a given of nature. This cannot affirm it, however. Not only because it uses already constructed objects but also because, in reality, like a reflection of its object, it is itself an object which has already been constructed.

If our argument is plausible (De Giorgi and Luhmann 1992), it is easy to see that theory is part of the object that it describes. 'Object' and 'theory' imply each other. The theory is a process of reflection of the object, which, acquiring materiality through its theory, is no longer only a semantic construction and becomes an object. Object of theory: 'What?'.

In reality, the fact that the object becomes something objective has the function of concealing the reflective nature of the theory. Precise semantics are established and refined which transform the circularity into opposition. The theory usurps the object because the object opposes the theory. In German, one says *Sachlichkeit*: this refers to the materiality of things. Perhaps, however, *Gegenständlichkeit* is an even better expression that describes the nature of that which opposes, that which is separate, or that which is external. At last the object exists. It has a body. Now we can ask: 'What is it?' (Watzlawick 1981).

Circularity

A theoretical framework talks about its object. It identifies it through the use of meanings attributed to the object. When we point to something as an answer to the question, 'What is it about?', in reality, a meaning is differentiated. A meaning always refers to other possible meanings but because it can serve as a qualifying framework for an object that meaning cannot be questioned within its own application. It must reflect its prerogative and for this reason is self-evident. In reality, in the historical semantics of opposition, theoretical reflection is always at work to make meanings univocal: it establishes them, and defines them as the sole qualifications of objects. Semantics conceals this circularity, making use of this obscuration. The artificial unambiguity of the meaning of the object makes sense only from within the logic of the opposition between theory and the object of the theory.

It seems self-evident that geography is concerned with the conformation of land and that history is concerned with the actions of individuals and communities. It would be useful, though, to recall that the distinction between history and geography was a great development made by Melanchthon as late as the sixteenth century, while the universal history of Orosius or the *Weltchronik* by Otto von Freising did not recognise that distinction at all (Goetz 1958: 36, 111, 258).

The idea of *guilt*, as an object of observation, makes sense – that is to say, it exists – only within the framework of the theology of salvation. Just like *intention* and *will*, as objects of observation, make sense or exist only within the framework of the theory of action. The meanings through which we observe the objectivity of the objects of theories have rich semantic value. They are the result of complex philosophical elaboration, but when they are assumed as references for theoretical constructions, they are isolated because their exclusivity, or their difference, is never questioned. They are considered self-evident. At this point, no one wants to question that theory is concerned with its object, for example, that criminology is concerned with criminality.

Meanings, however, are not only not self-evident but they stem from philosophical traditions which have produced conceptualities that are so well established that they can be considered as self-evident. The concept of *guilt* in penal law, like that of *malice*, for example, is the result of deep theological and philosophical elaboration. The principles of *intention* and *will* derive from typically modern philosophical constructions. The idea of the *subject of action* is a philosophical construction and, this one too, quite recent. The same idea of *action* is the result of a complex semantic evolution and it was only in the nineteenth century that it entered into the dogma of crime: from that moment onward a crime could only be qualified in relation to the idea of action.

A modern law text book could be replaced with whole passages from *Critique of Pure Reason* (Kant 1977a) and *Critique of Practical Reason* (Kant 1977b), or sections from Hobbes or other nineteenth century psychological theories. The modern principle of action – central to the dogma of continental penal law, and to an extent also to the practice of Common Law – has much less to do with the nature of man than with the philosophy of Kant (and also the thought of Hegel). In fact, the conceptual elaboration of that principle originated from the Kantian invention of the subject and its philosophical elaboration which was further developed by Kantian school theorists (von Bübnoff 1966). On the other hand, this is nothing to marvel about: even the idea of nature is treated as natural while we know with certainty that it is a philosophical construction.

All this is true also for the same theoretical constructions: both because they are constructed using processes constructed from resources (philosophical and semantic) which are elaborated outside and separate from their objects, produced in other places and other times of social communication, and because they are reflections of their objects. On the other hand, because they cannot be described as both '*virgins and mothers*', *subject* and *object*, they are justified by nobility of their birth, or for their 'epistemological foundations', as philosophers would say with careful affectation. A justification formulated in this way provides cover for theories as it allows the reality of those foundations to be hidden: if the guise of nobility is removed from them it is easier to see that they are only philosophical assumptions about humans and their world, or society, or good, or evil. Theories, therefore, justify their right to speech by celebrating their collusion with the universal competence of philosophy in shameful silence (Marquard 1981: 4–38).

This way of proceeding from theories has at least three relevant consequences; each one of them repeats the construction framework of the other. It naturally means that each of them reproduces the construction of the others. And, since the difference between the theoretical constructions is justified by the criticism of other theories, each theory considers itself as a higher level construction, more complete, more appropriate and fitting, better developed. In fact, it is common to hear that science develops precisely in this way. In reality, since these theories are developed by using recycled pieces of other theories, that which is called scientific development is nothing more than the accumulation of spare parts; recycling, but of a kind which contaminates the environment by disseminating rusty pieces.

Difference

We need to make yet another consideration. The framework of theoretical knowledge of a phenomenon is said to presume a difference between subject and object, that is, between the subject of knowledge and the object of knowledge. A difference between objecthood. A difference between different ways of being object.

Cognitive activity is, in traditional Western thought, the bridge that joins the subject of knowledge to its object. This presupposes difference. If it is true that the object acquires different characteristics depending on the theory that acknowledges it, or that those characteristics are knowable only through the cognitive activity of theory, it will also be true that difference is a component of the object and without the theory which acknowledges it – from the point of view of the theory – or which determines it through knowledge, it would not exist. But – from the point of view of the object – difference is also a constituent of the theory which, without the object, would not be the subject of knowledge; it would be, as Kant says – and he had some experience regarding these questions – like *a head which may be beautiful but which, unfortunately, has no brain* ('*ein Kopf, der schön sein mag, nur schade! dass er kein Gehirn hat*') (Kant 1982: 336).

If that which constitutes difference is the fact that one part is the other part of the other part, the foundation of the construction – that which makes the difference – cannot be other than the difference. This is the same condition of possibility of difference; it is that which cannot be the object of observation, that which cannot be seen. In fact, this is not a foundation, but it is the unity of difference, the unobservability of that which is not distinct. This is the reason why unity cannot be indicated; the reason why unity will not show itself.

We get closer to the core of the question: modern thought uses and universalises a construction procedure that manipulates social communication *obscuring the unity of difference which thought itself constructs in order to produce that which it employs as reality*. It is a process for constructing reality, or more precisely, a construction process of that which is *employed as reality*. It is exactly that which ill equipped novices to contemporary realism cannot observe and that leads them to transform into metaphysics what Marx opportunely called *vulgäre empiria* (Marx 1956–90: 203–335).

Then there is another process which modern thinking resorts to in order to manipulate social communication. It is a process of violence and exclusion, of the construction of artificiality that can, in turn, become stable and achieve structure. It is the violence that structures of social systems exercise over the unobservability of communication (Luhmann 1984: 148 ff 191 ff) by means of the interruption of its continuity, or by the introduction of numerous and differentiated external temporalities. The invention of the event makes this possible (Koselleck 1979: 144–57).

These are two processes which characterise modern thought. We are concerned with them here because they have produced highly relevant consequences: the first has civilized the social sciences, the second has civilized penal law.

Now, this representation of differences – just like the very same use of differences – is not exclusive to theoretical practice. It is widely practiced in modern society and is part of a semantic heritage that this society has been bequeathed in the form of the social differentiation characterising the society which preceded it, that of *stratification*. Modern society has taken evolutionary advantage of that semantic heritage to produce functional substitutes for the differences which constitute stratified society: the difference between *inferior* and *superior*. *Subject* and *object* are two modern replications of that difference. Cartesian thought taught us to read the modern world through an appeal to that difference. From that point on it established itself, it is dealt with like something objective and has made it possible to pass off a concatenation of other differences which are connected to it as objective: *reason* and *nature*; *order* (of actions) and *disorder* (of society); *rules* and *facts*.

These are differences in which the two constituent parts function as opposites for their own preservation, like complimentary negations. They work to maintain their identity and to endure through time. This mechanism is necessary not only because it renders the unity of their differences invisible, but also because the continual occurrence, its recurrence, its normalisation, renders the two different parts asymmetrical. This asymmetry of the two parts simplifies the world, making it accessible and controllable. One of the parts is considered *superior*, the other *inferior*; the former associated with *privilege*, the other with *exclusion* or *negation*. One must affirm itself, be recognised as *knowledge*, as *truth*, as *good*: the other, on the other hand, must be recognised as that which *resists knowledge*, as the *unknown*, as *falsity*, as *evil*. It is in this way that reason has the privilege of dominating nature, that order is the negation of disorder and that *rules* control *facts*. That the *ought* includes within itself values, goals, good, just, while *being* condenses within it, once again, the *vulgaere empiria*. The chain of differences is long: within it we can find the difference between *rational* and *irrational*, between *legal* and *illegal*, between *conformity* and *deviance*.

Reality

We would not have been so concerned with analysing the structure of difference if that structure did not give rise to consequences that determine the construction of what is used as reality in such a decisive way. Let us take as an example the difference between *conform* and *non-conform*. Observing social behaviour from a scientific point of view, that which should be explained (because it is not self-evident) is: 'How is conforming behaviour possible?' (De Giorgi and Luhmann 1992: 105–68). *Conforming* behaviour means that the offer of meaning that is made through social communication is accepted. Why should *the other* party to the communication accept the meaning that is being offered? Why should he/she be disposed to continue the communication without being motivated to do so? This is the reason why the structure of social communication is supported by the activation of complex technologies that serve to reduce the probability of rejection and to reduce the improbability of conformity. In social communication this form of behaviour cannot be the object of expectation in the same way that acceptance of the communication and its continuation cannot be the object of expectation. Without the support of complex communication technologies, capable of using artificial resources, the structure of expectations actually directed at the acceptance of communication would be extremely insecure because they are continually exposed to disappointment. Expectations of acceptance do not function because they *contain reality* but because someone (or everyone) presumes that others presume that others have the expectation of acceptance or, in other words, conforming behaviour. This complex web of presumptions is the result of the activation of those resources. Social communication has no knowledge of conformity that makes the expectation of the respective action possible. *Threats, force, the sacred, power, rules, money* are all artificial resources that can be used in different ways and with different effects to construct and to generalise about those presumptions.

If we consider the fact that individual perspectives of social communication diverge, and that the simultaneity of divergence manifests itself through communication and can only be addressed through communication, then we can easily see that what is unlikely to occur is *comformity*, not *non-conformity*. Only a *theory of society* that is able to explain what the social technologies are that allow for the production of such limited conformity rates that society presumes to have in order to operate, can be considered a realistic theory of action.

Considering these conditions, the *dominant* place in the difference between *conformity* and *non-conformity* is certainly that of *non-conformity*. Non-conformity is actually the prevailing part of difference. *Non-conformity* is actually the object of expectation. It may not be the value of preference but it is certainly the *real* value from which scientific reflection and the description of society should start. We can say that a certain concern regarding this was already evident in Weber's thoughts (1956: 1–30) and in those of Parsons (1949). Now, in modern society – whose evolution has made divergences of the perspective on action a central concern – the network of artificial resources now constitutes constant support for expectations. This society, indeed, exposes action to a generalised and institutionalised violence, through which it protects, from divergences, the artificialities with which it controls the likely rejection of the offer of meaning and the resistance to its continuation. This society considers that which is *artificial* as *natural*, that which is *contingent* as *necessary*, that which is a *normal object of expectation* as *non-conforming* and that which is an *unlikely object of expectation* (simply because it is a result of complex social technologies) as *conforming*. And since modern society is left to its own devices and the reality with which it continually measures itself is a reality of divergence of representations of reality, the means of constructing what will be used as reality are made ever more complex, ascribing the consequences of non-acceptance (of that which is used as reality) to the outside. Morality can be considered one of those means, together with religion and science. These means are established as structures of social systems once they acquire structure and reach a high level of specification. The law of a modern society is a structure of this type. It has the function of normalising the presumption of conformity.

The law makes use of the difference between *legal* and *illegal*. The codification of these two values or their universalisation, allows us to qualify what occurs as legal or illegal, conform or non-conform (Luhmann 1993a). Both these values are juridical values. They are both ways of the law. They are both ways through which we can see the world. They are legal qualifications, but they are not qualities of the world. They are not a part of the world. They are a part of law. In other words, law is the *unity of their difference*, it is the system that observes and operates via the oscillation between one value and another. Because both values are law, there is no value of preference, the law does not pursue one end which would fulfil its programme. Suffice to say that without violation of the law, the law would cease to operate.

In reality, the law is identified by only one of the two values: *legal*. As a consequence, non-conforming action is not regarded as its other value, but rather as a violation of the law. Given these conditions, the codification of the two values has made the construction of conditional programmes possible which are always activated when action resists acceptance of the offer of meaning and the rejection of the expectation prevails. Law, at that point, recodifies itself as the *law of the practice of law* or as *the law of sanctions* (Binding 1872). This difference makes use of the distinction between conformity and non-conformity for each of its parts. In the first instance it is considered from within the law, as a duality of the forms of the practice of law, or as the right to the law. This is why we talk about *private law* or private individuals' *freedom* (Cesarini Sforza 1963; Giosuè Solari 1959; Stefano Rodotà 1990). In the second case, on the other hand, the same difference is externalised; conformity or non-conformity are considered qualities of action: conformity becomes the positive value while non-conformity is not only a negative value but is considered a negative power, an external force and something outside the law. This value, moralised as a value of rejection, is customarily called *deviance*. The old distinction is replaced with the other, the distinction made by the secondary codification of the law: *conforming* and *deviant*. Deviance is the action whose consequence is punishment. The action is deviant. This means that the *juridical qualification* of action is transformed into a *quality of action*. This act could also be called *criminal action*, because the law defines it as a crime. Concealing the unity of difference, it is possible to forget that the criminal issue is the issue of law: the same story told from a different perspective. Exactly as occurs in José Saramago's splendid narration in *Levantado do Chão* (2014) where the story of the large estate is told as the *story of another people, abandoned and wretched, people who come with the land, people who are not recorded in the contract, dead souls, or perhaps they are still alive.*

Criminology

In an article by Henner Hess and Sebastian Scherer entitled 'Theorie der Kriminalität' (2004: 69–92), a work which has been rewritten various times, but which maintains its topicality and the rare quality of clarity and coherence, the two German criminologists attempt to elaborate a general theory about criminology. The authors affirm that such a theory should explain not only *the rates of criminality but also the criminal acts and the criminalising acts of individuals and – in a radical extension of the role traditionally attributed to a criminologist – it should make all the phenomena that receive (erhalten) their social meaning from the category of crime an object of explanation.* This general theory about criminality should consider, other than the committing of criminal offences, also the prerequisites and the consequences of criminality as an action, starting from the point of view of the law (Rechtssetzung) and including discourse concerning crime and criminality. The authors claim that the *'criminality of society'* is a combination of actors and actions, institutions and movements, social networks and juridical rules, relationships of power and conflict, but also of feelings, fantasies, discourses and stories.

It is difficult to accept a perspective as universal as that of the authors. More than the realm of a theory, one has the impression of dealing with a heterogeneous complexity of elements which we can certainly not attribute as object of a theoretical construction or object of knowledge. The authors must have been aware of this risk as they are quick to point out that what holds together this heterogeneity is the fact that all these elements derive their social meaning from the category of crime. More precisely: all the phenomena that gain their social meaning from crime, constitute the realm of criminality and the confines of this domain of meaning are also the confines of the object of a really general theory of criminality.

Let us move on to the general framework of this theory. The authors claim that social order is made up of actions by individuals to which, however, nature did not give uniformity of behaviour that guarantees a social life, cooperation and security of expectation (as Gehlen already knew). For this reason they must be imposed in the form of social order. Since this order limits the natural freedom of individuals, it is from here that the contradiction between individual and society, which poses a risk to the order itself stems. Another threat to the order is added to this: that of the opposition between dominant and dominated.

The actions that are perceived as threats to order are contrasted with measures of social control, those forces which are concerned with the maintenance of order. The actions that threaten order, depending on the circumstances, can be stigmatised as sin, disease, revolt or as criminality, and their treatment can be carried out by specialised institutions. According to Hess and Scherer, behind the definition of criminality, first and foremost, there is interest in the maintenance or furtherance of existing power relationships. Of particular interest, the two German authors note, is the consideration that contrary to what happens in the case of 'accidents' or 'illness', criminality makes a public debate between *authority* (*Herrschaft*) and *subject* (*Untertan*) possible, while its treatment and elaboration in a legal case – which in the end produces the result that the risk is personalised, that the person is isolated and that their personal revolt is publically repudiated – demonstrates the factuality of power and reinforces its legitimacy.

The power of definition – that can elevate some threatened interests to the category of protected legal rights – is vested in penal law. In virtue of criminal law's power to define (*Mittels dieser Definitionsleistungen*), criminality consists of actions which are perceived as risks to the social order or as an injury to protected legal rights or as a threat to them.

Lastly, the authors distinguish *theoretical criminality* (that defined by penal law) from *true criminality* (shown to be and stigmatised as real in contrast to other instances interpreted as *moral instances* (*moral-unternehmerisch*)) and *formal* and *informal* criminality, depending on whether or not it is concerned with a crime that has been classified by the authorised institutions.

Criminality is action: this point is central to the work of Hess and Scherer. Criminality is action by individual actors. Since extremely heterogeneous forms of action – sexual violence, tax evasion, threats to public safety or theft – can all be classified within the category of criminality, that which unites them is that fact that they are all prohibited under the law and that those who violate the law act with knowledge of the prohibition: action, thus, with the addition of an *ulterior force* (*Mehraufwand*) of a material or immaterial nature, psychic or physical. Lastly, Hess and Scherer write that criminology has the job of concerning itself with actions that fall within the category of criminalisation. Since this categorisation is made by those who act, we can without doubt say that on the basis of the subjective meaning that the actor associates with the action, those actions constitute criminality from the beginning.

About 'about'

The linearity of Hess and Scherer's construction is truly disconcerting. In their general theoretical suppositions regarding criminology there are all the conceptual apparatuses through which penal law constructs what it uses as reality. There is the opposition between law and crime, the exteriorisation of crime in relation to the law, there is the power of the definition of penal law, the individual act, the sense of subjective intent, protected legal rights, social order, the threat to order and the conflict between the individual and society. There is everything. This criminology, then, is nothing more than a reflection of penal law on itself. All the other ingredients, including the finer elements, that are used in the construction of more modern theories of criminology can be added; and Hess and Scherer do this (Baratta 1982): the *criminal career, labelling, social determination, class differences, criminal subcultures*.

Criminology will always be a theory of reflection, a reflective exploit by which penal law tests itself and constructs what it accepts as reality. But there is nothing to turn a theory of the reflection of penal law into an action theory and claim that the prerequisites for its construction can be transformed into the prerequisites for an action theory. The 'criminological' meanings that are considered as the meaning of action are constructions of penal law, not constructions of the subject of action: those meanings are not properties of action, but meanings which belong to penal law. If, on the other hand, they were constructs of non juridical social communication, they would no longer be relevant to penal law.

Criminology: What is it about? It is about penal law. It is a reflective theory of penal law

Yet again, as both criminal lawyers and criminologists recognise, meanings are constructions which have their origins in the power to define penal law. Kelsen (1934) already warned against confusing the juridical definitions of action or event (*Deutungsschema*) with the qualities of action or events of a different nature.

A theory that is concerned with these definitions is a theory of law, not a theory of the object (defined). A theory that has action as its object, is concerned with the determination of the qualities that it regards as qualities of its object. Obviously, these cannot be elucidations of meaning constructed external to the theory.

Criminology: What is it about? It is about the power of penal law to define. It is a theory of definition

If the power to define penal law, and therefore the determination in legal terms of action, derives from the conflict between rulers and those who are subject to the rules, and if this has the function of stabilising power and expressing its force, that which we insist on calling criminology cannot reasonably be considered a theory of criminal action but, rather more correctly, a theory of power. Indeed, as a theory of power, it could describe the ways in which power, as the power to define, constructs its reality.

Criminology: What is it about? It is about power. It is a theory of power

Yet again, if criminal action is defined as such by virtue of a decision – a decision by any one of the jurisdictions of power: political, moral, legal – a theory which makes action its object (in this case a criminological theory) cannot consider itself an action theory, but will be a political theory, or a theory of moral or juridical decision.

Criminology: What is it about? It is about decision. It is a theory of decision

Lastly, if that which characterises action as criminal action is the presence of a subjective sense of intentional violation of the law, and if only by virtue of this characteristic, action becomes the object of criminology, then criminology becomes a rough kind of criminal psychology. This really seems unacceptable.

Criminology: What is about? It is about psychical intentionality

And again: criminal lawyers and criminologists talk about protected legal rights.[2] Who is the observer? Who observes rights and defines them? The powers that be? Judges? Subjects? If rights do not represent natural objects but are, instead, social constructs, exactly who the observer is that observes the objects indicated by their name *protected legal rights* needs to be stated. It can be noted that the observer is penal law. So, we are back at the starting point, that is: criminology as a theory of reflection. In reality, there is more. It is said that protected legal rights are those rights that require legal protection because their violation would constitute a grave injury to society in as much

---

2 See the point made by Knut Amelung, *Rechtsgüterschutz und Schutz der Gesellschaft* (1972), a classic in the history of the dogma of protected legal rights and social damage of crime. The second title of the work is particularly meaningful: *Untersuchungen Inhalt und zum Anwendungsbereich eines Strafrechtsprinzips auf Dogmengeschichtlicher Grundlage. Zugleich ein Beitrag zur Lehre von der 'Sozialschädlichkeit' des Verbrechens* (Research into and Applications of Penal Principles based on Dogmatic Foundations. Contributions to the Doctrine of the Socially Damaging Nature of Crime).

as these rights have an intangible, universal nature integral to social coexistence. Since these protected legal rights cannot all be protected in the same way and at the same time, a hierarchy must be established. The hierarchy is not a given of nature. It is constructed and reconstructed with every juridical decision. It has the function of justifying and making decisional incongruence acceptable.

Criminology: What is it about? It is about congruence of what cannot be congruent

Criminal lawyers and criminologists should answer the question, 'Criminology, what is it about?', by saying: it is the end product of the transformation of a juridical qualification – the attribution of meaning, the accusation of action – into a quality of action, an empirically observable quality of acting understood as a result of a sense of subjective intent. Criminologists in the mould of Hess and Scherer swap the Kantian conditions of possibility of thinking of the action with the action itself; they seem to confound the operations through which penal law constructs what it uses *as* reality, with the reality of reality. They also seem to confound the activity of reflecting a system – the law – onto itself, or the practice through which observers observe themselves in order to differentiate themselves from the world, with a theoretical observation of the world, or a practice with the possibility of producing knowledge about the world. Now we have to interrogate the philosophical background from which criminologists such as Hess and Scherer mobilise the concepts they use.

'Was ist der Fall?' und 'Was ist steckt dahinter?'[3]

Philosophical thought at the end of the eighteenth century and the beginning of the nineteenth century made a significant contribution to the civilisation of penal law. Hobbes' question of order, or, according to Parsons's definition, the problem of how social order is possible, has at last found a coherent response and a modern solution. This solution would have freed the idea of order from medieval ideas of the ontology of the present and the preservation of substance; ideas that had made the representation of social stratification possible, like the form of differentiation that had preserved the world, protecting it from a future of decadence, corruption and damnation. The representation of time changed and the idea of causality was represented by Kant in a new way: 'causality', he says, 'leads to the concept of action, and this to the concept of force and, by way of this, to the concept of substance'. 'Action', he continues, already means 'a relationship between subject and

---

3 This is the title of the last lecture that Niklas Luhmann gave at the University of Bielefeld, on 9 February 1993 (Luhmann 1993b: 245–60). Translated: 'What is the case?' and 'What is behind it?'.

causality with effect'. Substance, which was called *das Zugrundeliegende*, an old Aristotelian idea, is the subject which turns objects into potential objects of knowledge by way of the transcendental action of the intellect and, further, by way of practical action affirms its transcendental freedom. The subject is the substance which is always aware of itself: *I think, therefore I act*. I act means I construct the world of my freedom like the world of freedom of others. By its action, the subject becomes *intelligible reason*: it becomes that from which we begin, or from which movement begins. This movement – yet again, an Aristotelian idea which had already been taken up by Hobbes and Leibniz – has a particular nature: it is, in reality, the preservation of reason, because action is immediately part of reason. It is because of this that action is self initiating, because, like reason, it is removed from time. 'Reason', Kant says, 'has the power to initiate from itself a series of facts'. In another work (De Giorgi 2006: 113), we have described the phenomenology of reason like this: in the realm of reason, action is an idea, like freedom. Reason, as the unconditional condition of every voluntary action does not allow for conditions which precede it in time. Every action, Kant concludes, regardless of the relationship it has with other phenomena, is the immediate effect of the lucid nature of pure reason that functions, therefore, freely, without being dynamically determined within the chain of natural causes of internal and external principles, but antecedent in time. Locating itself beyond time, the causality of acting is a transcendental causality, an immediate causality of reason, a causality through freedom.

Kant described the conditions of possibility of the subject, which, being free, as von Förster would have said (1982, 1985), can at last serve as a reference for the imputation of action. The action must be able to be ascribed to the subject independent of empirical experience on the basis of which it is possible to observe the concatenation of outward causalities of which the action is part.

This action is not an event which opposes the passing of time and its *Vergänglichkeit* (Koselleck 2000) to its transience; this action has no past. It has no time. It is part of the timeless space of reason. This transcendental reduction of action constitutes the Kantian nucleus around which all modern theories of action are developed. In particular, it forms the semantic nucleus around which the Kantian school of penal law – Paul Anselm von Feuerbach (*Revision der Grundsätze und Grundbegriffe des positiven peinlichen Rechts*, Teil I) (1799 [1966]) and many others – reorganised penal law dogma (De Giorgi 1984: 15 ff). It would take von Liszt (e.g. De Giorgi 1984: 23 ff) until the end of the 1830s before, in particular, action was included within the dogma of crime. The question of attribution, on the other hand, with which the school of Hegel was concerned, was clarified by Radbruch (1904) at the end of that century.

Lastly, the distinction between individual and action was established. The individual is the singularity (*das Einzelne*) to which the action may be attributed. This distinction developed the paradox of the rationality of reason. Reason presumes itself as the beginning of action movement. The person becomes visible as subject and the subject as rational through this movement. Successful action is the movement in which reason is preserved and the preservation of reason is also the preservation of the subject, which is the subject of reason. Since every subject aspires to self-preservation, the movement of the action of individuals manifests itself in the self-preservation of society as a result of the correlation of the actions.

Even Weber (1985: 562–65) interpreted action as movement but subjected the causality-rationality of the movement of action to meaningful understanding (*Verstehen*), because it presupposes that the direction of the movement is that of the subjectively intentional sense. In order to observe the act, however, Weber resorts to the artificial regularity of actions and to the objectification of meaning. He externalises reason as socially established rationality. The sense of acts can be observed on the basis of the consensus to comply. The subjective space of instrumental rationality is defined by faith in the fact that the conditions of everyday life (of the individual: *des Einzelnen*) are fundamentally of a rational nature and by faith in their rational function, that is, it conforms to well known and rational rules. We can understand the neurosis of the individual (De Giorgi 1984: 118). We also understand why what we usually call *compliant action* is highly unlikely while what we call *deviant action* is highly probable.

Criminology, as a theory of the reflection of penal law, considers itself as its object. While penal law has made use of empty Kantian formalism to construct a conceptuality that allows it to operate, criminology in the mould of Hess-Scherer exchanges the transcendental idea of action and subject as an empirical reality, while it talks about itself, believing that it talks about objects or things. These are questions of faith.

Conclusion

We were posed a question. The question presumes that in a more or less refined way, with recourse to theoretical references or critics, we would give as our answer a version of the idea that criminology has an object and that this object is deviant action, one of the many variations on the one theme which is eternally repeated: the principle of Hess-Scherer. The ingredients are all there: the subject, action, intention, compliant acts, deviant acts; penal law, social peace, order of actions, the protection of legal rights, the threat to protected legal rights; the power to define penal law, instances of criminalisation, guilt, punishment; labelling, cultures, subcultures; first the crime then the punishment; first the law then the fact; first the blame then the penance.

We were asked a theoretical question. We have taken it seriously; we have described how to construct the objects of theories and how to construct the theories of objects. The question presumed that criminology is a theory which claims to have an object. Subject and object. We have described the circularity of this construction, we have seen how this circularity is interrupted by the distinction of two parts and we have described the function of difference which allows us to construct that which we can use as reality. We have seen that we are dealing with a practice that is widely used and which has the function of obscuring the unity of difference that is constructed. We have also seen that this practice is not innocuous. The function of making unity invisible renders it possible to depict the other as the negation, as the opposition, as a wild exteriority that has to be combatted: evil, disorder, crime. It is represented as that which is outside. Lastly, we have seen the philosophical origins of this representation in the semantics of movement, reason, and that of action. We have discussed the Kantian legacy that transforms transcendental causality into material causality and that turns the conditions of possibility to think of the object into the object itself. Just as language does not permit us to know the reality that it describes, but uses language as its own reality, in this way criminology does not allow us to know the deviant action that it describes, but uses the meanings of penal law as meanings of reality. For this reason, criminology *à la* Hess-Scherer offers no knowledge of reality but reflects penal law, by using, like the the law itself, a rudimentary, recycled conceptuality.

Let us, however, imagine a knowledge of exclusion, that starts with an awareness of the unity of difference that produced it and uses it as a negation of what is included; a knowledge of what is repressed, that begins with the certainty of the unity of difference that produces it and uses it as a negation of that which must emerge; a knowledge of what is renegade that begins with the force of the unity of difference that produces it and uses it as a negation of that which must be imposed as truth; in other words: knowledge that is capable of describing the production of what Hegel called *the spurious infinity* (*die schlechte Unendlichkeit*) as the other part of the production of *compliance* and both parts as the reality of the unity of difference of the constitution of meaning: such knowledge could be said to be part of its object and could be called indifferently a theory of conformism acts and a theory of deviance. With such knowledge, the question, 'What is it about?' would be reformulated as the question that, as we have seen, Niklas Luhmann posed in his final lesson: 'What is behind it?' (*Was steckt dahinter?*) (Luhmann 1993b).

So, as he would have done, *watch from the side lines your own shadow with invisible eyes and smile while the people look, perplexed, at where there is nothing* (Saramago 1987).

Notes

This chapter is for Alessandro De Giorgi, on his fortieth birthday.

Although this chapter is the result of a collaboration between the authors, we can attribute the paragraphs entitled 'Object: What it is about?', 'Circularity', 'Criminology' and 'About "about"' to Raffaele De Giorgi, and the paragraphs entitled 'Difference', 'Reality', '"Was ist der Fall?" und "Was ist steckt dahinter?"' and 'Conclusion' to Luciano Nuzzo.

Bibliography

Amelung, K. (1972) *Rechtsgüterschutz und Schutz der Gesellschaft*, Frankfurt a.M.: Athenaeum Verlag.
Baratta, A. (1982) *Criminologia e critica del diritto penale*, Bologna: Il Mulino.
Binding, K. (1872) *Die Normen und ihre übertretung. Eine Untersuchung ueber die Rechtmessigehandlung und die Arten des Delikts*, Leipzig: Verlag von Wilhelm Engelmann.
Bübnoff, E. v. (1966) *Die Entwicklung des strafrechtlichen Handlungsbegriffes von Feuerbach bis Liszt unter besonderer Berücksichtigung der Hegelschule*, Heidelberg: Carl Winter- Universitaetverlag.
Cesanini Sforza, W. (1963) Il diritto dei privati. Milano: Giuffré.
De Giorgi, R. (1984) *Azione e imputazione. Semantica e critica di un principio nel diritto penale*, Lecce: Milella.
De Giorgi, R. (2006) 'Azione come artefatto', in R. De Giorgi, *Temi di filosofia del diritto*, Lecce: Pensamultimedia.
De Giorgi, R. and N. Luhmann (1992) *Teoria della società*, Milano: Franco Angeli.
Feuerbach, P.A. v. [1799] *Revision der Grundsätze und Grundbegriffe des positiven peinlichen Rechts*, Teil I, Erfurt; (2nd edn, 1966, Aalen).
Förster, H. v. (1982) *Observing Systems*, Seaside, CA: Intersystem Publications.
Förster, H. v. (1985) *Sicht und Eisicht, Versuche zu einer operativen Erkenntnistheorie*, Braunschweig/Wiesbaden: Springer Fachmedien.
Goetz, W. (1958) *Translatio Imperii: ein Beitrag zur Geschichte des Geschichtsdenkens und der politischen Theorien im Mittelalter und der frühen Neunzeit*, Tübingen: Mohr.
Hess, H. and S. Scherer (2004) 'Theorie der Kriminalität', in *Kölner Zeitschrift für Soziologie und Sozialpsychologie*, Sonderheft 43: *Kriminalsoziologie*, herausgegeben von S. Karstedt/D. Oberwittler.
Kant, I. (1977a) *Kritik der reinen Vernunft*, in Kant, I., *Werkausgabe*, III/IV, Frankfurt a.M.: Suhrkamp.
Kant, I. (1977b) *Kritik der praktischen Vernunft. Grundlegung zur Metaphysik der Sitten*, in Kant, I., *Werkausgabe*, VII, Frankfurt a.M.: Suhrkamp.
Kant, I. (1982) 'Die Metaphysik der Sitten, Rechtslehre', in *Kant Werke Ausgabe*, VIII, Hrsg. von Wilhelm Weischedel, Frankfurt a. M.: Suhrkamp.
Kelsen, H. (1934) *Reine Rechtslehre. Einleitung in die rechtswissenschaftliche Problemtik*, Wien: Franz Deuticke Verlag.
Koselleck, R. (1979) *Vergangene Zukunft. Zur Semantik geschchtlicher Zeiten*, Frankfurt a. M.: Suhrkamp.
Koselleck, R. (2000) *Zeitschichten, Studien zur Historik*, Frankfurt a. M.: Suhrkamp.
Luhmann, N. (1981) *'Identitätsgebrauch in selbstsubstitutiven Ordnungen, besonders Gesellschaften'*, in N. Luhmann, *Soziologische Aufklärung 3*, Opladen: Westdeutscher Verlag, pp. 198–227.
Luhmann, N. (1984) *Soziale Systeme. Grundriss einer allgemeinen Theorie*, Frankfurt a. M.: Suhrkamp.
Luhmann, N. (1990) 'Identität – was oder wie?', in N. Luhmann, *Soziologische*

Aufklärung 5: Konstruktivistische Perspektiven, Opladen: Westdeutscher Verlag, pp. 14–30.
Luhmann, N. (1993a) *Das Recht der Gesellschaft*, Frankfurt a.M.: Suhrkamp.
Luhmann, N. (1993b) '"Was ist der Fall?" und "Was ist steckt dahinter?". Die zwei Soziologien und die Gesellschaftstheorie', *Zeitschrift fur Zoziologie*, 22 (4): 245–60.
Marquard, O. (1981) 'Abschied vom Prinzipiellen. Auch eine biografische Einleitung', in O. Marquad, *Abschied vom Prinzipiellen*, Stuttgart: Reclam, pp. 4–38.
Marx, K. (1843) [1956–90] 'Kritik zur Hegelschien Staatrechts (§§ 261-313)', in *Marx-Engels, Werke (MEW) 43 Bde*, Berlin: Karl Dietz Verlag, vol. 1, pp. 203–35.
Parsons, T. (1949) *The Structure of Social Action*, Glencoe, IL: The Free Press.
Radbruch, G. (1904) [2010] *Der Handlungsbegriff in seiner Bedeutung für das Strafrechtssystem. Zugleich ein Beitrag zur Lehre von der rechtswissenschaftlichen Systematik*, Berlin: Kessinger Pub Co.
Rodotà, S. (1990) *Il terribile diritto. Studi sulla proprietà privata*, Bologna: Il Mulino.
Saramago, J. (1987) *O ano de 1993*, Lisboa.
Saramago, J. (2014) [1980] *Levantado do Chão*, Porto: Porto Editoria.
Solari, G. (1959) *Individualismo e diritto privato*, Torino: Giappichelli.
Spencer-Brown, G. (1969) *Laws of Forms*, London: George Allen and Unwin.
Watzlawick, P. (ed.) (1981) *Die erfundene Wirklichkeit*, München: Piper.
Weber, M. (1956) *Wirtschaft und Gesellschaft*, Tübingen: Mohr.
Weber, M. (1985) *Gesammelte Aufsätze zur Wissenschaftslehere*, Tübingen: Hrsg. Von Johannes Winkelman.

Part II
Themes

Chapter 6

Individuals and groups of individuals breaking laws

Anthony Amatrudo

Introduction

This chapter begins by briefly setting out the contemporary understanding of gangs in criminological literature before moving on to suggest that what is missing from that account is any serious technical understanding of the role of action and intention in the understanding of groups. It focuses almost entirely on the philosophical literature, given the focus of this book. In addressing the issues that flow from the existence of gangs, the approach taken has typically used sociological, psychological and economic criteria and neglected insights from contemporary philosophy, legal and political theory. Moreover, the *polluting* influence of funding from the police and a range of government agencies has meant that criminologists have had little incentive to be unduly critical of the basic ontological settlement around gangs. At a time of rapidly falling crime and the gentrification of many of our inner cities, we witness more and more emphasis upon the gang in criminological and social policy literature. The gang is typically seen as a straightforward and obvious association which relates to criminal behaviour, over time, in a set territory and which has certain structural features. The treatment of gangs within the discipline of criminology is not so much wrong so much as it is deficient in that it lacks a connection with more technical writing, drawn primarily from philosophy, but also including legal and political theory, which addresses issues of individual and group agency. When this is done, we see how the entire debate is both opened up to new possibilities, new questions and new understanding. Individuals contribute in varying ways; and that because different individuals are likely to be differently responsible it is preferable that they are held to be differentially responsible. We can see that cases of joint criminal venture inevitably tend to a position which plays down the social fact of individual agency. The widespread use of joint criminal venture seems to offend against commonly held contemporary conceptions of equal treatment and individual treatment. What we have shown is that it is possible to develop a mechanism which allows us to balance the claims of individual and collective action. However, what I hope will become clear is that holding individuals responsible for their actions, as individuals and not as members of a group, is a more straightforward procedure. This is not to deny the action of groups, only that if we say groups are responsible for action, *qua* group, then this would seem to make it far more difficult to detail how individuals are responsible for their actions, *qua* individuals. It may be possible to disaggregate individuals from groups: but better still to focus on individual action, where responsibility is more straightforwardly allocated, than to speculate upon the metaphysics of group responsibility, or guilt. The basic line of reasoning on collective action will throughout follow Michael Bratman's work which maintains that we share an intention to act *only* if:

(1) You and I intend that we *J*;
(2) You and I intend that we *J* in accordance with sufficiently meshing plans;
(3) I intend that we *J* partly because you and I intend so, you intend that we *J* partly because you and I intend so;
(4) It is common knowledge between us that the above conditions apply (Bratman 1999).

Gangs: the recent UK treatment

In terms of how the academic study of the gang views the issue it seems we have not travelled so far from the work of Thrasher back in the 1920s, and it is still characterised by descriptions of loose associations of adolescents 'living on the streets' and enjoying a feral socialisation of bonding through a street-life of conflict and ritual and, surely, crying out for some hearty Durkheimian social regulation (1929). The gang being understood as little more than a rough measure of the levels social disorganisation in a society which is 'itself in a state of economic, political and moral de-regulation' (Sumner 1994: 47). From such beginnings two meta-ideas have established themselves in the study of gangs: on the one hand there are those who focus upon criminality and on the other there are those who take a more appreciative and ethnographically focused stance (Matza and Sykes 1961). What is persistent, to use the title of a recent Home Office study, is that both schools of thought tend to see the issue overwhelmingly in terms of *delinquent youth groups* (Home Office 2006). The entire discussion is almost entirely unconcerned with any serious analysis by way of reference to issue of action and intention set in philosophical terms. This is a major issue at a time when almost any youth, but notably ethnic minority youth, on the streets is liable to be *labelled* a gang member and subject to the fierce *regulatory* powers of the statutory authorities as brilliantly set off by Smithson, Ralphs and Williams (2013).

The recent spate of gang typologies by criminologists seems wilfully to overlook the primacy of criminal action in the criminal law in favour of a descriptive focus upon the social organisation of groups of persons already identified as somehow problematic. Hallsworth and Young set out a three-point typology that sets out peer groups, gangs and organised crime groups (Hallsworth and Young 2004). Gordon sets out a typology of youth movements, youth groups, criminal groups, wannabe groups, street gangs and criminal business organisations (Gordon 2000). Klein and Maxson set out a typology detailing traditional gangs, neo-traditional gangs, compressed gangs, collective gangs and speciality gangs (Klein and Maxson 2006). However, there are many other such typologies all with their own adherents and critiques and attendant academic literature. In university examinations students are often asked to compare and contrast such typologies. The emphasis is upon a list of attributes, not upon criminal action *per se*. I find this treatment intellectually unsatisfying and even, morally, suspect in that it is often focused on working class and ethnic minority youth making them the subject of moral regulation by the state. What I propose is a wholesale shift towards an examination of action, intention and an adoption of criteria for this from the existing philosophical corpus. It is actions that are typically the subject of the criminal law, not existential states or the ontological and cultural status of persons. What this chapter does is to set out a range of philosophical approaches that relate to collective action in order that others can usefully relate them to the applied reasoning typically found in criminology.

Collective action: the central problem

In practical terms this chapter is aimed at re-orienting the contemporary debate concerning gangs and joint criminal venture towards an expanded concern for *individual* action as the basis for legal responsibility and away from straightforwardly reductive collectivist accounts. In so doing it argues that the issue of culpability become much clearer. The law must be centrally concerned with the wilful action of *persons*. The sort of thing I have in mind to take issue with is well-illustrated by the treatment of the war criminals in contemporary scholarship where there is an overemphasis upon the structural situation of the actor as opposed to her or his role in action (Harding 2007).[1] I readily concede that the place that an individual occupies in an organisation, or social group, has implications for their likely actions and that it is obviously important for criminal investigators; also that membership of proscribed organisations may be culpable in itself. The point, however, is surely that culpability *primarily* relates to the actions of individuals, and groups made up of individual actors: it is crucially not a structural or ontological issue. This is true of war criminals, bank robbers, rioters or street gangs. What crucially matters are the actions persons undertake even where there

---

1 Cf. Harding 2007: 247–48. Adolf Eichmann is discussed in relation to his position in a *criminal organisation* (the RSHA Department for Jewish Affairs) rather than his actions and intentions, as such, criminal though they were.

may be common agreement about the nature of the group and its overall intentionality. The person who wields the knife is surely more culpable than the fellow traveller in the gang. Moreover, issues of deliberation, goal setting and intentionality cannot be marginalised when looking at criminal action and criminal actors. In recent years, joint criminal venture prosecutions have risen in the UK. This chapter will set out how best to understand the action of individuals and of groups and it will examine how persons set goals and deliberate. This is important because it is intentional action that persons are responsible for. There is a need to deconstruct many of the taken for granted arguments advanced and to determine what action is in *technical* and philosophical terms. Scholars need to examine carefully what the law does when it applies the labels joint criminal venture and gang activity to the actions of persons. To claim that persons are acting in unison, or with common purpose, is a difficult determination. I do not claim collective action is impossible only that it is always a complex determination.

The important thing to note about collective action is that persons can self-impose constraints upon their own deliberation, that these constraints usually take the form of intentions and goals, and that these self-imposed constraints do convey some normative force. Collective action, then, occurs only when each of a group of individuals accepts the same set of constraints upon their personal deliberation, in order that they are then committed to causing (i.e. bringing about) some element of a common range of collectively acceptable outcomes. This model of deliberation is essentially *individualistic* as each individual person makes their own deliberation. The difference between deliberating on one's individual goals and deliberating on *collective* goals, I argue, is in the sort of goals set. We need to understand that a collective goal always focuses upon the *individual's* moral agency. Throughout the chapter the notion of individual, as opposed to collective, responsibility will be prioritised. Furthermore, it will be presupposed that actions imply a level of *personal* responsibility not reducible to ontological membership.

Any study of *collective action* must note how actions are related to both collective goals and collective reasoning, and must remember that groups are always themselves comprised of individuals. There is no way to ignore this. The issues of legal responsibility, criminal culpability and group membership are to be understood in terms of the way that the law accounts for *collective action*, i.e. where action is deemed unacceptable in law. However, it always has to work with a certain amount of individualism: 'There is no need to speak of degrees of responsibility. All that is required is the minimum voluntariness: that the person could have done otherwise' (Amatrudo 2010). This chapter develops a view which relates culpability and responsibility for *individual* actions cannot be reduced because of a prior, or existing, group membership. Moreover, it upholds that group membership should always be understood in relation to collective action. We should allow that groups may collectively engage in irrational actions, such as crime. Collective action may promote actions which are themselves destructive for the group itself. Indeed, for our purposes groups can, and do, collectively participate in wholly undesirable and immoral action. Bank robbers will rob banks through their collective actions and tyrants can commit genocide. The major assumption I make throughout, of course, is to think of criminal action as a just another form of action. Criminologists need to think of criminals as rational actors making rational, though morally and normatively derived, wrong decisions and often working with others to advance their own ends. What is crucial is that when we settle the issue of collective action, responsibility for action, both individual and collective, becomes a more rational enterprise. In any case it cannot be ascribed straightforwardly it must be arrived at through a rational process of reasoning.

However, whether collective actions are themselves beneficial, or not, is not the point for our purposes. All the same, it is worth looking at the rational choice, namely literature associated with the prisoner's dilemma (PD). List and Petit have recently set out the PD literature in terms of group agency (List and Petit 2011).[2] PD is just one of a number of theoretical games as Skyrms has shown in relation to out the stag hunt[3] in understanding the rise of social co-operation, notably in evolutionary contexts (Skyrms 1996, 2004). PD, of whatever sort, always follows a specific form, in which the dominant strategy is defecting due to the costs of social co-operation. Although we can all cite examples of co-operation that do not require either that the dominant strategy of defection or argue that co-operation is sometimes costly vis-à-vis defection. There are many times when co-operation is the rational and best thing to do even in terms set by rational choice theorists. Outside game theory there is a wide array of socially co-operative models. However, PD should not be overlooked because focusing upon it illustrates two important points. It shows that there are, indeed, instances of genuine collective action even where it seems not always to suit the best interests of all those co-operating. It also shows that individuals who contribute to collective action can justify their actions in terms of the pursuit of certain goals; in other words, that persons can see the *rational* aspect of collective action (McMahon 2001; Hollis 1998). PD games, moreover, have shown outcomes as typically being co-operative outcomes and since PD games are modelling the real-world that individuals have, it supposedly models real-world collective action happening even

2 See also Gauthier 1986, and Medina 2007.
3 In contemporary game theory a stag hunt being a game which describes a conflict between the two competing values: those of safety and social co-operation. It has its roots deep in the eighteenth century and was employed in the work of Rousseau. In short, each player must choose a course of action without the full knowledge of those he is co-operating with, even though to successfully hunt a stag, co-operation is necessary. The player's knowledge is incomplete with regards to others on the stag hunt. An individual may, alone, catch a hare without co-operation but this is worth far less than a stag. The stag hunt is then an important idea, or analogy, employed when thinking about social co-operation. How does one co-operate with imperfect knowledge?

when, arguably, individuals have reasons not to engage in it. This form of co-operation may be puzzling on one level but nonetheless it shows that collective action can occur for a variety of reasons. Collective action, like those which are shown up in PD games, may be justified by individuals in two ways. Individuals can either justify the collective action in its overall terms or in terms of their own contribution to collective action by way of performing a specific task or action.

For now, let us agree that collective action happens and that there is something rational in participating in collective action. Of course, some collective action is not deliberative, as is the case with dancers; but usually collective action is characterised by deliberation. Every individual person involved in collective action must deliberate about how to satisfy the group's goals either collectively and/or individually. Deliberation is the typical case in collective action. Deliberative collective action is the main issue for our purposes: the ways in which a group of individuals comes to analyse a problem and resolve it through co-operative means. If we are to understand gang activity and collective criminal action more generally, this would seem a more fruitful procedure than relying on external attributes and typological demarcation.

The focus should surely be upon deliberative collective action since such a focus is the best way to confirm that we are concentrating upon collective action rather than upon collective behaviour. Action being best understood as forms of behaviour undertaken for a specific reason, i.e. behaviour which is, at the time of the action, rationalised by the individuals performing it. On this reasoning, deliberation is the active consideration relevant for a decision given by the individuals undertaking it. Therefore, it is the case that when, by a deliberative process, a person X decides that the performance of an action x is most in accord with his or her reasons, then X will likely perform action x. In other words, when X performs x, he or she is engaged in *action* rather than behaviour. The rationale for such a position is the acknowledgement that when individuals commit to collective action they do so in terms of collective goals. Of course, collective goals could themselves be pursued deliberatively or non-deliberatively, but since we are concerned with ideas useful to the examination of *culpable* criminal behaviour I shall confine myself deliberative cases.

How do we account for deliberative collective action? There is a metaphysical aspect to this question for it presumes a difference, in kind, between individual and collective action. In problem-solving terms, what is the difference in a problem being solved individually and being solved collectively? For it is surely the case that some sets of action may themselves, in turn, be demarcated as a set of individual actions or a set of collective actions. This metaphysical aspect is furthermore entwined with the description of collective action itself. The metaphysical determination sets out what the collective action is but not what it ought to be, given the existence of a pre-existing collective goal. If we are to examine the normative aspect of collective action, we need to tackle the deliberative aspect of the problem. If, for example, we posit a rational person who, faced with a decision problem, intends to engage in collective action with other individuals. How then *should* such a person's own deliberation reflect his or her intention to undertake collective action? What *should* this person do if he or she intends to act collectively?

Collective action

A theory of collective action needs to provide a rationale for both the metaphysical and normative aspects of the problem. In practice, this means falling into one of two camps: either they will appeal to a *set of individuals*, all of whom act and deliberate on the basis of their own individual state of mind, or they will not. In technical terms, those that do are called reductive theories of collective action and those that do not are called non-reductive theories of collective action: both sorts of theory come in a variety of forms.

Addressing reductive theories

The definition of a reductive theory relates to the claim that every individual acts on the basis of their *own* will, or mental state, and that we can, accordingly, say that all collective actions may, in turn, be *reduced* to a sub-set of individual actions, each enacted by persons in terms of their own will, or mental state. Thereafter, the question arises as to the precise nature of these individual wills, or mental states. Here philosophers are divided as to the extent of the reductive element in accounting for collective action. The point to hold onto is that those who hold to a reductive theory of collective action view it as the sum of a set of individual actions enacted by a sub-set of wills, or mental states. Moreover, if we believe that the actions of individuals can be explained in terms of the various beliefs, desires and intentions of individuals, then a reductive theory would view collective action similarly. The content of the wills, or mental states, that explain individual action also holds for the content of the wills, or mental states, that explain collective action. In other words that individual wills, or mental states, explain both individual and collective action. This reasoning concerning a theory of collective action is typically expressed within rational choice theory, including those that prioritise an analysis informed by game theory, as with Gauthier (1974).

The team preference approach

Of course, a theory of collective action does not have to be fully reductive but which might allow some element of non-reductive reasoning within it. For instance, it would be possible to advance a theory of collective action which although the same sorts of wills, or mental states, are appealed to, their individual content is different; in other words, the theory would not be reductive as to the contents of the individual wills, or mental states, with regard to collective action. The collective appeal would be non-reductive with regard to individual preferences. Preferences are generally understood, notably in rational choice theory, as those things which rationalise both actions and goals. They provide a justificatory element for why some goal or goal is sought. We might say that collective action happens when a group of individuals rationalises their behaviour (i.e. action) according to a collective preference rather than their own individual preference. The recent history of analytical philosophy can furnish many examples of where this has been advanced. This view of collective action is usually termed team preference theory (Bratman 1992). The appeal of team preference theory in explaining collective action is in its appeal to the underlying process of reasoning in understanding collective action.

We-action theories

Anyone accounting for individual action will, however, be more likely to focus upon individual intentions rather than individual preferences, and ask questions relating to the relationship between intentions and the ways they are alert to the underlying reasons that individuals possess. We might argue that a theory of collective action should posit that the individual will or mental state of persons is of less significance than their content, and that such content is understood in terms of intentions and not preferences. In this case, we could understand collective action in terms of a sub-set of individuals all of whom intend a collective action; and not a set of individual actions. The intentions of the group would be on the same basis as that of its individual members. The underlying intentional basis of the group and its individual members would be the same, though the content of individual wills, or mental states, would reflect that the action is collective. This form of reasoning is termed *we-action* theory and it departs from fully reductive theories in regard to the way it understands the content of intentions. A fully reductive theory must necessarily always confine its explanation of collective action to the same form of content it utilises in explaining individual action. This is not the case with *we-action* theory since it builds upon the differentiation of collective and individual actions, with regard to their intentional basis, i.e. their intentional content. In other words, individual actions are formed of persons whose intentions have the content of individual action that collective action is still and collective actions display intentions that have as their content collective action. However, *we-action* theory is still reductive since it understands collective action as reducible to a sub-set of individual, though interrelated, actions. The most well-known *we-action* theory is given by Bratman (1992, 1993).

We-intention theory

As with other reductive theories of collective action, *we-intention* theory holds that all collective actions are enacted by individuals who act in terms of their own will or mental state. *We-intention* theory, however, is concerned with highlighting the difference between wills, or mental states, in collective and individual actions. The emphasis is still firmly upon the will or mental state of individuals involved in action, as with *we-action* theory it underscores that the determination as to whether persons are involved in collective action depends upon the individual intentions they have. However, the specific form of the intention that individuals possess and then act on in collective action is of a different sort from the type of intention that they act on when engaged in individual action. This is where the term *we-intention* comes into play and is contrasted with *I-intentions*. In other words, when a person performs an individual action, he or she is deemed to be acting with *I-intentions* and where a person is engaged upon a collective action, he or she is said to exhibit *we-intentions*. *We-intention* theory of collective action is not fully reductive as it appeals to non-reductive elements in its account. In *we-intention* theory there is a non-reducible determination in terms of collectivity which is in terms of the form of the intention. Collective actions can only be enacted by individuals who hold *we-intentions*, which may not be subsequently reduced to *I-intentions*.

Other types of reductive theory

It would also be possible to uphold a form of reductive theory that appeals to irreducible types of collective intentions and irreducible collective content within such intentions. One could argue that either collective intention or collective content could explain any version of collection action. Moreover, one might posit forms of collective action that might be explained in terms of a combination of differing sorts of irreducible collectivity within wills, or mental states, and some variation, or combination, of intentions and preferences. Such hybrid theories are not generally advocated, though one could foresee ways they could be.

Theories of plural subjects

What is clear is that, with regard to explanatory force, more reductive forms of reasoning are generally preferred to less reductive ones in the contemporary philosophical literature. However, those advocates of a non-reductive theory of collective action maintain that all collective actions require what they term directed normative commitment between the parties to collective action; in other words, that reductive theory fails to account for such directed normative commitment in its account. However, any non-reductive theory of collective action has to explain why reductive theory cannot explain directed normative commitment. One version of a non-reductive theory accepts that the actions are performed by persons with their own individual wills, or mental states, but that the action-applicable wills, or mental states, need not be held by individuals themselves. In other words, that collective action can happen when individuals act at the will or mental state of another. The major exponent of this position is Roth (2004). Alternatively, proponents of a non-reductive theory could maintain that collective action is not performed by individuals at all but rather by a special version of the person, the *plural subject*, and Margaret Gilbert (2006) advances this view. The plural subject is a person and, like any other, can take part in rational action, but plural persons are, importantly, divisible to a sub-set of individuals (all with their own wills or mental states). The plural subject is made up of individuals but not reducible to individuals. Plural subjects are conceived of as independent individuals who act in the same way as individual persons do. Therefore, collective action is said to be performed not by individuals but by plural subjects. It is a theory of collective action. We note a difference between Roth's work with its emphasis upon collective action being performed by individuals and Gilbert's work which holds to a plural subject view. Nonetheless, they are both versions of a non-reductive theory of collective action since they both hold that it is not possible to explain collective action in terms solely based on the basis of individual wills, or mental states. In holding that individuals are able to act on the basis of a will or mental state of another person, Roth opens up the limits of individual and collective agency. It is possible to group Gilbert and Roth together under the banner of a theory of plural subjects, whist conceding that Roth does not actually use terminology of the plural subject. What is important to note is how both Gilbert and Roth deny that collective action is a problem that is straightforwardly reducible to individual agency.

Some remaining theoretical issues

If we want a theory of collective action, leaving aside issues of how reductive or not it is, then it must also be in accord with our common sense understanding of the nature of human behaviour. An example of this might be the composition of collective action where there can be no remainder once the action of individuals is subtracted from the action of the group. This is described technically as the compositionality criteria (Szabo 2008). This reasoning relates entirely to behaviour and not to action *per se* and so does not open up questions regarding collective action. Actions are unavoidably related to individuals and with reasons and, therefore, could prompt questions of non-reductivist theorists if one claimed that collective actions are, in turn, reducible to discrete individual actions. In the plural subject account, collective actions can only be undertaken by plural subjects since the action of any group is not reducible to a sub-set of individuals. Behaviour is a less contentious area as the behaviour compositionality criteria merely states that the behaviour of a group is reducible to the individual behaviour of individuals; or in lay language, that groups always act through the behaviour of individuals.

Throughout, there is an assumption concerning the reasoning, or deliberation, of the individual persons that make up the group; namely, that collective goals necessarily constrain the reasoning, or deliberation, of the individual persons that make up the group, or if you like, the collective. Individuals display behaviour towards the object of some collective goal, or end, and individuals may need to deliberate in regard to how to achieve the collective goal. This is sometimes called the distributive deliberation, and maintains that collective goals need distributed in terms of the deliberation of the individual persons that make up the group, or collective. Another assumption relates to the individual attitudes of the persons that make up the group that performs a given collective action, and that collective goals need to be related to the individual wills or mental states of persons. So that whatever the collective goal is, it must be embedded in the will, or mental state, of the individuals who make up the group. The technical term for this condition is individual possession.

If we take these various assumptions together, we might term them a theory of minimal individualism. Moreover, such a position can be both compatible with both reductive and non-reductive theories of collective action. It is a reasonable position to advance for it asserts only that collectives are only collections of individuals. Even when collective action is not understood as reducible to individual action, one may still argue that collectives, or groups, are nonetheless made up of individuals and, furthermore, that collective goals can be understood in terms of the individual psychology of persons. This falls short of methodological individualism: and Gilbert has an account of collective action that does not breach methodological individualism, although her view is compatible with a more minimal, or thinner, individualism as her account of plural subjects is able to detail how belonging to a plural subject does, indeed, affect an individual's will, or mental state, and that person's deliberation (Gilbert 2004).

A way forward

My suggested theory of collective action is of a reductive *we-action* type. It has a number of important features:

(a) All the individuals who take part in a collective action deliberate with regard to a collective goal.
(b) That the collective goal is not held by a plural subject but by individuals, and therefore has a personal psychological aspect.
(c) Collective goals are understood in terms of the will, or mental state,

possessed individually by each individual in a collective action. Moreover, collective goals substantiate the deliberation of individuals.

(d) When individuals act in pursuit of a collective goal, they are involved in collective action. This point is especially important in determining the criminal responsibility of individuals involved in collective action, as with membership of a criminal group. It settles the issue of the individual criminal responsibility of persons and not some notional construct, such as a plural subject.

Of course, the view I advance relies on the view that collective goals are akin to individual goals. Individual goals being produced by persons through an action able to be performed by an individual; whereas, collective goals are produced by a collective through a sub-set of behaviour performed by a collective. There is a proviso, the own action condition of action. This proviso is typically imposed upon theories of human action and demands that individuals may only intend, or produce, actions which are theirs. So if a collective goal is produced through a sub-set of actions performed by a collective, how may an individual then deliberate, corresponding to a collective goal, and not in that way contravene the own action condition? This depends on the nature of the goals and how we theorise them. If we hold that individual goals are also individual intentions, then things open up. We may understand intentions as having a constraint upon an individual's capacity for deliberation. In other words, it would be irrational for an individual to take any action which would result in an outcome contrary with his or her prior intention. It is also possible to represent any individual goal as an intention to produce either an outcome or an action. Whenever we represent an individual goal as an outcome intention, it must also be in a specified form. Moreover, any intended outcome must accord that the outcome is a direct function of individual agency, not the agency of others, in this case the agency of other individuals in the deliberative process. Collective goals, understood as intentions, are no more than a range of possible outcomes that any collective may generate. The difference being is that individual goals may be set in terms of either action intentions or outcome intentions, but collective goals must always be set in terms of outcome intentions. Collective goals unlike individual goals (which must always be rendered into action intentions) can never be. Collective goals, as with individual intentions, limit the deliberation of individuals in the collective. So when an individual deliberates in accord with a collective goal he or she thereby not only constrains his or her own deliberation but must also have confidence that the other members of the collective not only hold the same collective goal, as the individual, but that they are similarly constrained in their deliberations because of it.

It is essential that for any collective action that all the individual members of the collective deliberates in terms of a commonly held collective goal and that all the individuals perform actions that follow from their deliberation and that the sum of actions produces an intended outcome. Only when all the members of the collective produce an outcome compatible with their collective goal is the constrained individual's collective intention a success. This is important for collective action, for anything short of that, though possibly rationally justified, falls short of our definition of collective action.

Back to crime

We have set out a fairly comprehensive theory of collective action and addressed a range of contemporary scholarship, but how does UK law consider jointly authored crime? How best to understand such things as joint enterprise and common purpose law-breaking in relation to collective action responsibility? The Law Commission Report, *Participating in Crime*, published in 2007 was supposed to be something of a landmark in terms of addressing some of the technical issues surrounding the law relating to multi-person crime. However, it did not tackle the issue of *collective action*, as such, and it did not relate legal practice to current philosophical knowledge or social theory. It surprisingly does not develop the concepts of either collective action or even personal desert in group offending once throughout its 221 pages. In its defence, in Chapter 5 it argues that the technical issues involved in determining collective action ought to make us wary of employing joint criminal venture, and that it may be safer and simpler to look at individual action and responsibility for it: accordingly that there ought to be a radical diminution of the widespread use joint criminal venture prosecutions (Law Commission 2007). In other words, it ducked the difficult task of setting out a clear basis for collective action: though we might approve of the more individualised treatment of criminal responsibility it advocated. During the past eight years more than 4,500 individuals have been prosecuted for murder involving two or more defendants, almost 20 per cent of all homicides, using the catch-all joint enterprise legislation. Many of these cases involve gang-related activity in our inner-cities. To prosecute such a large number of persons without a rigorous account of action is surely something of a scandal.

The neo-Kantian treatment we find in desert theory (which is in any case a legal or at best socio-legal theory, not a criminological one) addresses issues related to personal desert criteria, the assumption is made that *individualised* treatment and proportionality are to be preferred. It has nothing to say about the role of individual agency in group offending cases. Andreas von Hirsch (1976) conceives the issue thus: 'If two offenders convicted of the same offence receive different sentences, is that disparity? That depends on what other similarities and differences there are between the offenders and how these relate to the aims of punishment.' This is arguably acceptable as a normative model of sentencing but as it is removed from any focus on collective action it is of little use when working out how to conceive of responsibility in group offending cases. Desert criteria must give justifying reasons for the form of punishment given to criminals, and also, that desert must relate to *personal* responsibility. Contemporary desert theories are tied to claims about *personal* responsibility. A person must deserve something, for example a punishment, and that is contingent on a minimal level of voluntarism, in terms of an act committed; and the action must be that person's. Punishment and desert must relate to the *individual's* action alone. This is all well and good but does not really address the issue of gangs on the street, nor does it provide any guide in terms of practical policing, though it was never conceived to be. What we are crying out for is a more technical treatment of action, in this case criminal action, before assigning responsibility for it.

Bratman and *Going to New York Together*

I want to end this chapter with the rather playful example of Michael Bratman's *Going to New York Together*, which illustrates his constructivist theory of collective action and which shows off some interesting features (Bratman 1993, 1999). Bratman outlined several prerequisites for shared intentionality. Persons X and Y may be said to be engaged in collective action when the *we-intention* condition is satisfied, they both intend joint action, that any sub-plans mesh and that this is common between the two persons. Bratman's, most famous, example is of two persons (agents) going to New York together (Bratman 1993). He sets out how by intending that one another's sub-plans mesh that both parties to the collective action further intend that the collective action is enabled through the intention of the other agent. Both agents must respect each other's agency, in other words. This enabled Bratman to exclude what are known as Mafia examples where both agents have the intention to go to New York but where one party is subject to coercion or where the agency of the other agent is circumvented in some way, like being placed in the boot of a car. We note here that Bratman's meshing sub-plans idea forbids any Mafia examples since they tend to a notion that the other agent's agency is to be worked against rather than respected and worked with. Moreover, we wish a reasonable, and legitimate, model of collective action, i.e. two agents both engaged in the collective action of going to New York together; but only so long as they both intend this and do so in terms of their own sub-plans meshing; and that this is also common knowledge between them.

This allows us a pretty comprehensive view of collective action, though we must be alive to issues around *we-intention* conditions. Bratman's other agent conditional mediation does not tell us why an individual intends that a group do some, or other, collective action. Bratman states that an intention which is conditional upon another individual acting in a certain fashion does not tell us why they intend some joint action, or actions (Bratman 1999). Although it seems reasonable that there, indeed, must be some intention which persons involved in collective action each possess and which is directed at a collective action, not just individual action. It is disingenuous, however, to say that an individual intention that a group perform some collective action, as it infers that the agent's intentions must necessarily impose a constraint upon the agents to enact the collective action. It is far better to say that the agents each possess individual (i.e. separate) intentions that the collective bring about some outcome. It is better still, and more straightforward, to reason that both agents consent to their deliberations being constrained by the goal the group possesses, and which they intend their actions to be constrained by, that is, the group's goal. This is the best way to interpret the *we-intention* condition; then we have a very robust version of collective action. We will then have a theory that shows agents involved in collective action, reasoning towards a collective goal and constrained in terms of outcome intentions, and we would have accepted the meshing sub-plans condition upon collective action. In terms of the *Going to New York Together* example, the agent's plans do, indeed, mesh since the outcomes are functions of the two agents acting together. There is a deal of difference between an agent locking another in the boot of a car to go to New York and the two agents both choosing to travel by train to New York together. The former being a violation of the collective intention provision and the latter being a fulfilment of it.

However, what if we suppose that the two agents share the exact same sub-set of plans, although they still mesh, do they hold the same collective intention? What if X preferred to take a bus rather than take a train to New York? If this holds, then X and Y would appear to be tied up in other forms of reasoning, though still co-operating. Of course, this sort of thing happens all of the time, for example, when playing various sorts of games, notably card games. Moreover, this example of a preference for this or that mode of transport shows clearly how collective outcomes may be satisfied in a whole variety of ways. There are many ways to travel to New York and this is not really the point; instead, we should focus upon the fact that X and Y agree on a way of getting to New York together. As long as there is agreement between them and providing they both constrain their deliberation in accordance with that, then both parties are involved in collective reasoning. There is no need to explicitly state Bratman's meshing sub-plans condition as it is part of the way we understand the outcomes as following the actions of agents. With regard to the condition that collective action is a product of the individual agency, this requires that each agent is both free to choose the action they perform and that the agency of others is respected. We also need to hold to the common knowledge condition, though it is best understood as a belief of common knowledge, rather than common knowledge. So long as both agents believe that the common knowledge condition is met, then it is. The important point here is that both believe that there is common knowledge and thereby they might hold a common goal. Bratman's main thrust is that any serious theory of collective action must be able to accommodate a variety of possible visits to New York together and also be able to exclude Mafia-type visits as examples of collective action. The rationale I have provided does both: it furnishes examples of genuine collective action, as in a trip to New York (together) and it makes clear why Mafia members fail so to do.

Conclusion

There is a real need for criminologists to address the issues of criminal action and responsibility in gang and group offending cases; drafting intricate typologies and undertaking ethnographies is no use in this task. There is a wealth of philosophical material available ripe for utilisation within criminology. Unless criminologists can say something meaningful *about individuals and groups of individuals breaking laws* in a more robust and technically sophisticated way, they will be doing good, but not very important, work. What I trust I have provided in this chapter are some technical accounts of collective action which cry out to be *applied* in real-world criminological cases.

Bibliography

Amatrudo, A. (2010) 'Being Lucky and Being Deserving and Distribution', *Heythrop Journal*, 51 (1): 658–69.
Bratman, M. (1992) 'Shared Cooperative Activity', *The Philosophical Review*, 101 (2): 327–41.
Bratman, M. (1993) 'Shared Intention', *Ethics*, 104 (1): 97–113.
Bratman, M. (1999) 'I Intend That We J', in *Faces of Intention: Selected Essays on Intention and Agency*, Cambridge: Cambridge University Press, pp. 142–61.
Gauthier, D. (1974) 'Rational Cooperation', *Nous*, 8 (1): 53–65.
Gauthier, D. (1986) *Morals by Agreement*, Oxford: Clarendon Press.
Gilbert, M (2004) 'Scanlon on Promissory Obligation: The Problem of Promisees' Rights', *The Journal of Philosophy*, 101 (2): 83–109.
Gilbert, M. (2006) 'Rationality in Collective Action', *Philosophy of the Social Sciences*, 36 (1): 3–17.
Gordon, R. (2000) 'Criminal business organisations, street gangs and "wanna be" groups: a Vancouver perspective', *Canadian Journal of Criminology and Criminal Justice*, 42 (1): 39–60.
Hallsworth, S. and T. Young (2004) 'Getting real about gangs', *Criminal Justice Matters*, 55 (1): 12–13.
Harding, C. (2007) *Criminal Enterprise: Individuals, Organisations and Criminal Responsibility*, Cullompton: Willan.
Hirsch, A. von (1976) *Doing Justice: the Choice of Punishments*, New York, NY: Wang and Hill.
Hollis, M. (1998) *Trust within Reason*, Cambridge: Cambridge University Press.
Home Office (2006) *Delinquent Youth Groups*, London: Home Office.
Klein, M.W. and C. L. Maxson (2006) *Street Gang Pattern and Policies*, Oxford: Oxford University Press.
Law Commission (2007) *Participating in Crime*, London: Law Commission.

List, C. and P. Pettit (2011) *Group Agency: The Possibility, Design and Status of Corporate Agents*, Oxford: Oxford University Press.

Matza, D. and G.M. Sykes (1961) 'Juvenile delinquency and subterranean values', *American Journal of Sociology*, 41 (6): 887–91.

McMahon, C. (2001) *Collective Rationality and Collective Reasoning*, Cambridge: Cambridge University Press.

Medina, L.F. (2007) *A Unified Theory of Collective Action and Social Change*, Ann Arbor, MI: University of Michigan Press.

Roth, A.S. (2004) 'Shared Agency and Contralateral Commitments', *The Philosophical Review*, 113 (3): 359–410.

Skyrms, B. (1996) *Evolution of the Social Contract*, Cambridge: Cambridge University Press.

Skyrms, B. (2004) *The Stag Hunt and the Evolution of Social Structure*, Cambridge: Cambridge University Press.

Smithson, H., R. Ralphs and P. Williams (2013) 'Used and abused: the problematic usage of gang terminology in the United Kingdom and its implications for ethnic minority youth', *British Journal of Criminology*, 53 (1): 113–28.

Sumner, C. (1994) *The Sociology of Deviance; An Obituary*, Buckingham: Open University Press.

Szabo, Z.G. (2008) 'Structure and conventions', *Philosophical Studies*, 137 (3): 399–408.

Thrasher, F. (1929) *The Gang*, Chicago, IL: University of Chicago Press.

Chapter 7

What is criminology about?
The study of harm, special liberty and pseudo-pacification in late-capitalism's libidinal economy

Steve Hall

Why criminology must break its chains

The non-conservative dimension of criminology is currently dominated by what we can describe loosely as the 'liberal left', the conglomeration of liberal humanism, 'new left' culturalism, identity politics and anarchism that grew in the 1960s as a multifaceted protest against the 'old orders' of conservatism, corporate capitalism, patriarchy, racism and failed state socialism. In the post-war era, liberal-left criminology has been evasive whenever it encounters the discipline's primary aetiological question of, 'why individuals or corporate bodies are willing to risk the infliction of harm on others in order to further their own instrumental or expressive interests' (Hall 2012a: 1). Conservative and classical liberal criminologists are less evasive, but their metatheory rests on the ancient and reductive ontological certainty of the human being as the intrinsically 'fallen' creature, which ignores Fredric Jameson's (1981) reminder that we should always historicise – by which he means periodise – the human condition and our attempts to understand it. On the other side of the divide, today's liberal left celebrates the possibility of radical indeterminacy, the notion that, should actors dissent and choose to act differently, things could always be different: by which they really mean 'better', even though they are normally shy of expressing such moral essentialism.

However, as it slowly dawns on the discipline's liberal-left wing that its core metatheoretical assumption of crime as misguided proto-political dissent expressed by the victimised actor has been a fatal category error (Hall *et al* 2008; Treadwell *et al* 2013), it is too easy for conservative critics to say, with some justification, that liberal-left criminology cannot recognise or explain its own principal objects of harm and crime, or explain why people do such things to each other. This is one reason why Western populations are currently abandoning any faith they might still have in liberal-left politics to 'deliver them from evil' (see Becker 1975), or, in plain secular parlance, prevent the harms caused by the sporadic and systemic crime, violence and corruption that can be found throughout the social structure.

This evasion creates a vacuum into which right-wing contenders flow to offer populist explanations and punitive solutions. When Western crime rates increased in the 1960s and 1970s despite increases in freedom and affluence and the (albeit temporary) truncation of social inequality, doubt was cast on the liberal left's rather tentative causal explanations of relative deprivation and repression. Subsequently, criminology entered its first 'aetiological crisis' (Young 1987). However, the liberal left, hamstrung by its proclivity to sneer at aetiology and marginalise theory in its educational and research programmes, preferring instead to strut its pluralist, deconstructive sophistication and put most of its effort into a long-running critique of punitive social reaction, still seems reluctant to accept the requirement for new ideas relevant to today's circumstances.

The liberal left is now a firmly established paradigm and resistant to new ideas. A clear example of such resistance can be detected in the philosophical kernel of the critical industry that grew around the global popularity of Slovene radical philosopher Slavoj Žižek, who provides us with new conceptions of ideology and subjectivity that are relevant to criminology (Winlow and Hall 2013; Hall 2012a). In this chapter I will present a brief counter-critique of this critical industry, followed by discussions of the emergent criminological concepts of *harm*, *special liberty* and *pseudo-pacification*, and ending with a brief synopsis of the new philosophical framework of *transcendental materialism*, based on the work of Žižek and others. This framework provides a new way of thinking about ideology and subjectivity, based on the subject's fundamental traumatic encounter with the Real and its compulsory solicitation of a coherent symbolic order driven by a pressing need for comprehensibility and coherence (Johnston 2008; Hall 2012b). If combined and developed, these concepts and frameworks could present criminology with a new explanatory perspective.

However, criminology is an importer discipline (Loader and Sparks 2010), and a reluctant one at that, therefore it must wait for new ideas to filter through the more established disciplines of philosophy, social sciences and the humanities. Whereas the conservative and classical liberal wing of the intellectual establishment has continued to act as expected, ignoring all new ideas and continuing to research the most effective ways of bolstering traditional institutions, the liberal-left wing's reaction to Žižek's ideas has been more interesting. It is founded on a concern that the ontological and ethical foundation of his particular form of cultural politics – drawn chiefly from Hegel, Marx and Lacan – discerns essential value in some traditional institutions, such as family, universalist philosophy, executive political power, the state, religion or socialism. For many on the liberal left, seeing any value in these slain dragons would return us to some variant of the old oppressive order and its normative structures such as statism, heteronormativity or patriarchy (see Braidotti 2002). Žižek's Hegelian-Lacanian conception of subjectivity has elicited the utmost concern from the liberal left; the claim that the subject is born in a trauma that makes its unbounded freedom an impossible burden. For Judith Butler, his concept of the originary trauma presupposes that kinship and sociality share a traditional structure:

> What he's doing is consolidating these binaries as absolutely necessary. He's rendering a whole domain of social life that does not fully conform to prevalent gender norms as psychotic and unliveable
> (Butler, cited in Osborne and Segal 1993: 37)

Butler suspects that such a theory of primal trauma is the road back to conservative oppression because it insists that subjectivity must be grounded in traditional kinship and social relations that, for her, are saturated with heteronormative assumptions. She was not the first to join the great collective knee-jerk. Dews (1995) accused him of denying the creative processes of reflexivity and intersubjectivity, although his position changed markedly in later work of more interest to criminology (Dews 2008). Holloway (2002) accused him of reviving a notion of totalising executive political power that we must consign to the dustbin of history because of the death and destruction it caused in the past. Ebert (1999) accused him of masking his actual cynicism with his analysis of cynicism, which throws the damp cloth of 'metacynism' over today's active and incrementally successful reformist identity politics. He has also been accused of a multitude of other sins (for a discussion, see Parker 2004).

Underlying this conception of subjectivity as trauma is the universalist philosophy that Žižek advocates. For the liberal left, such universalism would halt the march of piecemeal progress and return politics to an unwinnable ideological battle. Left liberals fear the return of the 'Law', the Oedipal relation that the child-as-subject must negotiate to enter civilization, the symbolic order that must enter the subject's unconscious if it is to recruit drives and desires to its transcendental ideals and ensure its essential maintenance and reproduction. For Žižek, however, this does not mean the return of traditional elite authority, its ontological certainty and its repressive system of control and punishment, but it does mean the return of symbolic reconstruction as the ultimate end of initial deconstruction and dissent. It is also dawning on some other thinkers that symbolic reconstruction and the return of the collective super-ego might be the essential prerequisites for the eventual downsizing of the repressive control system (Stiegler 2009; Crogan 2010).

Criticism of the symbolic reconstruction and unifying politics advocated by Žižek and other contemporary European thinkers has cooled off since the financial crisis in 2008 and the failure of the ensuing worldwide protests to coalesce into a political movement offering a genuine alternative. For some, as neoliberalism ploughs its destructive furrow with renewed conviction in the immediate wake of one of its most catastrophic failures (see Mirowski 2013), as recession, socio-economic austerity, relentless exploitation of cheap, expendable labour and the upward flood of wealth towards the neoliberal elite create precarious lives and increase fear and insecurity, yet no coherent oppositional politics can get off the ground, Žižek's cynicism is begrudgingly accepted (see Winlow and Hall 2013). Others, liberals and conservatives alike, conform to tradition and accentuate the positive – progress made in human rights and personal freedom, technological developments and so on. Criminology is stuck in a rather odd position across this divide between pessimism and optimism. The much-vaunted statistical crime decline in the West since the mid-1990s has nudged the discipline over onto the optimistic side almost by default. Conservatives and classical liberals are obviously celebrating the statistical decline as evidence that capitalism and its attendant institutions are back on track. However, whilst the liberal left remain circumspect and divided, established liberals such as Pinker (2012) also celebrate the statistical decline because they suspect it must be a result of a new fairness, sociability and gentleness as the people's rainbow alliance of piecemeal cultural struggles against the system's traditional iniquity bears fruit.

The recent statistical crime decline, although now coming under increasing critical scrutiny (see Parker 2008), has reinforced the notion that new ideas are not really required at the moment. Criminology's aetiological negligence is the result of both too much optimism from the liberal left, for which the crime decline is real and a gift from good people, and too much pessimism from the neoliberal right, for which it is a gift from the good state working effectively against bad people. The result is that the excellent criminological research currently in train is being starved of new ideas in its two primary dimensions: first, new trends in harm and innovative criminality, and, second, philosophy and theory, where conceptual tools needed to investigate the political, economic and psycho-cultural contexts underneath these trends can be created. For instance – just to refer to a small few selected from a large body – penetrative new ideas such as the 'depressive hedonia' and 'soft narcosis' (see Fisher 2009) currently pervading youth culture and driving young people into social and political withdrawal, all-purpose scavenging and soft criminality; 'post-politics' (Mouffe 2000); the 'crime-consumer couplet' (see Passavant 2005); the new 'super-ego injunction to enjoy' (see Žižek 2008); and the 'libidinal economy' (see Stiegler 2011), all of which depoliticise and desubjectivise young people, have been ignored by most criminologists.

Systematically ignoring this large body of new ideas and chaining ourselves to politico-philosophical concepts from the dawn of the 'new left' in the 1960s – such as 'moral economy', 'moral panic', 'imaginary solutions' and so on – allows criminologists to keep on conjuring up increasingly far-fetched notions drawn from the principle that crimes are misguided proto-political actions (see Taylor *et al* 1973). Thus we get the unlikely claim that the English consumer riots of 2011 were 'preconsciously' political (Akram 2014) because political urges are stored in the *habitus* of today's young people; we do not see them articulated or practiced, but they are there all the same.

Akram, however, entirely misunderstands Bourdieu, for whom *habitus* is an internalised guide to the *dominant* external logic of practice (Bourdieu 1990), and as such the most difficult aspect of the human psyche for reflexive thought to penetrate, not an internal source of oppositional pre-political impulses to be stirred into action at the first sight of unfairness (Hall 2012a). This convenient misunderstanding allowed Akram to fabricate this concept even as politics palpably failed to reassert itself in the midst of the most serious global economic crisis since 1929 and its destructive social fallout, and even as the absorption of potentially political young people into the depoliticising surrogate social order of consumer culture was painfully obvious (Treadwell *et al* 2013; Winlow and Hall 2012). The liberal left had no answer to why these young people chose to do harm to each other and their environment rather than engage in articulate politics, which again allowed the right to press their case for individual 'evil' disconnected from its underlying economic, social and cultural contexts.

Harm and the politics of aetiological revival

There is no consensual understanding of harm in criminology, but in a post-war era characterised by the increasing dominance of interpretivism and relativism, the ambition that this can be arrived at was somewhat marginalised. Criminology must return this debate to the centre of criminological education and research. The first step is to decentre legal definitions of crime and centralise a serious debate on harm. This will not be easy. The political philosophy behind each criminological faction prefers to depict the identity-group it represents as the innocent and oppressed victim. The two big players have the loudest voices; conservatives will resist definitions of business activity as harmful, whilst left liberals will resist definitions of drug taking or petty property crime as harmful. Libertarians will argue that our entitlement to define anything as harmful should be pruned as vigorously as possible. Relativists and constructivists acknowledge the existence of a core of consensual harms, but they tend to reduce this category to 'brutal violence' (see Henry and Milovanovic 1996). This definition is both too nebulous and too restrictive, the product of a resolute reluctance to open up a debate at the centre of the discipline. Such reluctance is the product of left liberalism's all-encompassing fear of what to them is the only real perpetrator of harm, the oppressive state bearing down on free individuals on behalf of the traditional normative order, and the concern that any expansion of the category of consensual harm, or indeed any prominent debate on the issue, will justify the equivalent expansion of modes of 'governmentality' (see for instance Ericson 2006).

However, perhaps a better first principle is that irrational fear from any political or cultural position should not rule criminological thought – everyday people's fear of overwhelming criminality, conservatives' fear of the 'working class mob', liberals' fear of the state and normative orders, or whatever – and it is wrong to attempt to close down the debate; wrong for the integrity of the criminological discipline and wrong for future generations who might want the opportunity to make their own decisions in the specific historical circumstances in which they find themselves. Harm cannot be limited to brutal acts of physical violence because it is an expansive and variegated category that contains an assortment of acts and experiential consequences. We will investigate this issue later as we encounter the concept of the *pseudo-pacification process* and consider the possibility that the culturally expansive and economically functional sublimation of harm from its raw form of brutal violence should be criminology's central concern.

Behind this intellectual evasion is the powerful post-war current of *political catastrophism*. We still live in the shadow of Stalinism and Nazism, the abhorrent products of Schmitt's (1985; see also Agamben 2005) 'state of exception', the self-conferred entitlement to suspend human rights in order to purify the social body and establish authoritarian political regimes. Agamben's *homo sacer* is the subject of the state of exception, an expendable individual victim who is neither murdered nor sacrificed, but cast outside all legal and normative categories to be killed with impunity. This historical abyss disturbed the liberal-left sensibility to such an extent that it attempted to dismantle collective politics outright in order to eliminate all risk of the return of institutionalised genocide (Jacoby 2005). To a large extent it succeeded in its mission, thus we now exist in an unprecedented era of *post-politics*, a self-induced political paralysis. Unfortunately, however, the continuation of war and genocide across the world and current signs of the return of the far right in the industrialised West suggest that this tactic did not achieve its goal (Hall 2012c; Winlow and Hall 2013).

Political catastrophism was over-extended (Žižek 2001). A large number of recent social scientific texts begin with grim warnings against totalitarianism followed by a brief genuflection to Foucault on 'biopower' and 'governmentality', then they proceed to place things like government healthcare warnings in the same category as gang violence, as discursive objects constructed to raise public concern, whip up 'moral panics' and increase state power over the individual (see for instance, Matthews 2014). However, this overextended reaction also helped neoliberals to destroy the credibility of the social-democratic regulatory framework, which allowed their philosophical mentors, the fanatical libertarian anarcho-capitalist right, to return from exile to the centre of politics and culture (Harvey 2007). Once established there they completed with ease the destructive task of crushing conservatism, communism, socialism and social democracy alike to unleash the forces of the neoliberal market upon us all. Now we find ourselves in a world of totalitarian neoliberalism, administered by a corporate oligarchy and plagued by widening social inequality, jobless financial growth, the economic marginalisation of youth, proliferating urban slums, ethnic and geopolitical tensions and the normalisation of global criminal markets. We also face the return of reactionary protectionism and an upsurge of resolute nationalism, ethnocentrism and racism.

In short, the traditional socialist left quit whilst the liberal left survived by acting as the reluctant under-labourer to the neoliberal right (Dean 2009). Now, as the tenured job fades from view and social welfare comes under concerted attack, the sole immediate solution to harm and crime is the security state, precisely what liberals wanted to avoid. In the absence of a feasible political alternative, harm, crime and their complex probabilistic aetiology are downplayed and customised to fit the only solutions on offer; from the liberal left a downsized and humanised criminal justice system embedded in a comprehensive welfare system, and from the neoliberal right a more efficient criminal justice system embedded in a downsized welfare system and a wealth-creating deregulated capitalist economy. This means, of course, that the 'problem' is being defined by the approved solutions, which both rest on the fundamental fallacy that harm and crime are, indeed, aberrant problems rather than, as we shall see later, the consequences of practicing normality in a specific way. The displacement of honest and penetrative criminological debate on aetiology is diverting attention from the reality that political intervention in the socio-economic field of a far more fundamental type is required if the criminogenic conditions of late capitalism are to be addressed (Currie 2010).

The culturo-political fragmentation of the left and the dominance of hardline social constructionism and relativism in its intellectual discourse have together led us into the impenetrable fog of *symbolic inefficiency*, which has infused not only criminology and social science but also politics and popular culture (Winlow and Hall 2013). Pulled along in the wake of Derrida and the cult of deconstruction, we find ourselves no longer able to establish meaning except for the short time required to deconstruct and destroy it. Embracing anti-statism, dissidence and subversion with no political purpose, the liberal left has permanently suspended any chance that real interventionist politics might return. Social movements come and go with little lasting effect apart from the entry of various cultural identity-groups into the system's interpersonal competition, whilst the precariat (see Standing 2011) grows, criminal activity mutates and the security state expands in the vacuum created by the withdrawal of substantial democratic forms of political intervention.

Subjectivity and special liberty

Whilst the liberal-left's 'critical criminology' faction pumps away with its traditional critique of state and corporate harms, it ignores the vitally important *cultural currents, individuals and forms of subjectivity* behind these harms. To broaden and deepen our view, we might want to consider the concept of *special liberty* (Hall 2012a). This cultural norm operates as a form of subjective permission to allow business operators to inflict multiple harms of varying magnitude on human beings and their environments, and as they do so justify their actions by defining themselves as essential to the continuation of progress and prosperity. However, this normative mentality is not restricted to a structural elite class; special liberty is a general cultural current. Since deindustrialisation, legitimate and illegitimate markets have expanded to attract numerous individuals, thus the permission and the inclination to risk inflicting harm on others – to simply 'get things done' in order that the competitive logic of business can be served – operates throughout the social structure, from corporate boardrooms to ghettoes. To the subject of special liberty, who regards himself as a miniaturised sovereign state, the everyday 'other' individual is a sublimated variant of *homo sacer*, a worthless unit not necessarily to be killed – although in extreme cases this does happen – but to be exploited with impunity in order to serve the logic of the market and the enrichment of the Master.

Harms are not restricted to the material dimension expressed in the standard culturo-legal terms 'person and property'. They can also be found in the environmental, financial/economic, social, cultural, emotional and psychological realms. To make intellectual and political progress in the midst of such diversity, and to offer philosophical aid to sub-disciplines such as green criminology and feminist criminology, which are attempting to address specific dimensions of harm, we could revisit the Hegelian notion of *social recognition* as a first step in an attempt to ground and unify harm as a working category (Yar 2012). The ethical demand that all those who act in the world should recognise the rights and empathise with the fundamental needs and emotional sensibilities of others is the foundation of this position. Although needs are multi-dimensional, for Honneth (1996) they can be reduced to the categories of material survival, love, rights and esteem.

However, first we must overcome a considerable obstacle thrown up by the reality of life in late capitalism. We can no longer use Hegel's formulation in its original form because in late capitalism's socio-economic order the social interdependency on which social recognition between the Master and Slave depends has been severed. As automated production and deregulated finance dominate the global economy, and the return on capital now exceeds the rate of growth in the real economy expressed in output and wages (Piketty 2014), the global oligarchy can simply dispense with the services of an increasing number of people and leave them to their own devices. Most of the Slaves, even those who hold on to precarious service work, are technically redundant, therefore the Master's recognition of the Slave and his need for the Slave's work, approval and consent are no longer compulsory. The organic relational and reciprocal source of the Slave's political power has receded into the past. The Master is now entitled to special liberty by default, which in turn enables and justifies narcissistic self-affirmation and the reduction of social recognition to an arbitrary choice.

As organic socio-economic interdependency unravels, the security state expands to enforce pacification, and seductive mass media and consumer culture recruit the subject to its fantasised surrogate social world, the Master finds himself under little pressure to respond to dwindling judgements and protests about multiple harms. The Slave, deprived of organic relational interdependency and class solidarity, finds that mimicry of the Master's business practices in brutal subterranean environments is one of the most reliable ways to guarantee material and symbolic survival. We cannot restore social recognition if we assume that a genuine democratic politics that can rearrange core socio-economic relations has even a partial existence in today's world. Criminology's recognition of harm and its grounding in post-politics and severed socio-economic relations can not only move the discipline forward but increase its political potency.

The pseudo-pacification process: how we made friends with special liberty and harm

In the liberal-capitalist system harm is not an aberration, a set of multiple hazards and problematic consequences to be obviated by minor policy tweaks. It is integrated in the system's dynamic core and reproduced in its conventional culture and subjectivity. Throughout its history, capitalism has not been a civilizing process but a *pseudo-pacification process* (Hall 2007, 2012a, 2014). Across the course of the capitalist project in the West, there has been a marked shift in the normality of harms. After the fall of the Roman Empire in Europe the social order was governed in the final instance by intimidation and physical violence (Tilly 1985), which also operated unofficially in a similar vein at the core of a criminal shadow-economy dominated by successful brigands (Hibbert 2003). However, in England, after the Norman invasion, proto-capitalists taking advantage of the Norman warlords' lax estate management noticed that a market economy can flourish when property rights are protected by reducing both violent governance and violent brigandage. They also noticed that the diametric opposite, socio-economic peace maintained by the cultural norms of ethico-legal regulation, altruism and sociability, also hampered the market's expansion. Proto-capitalists emerging amongst the rich peasant and merchant classes attempted successfully to arrange a 'third space' of 'orderly disorder', adjusting politics and law to reduce both physical violence and traditional ethics to create a *pseudo-pacified* social environment conducive to the rise of aggressive yet non-violent socio-symbolic competition and economic exploitation.

A politico-legal and culturo-economic environment of atomised individualism, exploitative business practice and aggressive socio-symbolic competition, in which success was signified by gentrification and conspicuous consumption, allowed the more brutal forms of physical violence that had permeated crime, governance and punishment to be reduced. Other European regions followed suit later in order to expand their own market economies, which, despite an earlier start in the Mediterranean region, had been hampered by violent brigandage and governance up to the sixteenth century. The United States found the conversion of physical aggression into sublimated socio-symbolic competition a little more difficult to achieve in its condensed period of economic development from the early nineteenth century. Its homicide rates undulated quite markedly and failed to reach the very low rates achieved in Europe.

From the twelfth century in England, cultural life was highly individualised. The main impetus came from legal change as the laws of primogeniture and entail, which applied only to the Feudal elite in Europe, were introduced throughout the social structure (Macfarlane 1981). All siblings apart from the eldest were effectively dispossessed, a traumatic experience which gave them little choice but to establish outside the family and community some sort of business operation upon which they could attempt to build some security and continuity back into their lives. The criminogenic cult of special liberty established itself in the desperate need to overcome obstacles. The family and community lost their places as the main economic and protective units. Insecure yet ambitious individuals were dispersed into the market economy just as cells split as the motor of organic growth. Early capitalism was a sort of socio-economic tumour, virulent and difficult to control (Hall 2012a). Newly dispersed and isolated individuals were compelled to adjust as subjects to competitive life in the nascent market economy, dependency on which was the primary factor that defines the epochal shift from feudalism to capitalism (Meiksins Wood 2002).

The growth of markets, and the normalisation of conspicuous consumption as the cultural means of anchoring social signification and subjective desire to the economy, coincided with the decline of homicide and violent brigandage. However, this decline correlated with a rise in property crime, fraud and associated forms of non-violent criminality. Increasing wealth was accompanied by declining honour, generosity and egalitarianism. Ethical values were displaced from the centre of socio-economic life and removed to the boundary to act as ascetic restraining mechanisms for the containment of the sublimated vices – greed, exploitation, deception, usury and socio-symbolic aggression – that had been installed as dynamic forces at the core. In this context pacification was neither a product nor a cause of civilized values but a functional condition propagated to allow the expansion of aggressive yet non-violent forms of economically functional socio-symbolic competition. Consequential harms became collateral damage, unwelcome but necessary. This is the rudimentary shape of the *pseudo-pacification process* (for more detail, see Hall 2007, 2012a, 2014).

This process reduced violent crime and harm but created a probabilistic environment in which non-violent crimes and a greater variety of harms were likely to proliferate. Analysis of the process requires a conception of modernist market-fixated subjectivity as dualistic, motivated primarily by methodically elicited yet ideologically disavowed aggressive drives, the collective of the 'obscene Real' and its stupid pleasures (Žižek 2008), which are pacified by internalised cultural codes and external means of control. However, these codes are dualistic insofar as they do not simply repress or eliminate but also stimulate and convert aggressive drives. This culturo-economic invasion and configuration of the chaotic, undirected drives at the core of subjectivity severed the connection between desire and the transcendental ideals that can attract and motivate the active social subject. Pacification, sociability and political participation thus became overly dependent on the constant gratification of drives and desires orientated to socio-symbolic competition.

Contra the Weberian liberal discourse on reflexivity and ethical constitutionalism, the reality is that most individuals in the capitalist continuum abandoned ethics and transformative rebellion for the sake of adaptation to capitalism's brutal yet rewarding interpersonal competition. Ethical realism and its politics were rejected in favour of pure pragmatism attended by the multiple gestures of ethical idealism manifested in fake 'sentimentalism' and 'benevolentism' (Eagleton 2009). In such a cynical epoch, the internalised consumerist envy – publically disavowed to be experienced privately as enjoyment – that energises the capitalist project, and the special liberty and exploitation it continues to sanction, is celebrated by the liberal right and criticised only sporadically and lightly by the liberal left, least of all by 'radical' criminologists who cling desperately to outdated notions such as the 'moral economy'. Deep critique of consumer culture and subjectivity seemed to be the preserve of an unholy alliance of now extinct conservatives and socialists. The likelihood that much economic and expressive criminality is the outcome of the twin desires to constantly gratify obscene drives that cannot be gratified, and simultaneously avoid the mundane labour and social obligations that once structured the lives of everyday people, is currently escaping us. Contributing by default of silence to the ideology that disavows these obscene drives, left-liberal criminological theorists cannot connect agency to structure or explain the motivations behind most forms of crime. On the other hand, by positing the 'malady of infinite aspiration' as a timeless and natural latent force, conservative control theorists along with traditional Durkheimians and Mertonians reproduce the fallacy that both protects the economic system and its subjects' exploitative activities and justifies the expansion of the control apparatus.

Elias's (1994) theory of the 'civilizing process' joins the criminological canon in ignoring the systematic promotion of sublimated rule-bound aggression in business and socio-symbolic life. There has never been a 'civilizing process'. Neither has there ever been a Foucauldian disciplinary regime of 'biopower' normalising the population and producing discursive subjectivity, rather, a system of regulatory practices sanctioned and reproduced *by the population itself* to control the socially and environmentally harmful overflow from the sublimely aggressive subjectivity they also sanction and reproduce. Sublimated aggression is cultural fuel required for the economic development and prosperity that the majority wanted and for which they continue to sacrifice their subjective freedom and tolerate an inherently criminogenic environment. This is the still the situation today; the normalised and fully sanctioned presence of sublimated aggression at the centre of cultural and socio-economic life, practiced every day by sublimely competitive individuals throughout the social structure and across the political divide, makes ideology's reproductive job rather easy.

Transcendental materialism

Perhaps, then, it is time for criminology and social science in general to consider the importation of a new philosophical perspective that rests on a combination of revived and innovative concepts. The upshot of this position is that capitalism has temporarily captured the majority of Western individuals at the deep psychological level of drive and desire as subjects of its ideology. All idealist theories based primarily on false consciousness, hegemony, language, symbolic interaction, discourse, interpretivism and ethical constitutionalism thus fail. The theory of pseudo-pacification can draw upon *transcendental materialism* to provide ontological foundations for its criminological argument that the fundamental purpose of this capture is to simultaneously stimulate and pacify the subject's drives in such a way that they obviate any form of collectivism and fuel consumer culture and economic expansion. This requires a reassessment of the mediatory relationship between biology, culture and ideology. The simplified upshot is that human drives are not hard-wired 'instincts' mechanistically attuned to survival and triggered by environmental phenomena, but, as the latest neuroscience suggests, activated by an assortment of sophisticated emotions (see Damasio 2003) that constitute an interface between weak, indeterminate instincts and the external realm of symbols and ideology (Johnston 2008; Malabou and Johnston 2013).

The trace of the experience of extreme abuse and neglect in early childhood can be etched firmly in the neurological system, which partially explains the motivations behind most of the relatively small amount of extreme and methodical violent crime (Bollas 1995), but most crime is committed by those who have not experienced such extreme terror. Some family regimes are excessively brutal, but the majority are merely tough, and some can combine tough discipline with care. Most forms of family socialisation are preparation for the individual's future life in capitalism's competitive individualist culture. Mainstream culture and its institutions work on behalf of the pseudo-pacification process to socialise tough individual competitors willing to play by the rules. Here we can see the rough initial shape of a conception of subjectivity and harm that is both scalar and formal: capitalism seeks ideal-type subjects willing to do harm to others as they pursue the commodifiable types of self-interest that fuel economic expansion, but the ideal-type harm is also scaled down to stop short of direct physical violence.

To justify the perpetration of activities that are harmful or potentially harmful to others – harms that range across a complex spectrum from loss of livelihood and diminution of status to physical intimidation and violence – the individual must enter a scalar mode of *dissociation* (Stein 2007; Sullivan 1953), a subjectivity that seeks to by-pass social language, morality and social obligations to *simply act* in accordance with drives and desires orientated to success in the socio-symbolic competition (see also Stiegler 2009). Dissociation allows the individual subject to imagine a personalised *state of exception*, granting himself *special liberty* to attempt – compulsively yet always unsuccessfully – to gratify the desires that connect drives to external objects and can range the norm of pseudo-pacified socio-symbolic ambition to the extremity of irrational hatred and prejudice. The ruthless businessman, the neighbourhood bully and the serial killer all operate with *scalar* rather than *qualitative* variations of special liberty. Freedom, of course, has nothing to do with special liberty, but exists beyond an initial escape from its underlying drives and desires.

Therefore, what separates the ruthless businessman from the serial killer is little more than a scalar variation in drives, desires and willingness to conform to the system's rules. The subject of special liberty, driven by consumer capitalism's obscene Real of envious and competitive drives, can operate throughout the social structure, from ghettoes to corporate boardrooms and governmental corridors of power. Liberal capitalism has never attempted to either 'liberate' or 'control' subjects, but to create and reproduce a third space created by the dynamic tension between both. Many would agree that the fostering of genuinely civilized emotions would lead to a more sociable and peaceful world, but the conundrum is that they would be economically and personally dysfunctional in capitalism's competitive socio-symbolic environment.

A criminological take on *transcendental materialism* begins with the connection between harm and loosely controlled drives and desires, but, unlike conservative control theory, it does not naturalise or trans-historicise them. Left liberalism, on the other hand, lacks a positive conception of harm as drive (Dews 2008). Overwhelmed by a constant fear of natural forces that threaten to overwhelm the autonomous ethical individual and the systems of symbolic negotiation on which its philosophy depends, liberalism can only posit the cause of harm as an aberration, a misunderstanding or a failure to negotiate meaning between the actor and the victim. *Transcendental materialism* is a term used by philosopher Adrian Johnston (2008) as he attempted to systematise the brilliant but often haphazardly presented work done by Slovene philosopher Slavoj Žižek (1989, *passim*) on the ontogenic formation of the subject and the relationship of its material being with ideology. This framework, based on re-readings of Schelling, Hegel and Lacan updated in the light shed by contemporary continental philosophy, psychoanalysis and neuroscience, moves us beyond the exhausted and politically ineffectual neo-Kantian idealism of Derrida, Deleuze, Foucault and Butler to present us with a path to more fertile ground by understanding the basic, universal human neurological system as an abyss of weak, undirected instincts shot through with conflicting drives. The simplified upshot is that the human being is hard-wired but only, paradoxically, for plasticity, and therefore malleable, in any substantive sense of the term, *only* at the *material level* (Johnston 2008). In our evolutionary, migratory history this malleability has been essential for survival in multiple physical environments that have changed in a variety of ways over time and have, until the widespread use of technology in the Anthropocene era of global human domination, demanded different forms of socio-economic organisation (Johnston 2008; see also Gilmore 1990). Symbolic systems, on the other hand, do not offer flexibility and transformative momentum but have evolved for the practical purpose of providing chaotic drives with the rigid communicative comprehensibility that social groups require to function as economic organisations.

Because pre-symbolic life is traumatic for the helpless child, de-naturalising the proto-self to create subjects of language and seek a comprehensible symbolic order inhabited by others who are committed to its shared meanings is also a natural act. This process, whether or not the neo-Kantians like it, is the formation of what we call subjectivity. Individuals must actively 'solicit the trap' of a rigid symbolic order – an ideology – simply to become selves and belong to a group as social subjects (Hall 2012c). However, the major and hitherto intractable problem is *deaptation* (Johnston 2008). Symbolic systems, which have usually been hierarchical as environmentally specific functional successes were translated into social orders, periodically become counter-productive in new environments. Ideologies tend to insulate themselves from major shifts in natural and socio-economic environments. However, on its own and with no reconstructive purpose in sight, constant dissent is counter-productive because anxious individuals cannot tolerate an existence in the absence of an ideology whose values, norms and symbols are shared by others; they crave a *unary order*. Identity that has been actively solicited by anxious individuals fleeing the primary trauma can be provided only by entry into a symbolic order, whose values, norms and symbols are returned inwards to be consolidated and temporarily *re-naturalised* in the body's neurological circuits. Of course wide pluralism in norms and aesthetics can be celebrated, but in the core, where social justice must be established, harms minimalised and unavoidable problems and sacrifices shared rather than unfairly distributed, universal ethics and politics are a necessity. In the absence of a coherent alternative, individuals will – actively or begrudgingly, it does not really matter – elect to stick with the one that exists and refuse to risk all in a transformative convulsion or even a period of rapid and substantial reform.

Ideology does not need to constantly naturalise itself by hegemonic means; the subject is the author of hegemony as it actively solicits re-naturalisation of the symbolic order as an escape from trauma. Today's ideology is *negative*; people have all sorts of *positive* opinions about this and that, which, on the surface of it, suggests that a dominant ideology does not exist (see Abercrombie *et al* 1980). However, the dominant ideology the vast majority share is 'capitalist realism' (Fisher 2009; see also Badiou 2002; Žižek 2001), the conviction, honed in the era of political catastrophism, that no alternative socio-economic system is possible. Capitalist realism's ideological function is to vigilantly repudiate the reality that, to truly transform itself at the level of drives and desire, the subject must risk another traumatic encounter with the Real of indeterminate drives, but refuse to stay in this dismal, fearful, permanently fragmented position of liberal-postmodernist, post-structural limbo where no alternative unary identity can be constructed and no real politics can take place. Rather, to regain sanity and increase the chance of potential collective survival into the future, the subject must re-enter an alternative ideology based on universal social justice and suited to the current environment. Transcendental materialism's ontological claim is that there exists neither an 'autonomous' nor a 'determined' subject, but a proto-subject who actively seeks a collective symbolic order in which he or she can become individuated; the choice between obsolete or new symbolic orders is the sole choice available.

Modernity's alternative unary political and socio-economic orders – socialism and social democracy – have disintegrated with no replacement in sight. Liberalism, on the other hand, does not exist as a unary political order, only as a clearing house for atomised individuals and plural cultures in a market economy and a political safety valve for the perpetually frustrated forces of structural change (see Hedges 2010). Violent criminality and both traditional and new forms of competitive, hostile tribalism grow in the vacuum created by the abandonment of the project to construct a new unary order. Examples abound in today's violent paraspaces and failed states, in disrupted former agricultural communities and communist states, in deindustrialised and economically abandoned areas of the old industrial world, and in the cut and thrust of global geopolitics and business competition (Hall 2012c). Only expansive securitisation and the rule of law, combined with the empty promise of increasing prosperity somewhere down the line when traditional capitalist economic principles can be revived, prevent further unrest and violence.

However, there is a further twist. Left-liberalism and neoliberalism, together with their classical liberal antecedents, are two variations of a liberal-capitalist system that is a historical exception insofar as it has never attempted to create solidarity and security, unlike preceding and intervening systems, which were failed attempts to do so (Jameson 2010). To promote aggressive competition between energetic asocial individuals it systematically stimulates the anxiety of a subject stranded in the limbo between trauma and the dream of a secure unary order that can never be realised. *Pseudo-pacification* was not a process seeking to adapt to a new environment. Rather, recognising the energising value of permanent dissociation and anxiety, it sought to expand and reproduce a novel and synthetic simulacrum, a post-social environment (Winlow and Hall 2013). The *pseudo-pacification process* is founded on the stimulation, democratisation and subsequent recapture in its active symbolic form of the obscene Real, whose drives are sublimated to fuel socio-symbolic competition and energise the economy. Therefore, from its inception the system was *fundamentally and functionally deaptive*, a form of *managed deaptation* fuelled by the seductive dream of constantly going beyond all ethical and natural limits, a Rabelaisian injunction to *do as thy wilt* and damn the consequences. For enthusiastic and reluctant recruits alike, pacification is dependent on continuous incremental increases in wealth and the ability to circulate the commodities and competitive opportunities for social status and the recapture of lost identity. The very core of the system is criminogenic, but, paradoxically, so far anyway, it has pacified populations insofar as traditional forms of acquisitive, expressive and governmental physical violence have been largely displaced by a far more expansive accumulation of variegated and hidden harms.

The present is characterised by automated production, resource depletion, climate change, slow economic growth and consumer saturation. The *pseudo-pacification process* is becoming truly outdated and dysfunctional. Our ability to keep the lid on crime and harm is currently over-reliant on an unsustainable combination; the constant expansion of both the external control system and the means of gratifying consumer desires. There are signs that some young people might be seeking an alternative unary ideology beyond left-liberalism's theatre of negative rights and politically aimless dissent, a truly adaptive socio-economic order that transcends the *pseudo-pacification process*. Others, less attuned to the hazards and possibilities of our current situation, retreat into *depressive hedonia*, an asocial, post-political realm of restlessness, nihilism and frustration, seeking temporary respite in the 'soft narcosis' of late-night TV, marijuana and the new round of cheap or free commodities (see Fisher 2009). In the most impoverished locales, many continue to drift into criminality. Perhaps criminology – if it allowed itself to take advantage of its clear view of the system's most deleterious and often tragic consequences – can investigate the pressing need for a new unary order in which it is possible to relax the pressure, to stop stoking anxiety and the sense of lack in the individual's psyche. Perhaps this would move us towards less disappointment and frustration, less crime, a return to the principles of citizenship and democratic politics and a diminished need for control.

Bibliography

Abercrombie, N., S. Hill and B.S. Turner (1980) *The Dominant Ideology Thesis*, London: Allen & Unwin.

Agamben, G. (2005) *The State of Exception*, translation by K. Attell, Chicago, IL: University of Chicago Press.
Akram, S. (2014) 'Recognizing the 2011 United Kingdom Riots as Political Protest: A Theoretical Framework Based on Agency, Habitus and the Preconscious', *British Journal of Criminology*, 54 (3): 375–92.
Badiou, A. (2002) *Ethics: An Essay on the Understanding of Evil*, London: Verso.
Becker, E. (1975) *Escape from Evil*, New York, NY: The Free Press.
Bollas, C. (1995) *Cracking Up*, London: Routledge
Bourdieu, P. (1990) *The Logic of Practice*, Cambridge: Polity Press.
Braidotti, R. (2002) *Metamorphoses: Towards a Materialist Theory of Becoming*, Cambridge: Polity Press.
Crogan, P. (2010) 'Knowledge, Care and Transindividuation: An Interview with Bernard Stiegler', *Cultural Politics*, 6 (2): 157–70.
Currie, E. (2010) 'Plain Left Realism: An Appreciation and Some Thoughts for the Future', *Crime, Law and Social Change*, 54: 111–24.
Damasio, A. (2003) *Looking for Spinoza: Joy, Sorrow, and the Feeling Brain*, Orlando, FL: Harcourt.
Dean, J. (2009) *Democracy and Other Neoliberal Fantasies: Communicative Capitalism and Left Politics*, Durham, NC: Duke University Press.
Dews, P. (1995) 'The Tremor of Reflection: Slavoj Žižek's Lacanian Dialectics', in P. Dews (ed.) *The Limits of Disenchantment: Essays on Contemporary European Philosophy*, London: Verso.
Dews, P. (2008) *The Idea of Evil*, Oxford: Blackwell.
Eagleton, T. (2009) *Trouble with Strangers: A Study of Ethics*, Chichester: Wiley-Blackwell.
Ebert, T. (1999) 'Globalization, internationalism, and the class politics of cynical reason', *Nature, Society, and Thought*, 12 (4): 389–410.
Elias, N. (1994) *The Civilizing Process*, Oxford: Blackwell.
Ericson, R. (2006) *Crime in an Insecure World*, Cambridge: Polity Press.
Fisher, M. (2009) *Capitalist Realism: Is There No Alternative?*, Alresford: Zero Books.
Gilmore, D. (1990) *Manhood in the Making: Cultural Concepts of Masculinity*, New Haven, CT: Yale University Press.
Hall, S. (2007) 'The Emergence and Breakdown of the Pseudo-Pacification Process', in K. Watson (ed.) *Assaulting the Past: Violence and Civilization in Historical Context*, Newcastle upon Tyne: Cambridge Scholars Press.
Hall, S. (2012a) *Theorizing Crime and Deviance: A New Perspective*, London: Sage.
Hall, S. (2012b) 'The Solicitation of the Trap: On transcendence and transcendental materialism in advanced consumer-capitalism', *Human Studies: Special Issue on Transcendence and Transgression*, 35 (3): 365–81.
Hall, S. (2012c) 'Don't Look Up, Don't Look Down: Liberal criminology's fear of the supreme and the subterranean', *Crime, Media, Culture: Special Issue: York Deviancy Conference 2011*, 8 (2): 197–212.
Hall, S. (2014) 'The Socioeconomic Function of Evil', in L. Ray and J. Kilby (eds) *Sociological Review Monograph: Violence and Society: Towards a New Sociology*, Chichester: Wiley.
Hall, S., S. Winlow and C. Ancrum (2008) *Criminal Identities and Consumer Culture: Crime, Exclusion and the New Culture of Narcissism*, London: Routledge/Willan.

Harvey, D. (2007) *A Brief History of Neoliberalism*, Oxford: Oxford University Press.
Hedges, C. (2010) *The Death of the Liberal Class*, New York, NY: Nation.
Henry, S. and D. Milovanovic (1996) *Constitutive Criminology: Beyond Postmodernism*, London: Sage.
Hibbert, C. (2003) *The Roots of Evil*, Stroud: Sutton.
Holloway, J. (2002) *Change the World Without Taking Power: The Meaning of Revolution Today*, London: Pluto.
Honneth, A. (1996) *The Struggle for Recognition: The Moral Grammar of Social Conflicts*, Cambridge: Polity Press.
Jacoby, R. (2005) *Picture Imperfect: Utopian Thought for an Anti-utopian Age*, New York, NY: Columbia University Press.
Jameson, F. (1981) *The Political Unconscious: Narrative as a Socially Symbolic Act*, London: Methuen.
Jameson, F. (2010) *Valences of the Dialectic*, London: Verso.
Johnston, A. (2008) *Žižek's Ontology: A Transcendental Materialist Theory of Subjectivity*, Evanston, IL: Northwestern University Press.
Loader, I. and R. Sparks (2010) *Public Criminology?: Criminological Politics in the Twenty-first Century*, London: Routledge.
Macfarlane, A. (1981) *The Origins of English Individualism: The Family, Property and Social Transition*, Oxford: Blackwell.
Malabou, C. and A. Johnston (2013) *Self and Emotional Life*, New York, NY: Columbia University Press.
Matthews, R. (2014) *Realist Criminology*, Basingstoke: Palgrave Macmillan.
Meiksins Wood, E. (2002) *The Origin of Capitalism: A Longer View*, London: Verso.
Mirowski, P. (2013) *Never Let a Serious Crisis Go to Waste: How Neoliberalism Survived the Financial Meltdown*, London: Verso.
Mouffe, C. (2000) *The Democratic Paradox*, London: Verso.
Osborne, P. and Segal, L. (1993) 'Gender as performance: An interview with Judith Butler', *Radical Philosophy*, 67: 32–39, retrieved 6/4/2011 http://theory.org.uk.but-ind1.htm
Parker, I. (2004) *Slavoj Žižek: A Critical Introduction*, London: Pluto.
Parker, K.F. (2008) *Unequal Crime Decline: Theorizing Race, Urban Inequality and Criminal Violence*, New York, NY: New York University Press.
Passavant, P. (2005) 'The Strong Neoliberal State: Crime, Consumption, Governance', *Theory and Event*, 8 (3) (online http://muse.jhu.edu/login?uri=/journals/theory_and_event/v008/8.3passavant.html, accessed 3 February 2014).
Piketty, T. (2014) *Capital in the Twenty-First Century*, Cambridge, MA: The Belknap Press
Pinker, S. (2012) *The Better Angels of Our Nature: A History of Violence and Humanity*, London: Penguin.
Schmitt, C. (1985) [1922] *Political Theology: Four Chapters on the Concept of Sovereignty*, translation by G. Schwab, Cambridge, MA: MIT Press.
Standing, G. (2011) *The Precariat: The New Dangerous Class*, London: Bloomsbury.
Stiegler, B. (2009) *Acting Out*, translation by D. Barison, D. Ross and P. Crogan, Stanford, CA: Stanford University Press.
Stiegler, B. (2011) *For a New Critique of Political Economy*, Cambridge: Polity Press.

Stein, A. (2007) *Prologue to Violence: Child Abuse, Dissociation and Crime*, Mahwah, NJ: The Analytic Press.
Sullivan, H. (1953) *Conceptions of Modern Psychiatry*, New York, NY: W.W. Norton.
Taylor, I., P. Walton and J. Young (1973) *The New Criminology: For a Social Theory of Deviance*, London: Routledge.
Tilly, C. (1985) 'War Making and State Making as Organized Crime', in P. Evans, D. Rueschemeyer and T. Skocpol (eds) *Bringing the State Back In*, Cambridge: Cambridge University Press.
Treadwell, J., D. Briggs, S. Winlow and S. Hall (2013) 'Shopocalypse Now: Consumer culture and the English riots of 2011', *British Journal of Criminology*, 53 (1): 1–17.
Winlow, S. and S. Hall (2012) 'A Predictably Obedient Riot: Post-politics, consumer culture and the English riots of 2011', *Cultural Politics*, 8 (3): 465–88.
Winlow, S. and S. Hall (2013) *Rethinking Social Exclusion: The End of the Social?*, London: Sage.
Yar, M. (2012) 'Critical Criminology, Critical Theory and Social Harm', in S. Hall and S. Winlow (eds) *New Directions in Criminological Theory*, London: Willan/Routledge.
Young, J. (1987) 'The Tasks Facing a Realist Criminology', *Crime, Law and Social Change*, 11 (4): 337–56.
Žižek, S. (1989) *The Sublime Object of Ideology*, London: Verso.
Žižek, S. (2001) *Did Somebody Say Totalitarianism?*, London: Verso.
Žižek, S. (2008) *Violence: Six Sideways Reflections*, London: Profile.

Chapter 8

Sartre on edgework

James Hardie-Bick

Introduction

Lyng's (1990) research on 'edgework' has proved to be particularly useful for exploring how individuals intentionally negotiate the boundaries that separate order from chaos. Lyng has provided a compelling social-psychological framework for understanding the phenomenological sensations associated with activities that seek to test the limits of human endurance and criminologists have found the literature on edgework relevant for their own research (Ferrell 2001, 2005; Hayward 2002, 2004; O'Neill and Seal 2012; Young 2003, 2009). This chapter has essentially two aims. First of all, I explore Lyng's arguments by comparing 'edgework' to Csikszentmihalyi's (1975) research on 'flow'. I aim to show why Csikszentmihalyi's research should also be seen as offering important insights in relation to the pleasures and sensations of voluntary risk-taking. The second aim of this chapter is to show how Sartre's existential philosophy has the potential to make an important contribution to this literature. This section specifically focuses on Sartre's early philosophy of self-knowledge and consciousness in both *The Transcendence of the Ego* (2004 [1937]) and *Being and Nothingness* (1998 [1943]). Using the philosophy of Sartre to explore some of the unacknowledged similarities between 'edgework' and 'flow', my overall intention is to highlight the relevance of both perspectives and to widen the current focus of criminological debates concerning high-risk behaviour.

Criminology, edgework and transgression

Criminology, Lippens argues, 'is about the shifting boundaries between those who are "in" and those who are "out"' (Lippens 2009: 124). These flexible and ever changing boundaries provide the focus for a range of divergent approaches to study crime, criminal behaviour, deviance, punishment and social control. This chapter aims to contribute to the increasing amount of criminological research addressing the phenomenological attractions of negotiating and transgressing the boundaries and margins of the normative social order. One of the most influential studies concerning the experience of crime and the positive attractions of engaging in criminal behaviour is Katz's (1988) *Seductions of Crime*. Katz's account of moral transcendence and his analysis of street crime criticizes 'rational choice' models of criminal behaviour and examines the subjective experiences of criminal action. By focusing on perpetrators' experiences of committing crime, Katz's research inverted traditional criminological concerns. Rather than primarily focusing on structural background factors such as class, poverty or unemployment to explain why people resort to criminal behaviour, Katz's study demonstrated the need for criminologists to understand the sensual and emotional foreground factors involved in violating social expectations and committing criminal acts. It is precisely the quest for adrenalin, excitement and feelings of transcendence generated by criminal endeavours that serves to motivate further criminal acts. Katz's original study encouraged criminologists to concentrate on the experiential foreground and successfully highlights the seductive sensations of engaging in criminal behaviour.

Criminologists have recognised the similarities between Katz's phenomenological research and Lyng's theory of edgework (Ferrell *et al* 2008; Presdee 2000; Young 2003). Whilst not restricted to criminal experiences, Lyng (1990, 1993, 2005, 2005a, 2005b, 2008) also focuses on encounters with boundaries and edges and examines how experiences of negotiating the edge provide a powerful contrast to the standardised routines of modern life. Originating from an empirical research project on skydivers (Lyng and Snow 1986), his research provides a theoretical framework for understanding why people engage in activities where a lack of preparation or concentration could have disastrous consequences. In leisure pursuits such as skydiving or climbing, participants confront intense emotions and the dialectic of fear and pleasure has to be controlled (Le Breton 2000). In order to survive the experience, high-risk enthusiasts need to maintain high-levels of concentration and avoid being overcome by fear. The edgework perspective has influenced a variety of empirical projects that examine why people deliberately choose to place themselves in situations that could result in the ultimate sanction of death (Vanreusel and Renson 1982).

Lyng's research on edgework can be applied to any activity that has the potential to transgress everyday boundaries that separate life and death. The concept of edgework is taken from the late Hunter S. Thompson (1967, 1980, 1993), who used the term to describe a range of intensely fearful, often drug induced, human experiences. Lyng borrows this concept to describe those who participate 'in life threatening or anomie-producing activities' and manage to 'successfully negotiate life-and-death situations' (Lyng and Snow 1986: 169). The significance of the edge is reflected in how edgeworkers seek to get as close to the edge as possible without actually crossing it. As Lyng states, edgework requires skilled performances and failing to successfully 'meet the challenge at hand will result in death or, at the very least, debilitating injury'

(Lyng 1990: 857). Indeed, for many participants, having the opportunity to test and challenge their individual skills and capabilities is claimed to be one of the most rewarding aspects of the overall experience. Skydivers, for example, learn how to perform increasingly complex manoeuvres during freefall together with the highly specific skills required to deal with a variety of life threatening contingencies that could realistically occur during their decent. Participation allows individuals the opportunity to develop their skills, overcome dangerous situations and experience 'intense sensations of self-determination and control' (Lyng 2005a: 5). The challenge is to maintain high-levels of concentration in order to control life-threatening situations that many would consider uncontrollable.

Sociologists and criminologists have used the edgework perspective to investigate a diverse range of social phenomena including armed robbery (Matthews 2002), juvenile delinquency (Miller 2005), drug use (Reith 2005) and financial risk-taking (Smith 2005). More recent research has focused on ultimate fighting (Lyng *et al* 2009), sadomasochism (Newmahr 2011) and probation work (Mawby and Worrall 2013). Although the 'uninitiated' may adamantly believe edgeworkers to be immature and unfocused misfits who are 'intent on their own imminent destruction' (Ferrell 2005: 77), an increasing amount of criminological research suggests that individuals are attracted to high-risk behaviour for the qualitative experience that is its central feature. As Ferrell (2005) points out, participating in activities that can be conceptualised as edgework often incorporates far more than the pleasure and excitement that accompanies such activities. Not only do edgeworkers receive 'a body blast of intense pleasure' but participation in such activities can literally invert 'the usual hierarchies that govern daily life' by constituting '"visceral revolts" against the order of things, sensual uprisings against boredom, tedium, alienation, and regulation' (Ferrell 2005: 84). In this respect, the activities of those attracted to extreme experiences offer a type of resistance to the constraints of living in a homogenised and rationalised social world (Mitchell 1988).

A sense of flow

Edgeworkers maintain that when they participate in these activities they 'experience themselves as instinctively acting entities' and as a consequence they experience 'a purified and magnified sense of self' (Lyng 1990: 860). The claim that engaging in high-risk activities involves 'alterations in perception and consciousness' (Lyng 1990: 860–61) and produces a sense of self-realisation is also documented in Csikszentmihalyi's research. Csikszentmihalyi (1975, 1988, 2002) provides an alternative theoretical framework to understand the attractions of voluntary risk-taking. Csikszentmihalyi studied a range of individuals including athletes, artists, surgeons, rock climbers and composers and developed his theory of 'flow' to explain the state of being produced by totally engaging in these activities. The concept of flow refers to 'the state in which people are so involved in an activity that nothing else seems to matter; the experience itself is so enjoyable that people will do it even at great cost, for the sheer sake of doing it' (Csikszentmihalyi 2002: 4). Csikszentmihalyi examines a range of pleasurable and challenging activities that have the potential to generate a sense of flow, but his research on rock climbing also suggests that flow captures some of the main attractions of engaging with high-risk activities. His research deserves more attention from criminologists as he argues that experiences involving physical danger offer an 'outstanding example of a particular class of flow activities' (Csikszentmihalyi 1975: 74). Participating in high-risk activities requires high levels of focused concentration that narrows the stimulus field and overrides self-awareness. According to Csikszentmihalyi, it is due to achieving the sense of 'flow' that motivates participants to engage in such activities.

To achieve a sense of flow the activity has to provide a combination of the following components: opportunities for action, feelings of competence and control, deep involvement and focused concentration, a merging of action and awareness, a sense of time being distorted, a loss of self-consciousness (or self-concept) and the emergence of a stronger sense of self after the activity. He found that a combination of these factors causes deep feelings of creativity and enjoyment. In contrast to Lyng's research on edgework, to experience flow the level of danger needs to be proportionate to the participants' skills and ability. Csikszentmihalyi therefore challenges Lyng's notion that physical danger is a 'dominant preoccupation' of those who engage in these activities. During his research with climbers only one of his informants claimed to climb for 'for cheap thrills' and no other informant 'gave any indication of pursuing danger for its own sake':

> 'Danger', as one put it, 'is not a kick'. Rather, danger is accepted and utilized as a part of the gestalt of climbing, in which feelings of control and competence predominate over voluntary risk in the figure-and-ground relationship.
>
> (Csikszentmihalyi 1975: 83)

Other studies on high-risk pursuits support Csikszentmihalyi's findings and suggest that the majority of participants do not intentionally increase the dangers. Whilst some individuals do seek out 'cheap thrills', my own research on skydiving showed how participants often refused to jump with those who took 'irresponsible' risks (Hardie-Bick 2011a). Hunt's (1995) research with deep wreck divers also found that those who engaged in excessive risk taking were often the subject of rumour and gossip and considered to be unsafe. Celsi *et al*'s (1993) research on skydiving and Mitchell's (1988) research with rock climbers and mountaineers both describe how high-risk participants aim to limit dangerous circumstances to a manageable level.

These studies suggest that participants explore and test their own personal boundaries but they do not deliberately attempt to seek out situations that are beyond their level of experience. As Csikszentmihalyi (1975) observes, participants search for new challenges that are generally approximate to the individual's level of ability.

Anxiety, chaos and uncertainty

Lyng (1990) acknowledges Csikszentmihalyi's work has many similarities with his theory of edgework. Nevertheless, he also argues that there are important differences. The first difference refers to the 'structural parameters of the two experiences' (Lyng 1990: 863). In order for flow to occur the activity must be proportionate to the individual's level of ability and strike a balance between the extremes of boredom and anxiety. Boredom results from engaging in non-challenging situations whereas anxiety occurs if the situation requires skills beyond their level of experience. For flow to occur, the situational demands should not over-tax or under-tax their personal level of ability. According to Lyng, as these activities take place between the poles of boredom and anxiety they cannot be described as edgework. Lyng argues that edgeworkers seek out risk as 'an end in itself' (Lyng 2005a: 5) and attempt to maximise risk in order to increase their chance of experiencing a unique high. Lyng describes the edgework perspective as a 'theory of *uncertainty* seeking' (Lyng 2008: 109) that produces high levels of anxiety and chaos that would disrupt the experience of flow. Another important difference concerns the phenomenological experience itself. Lyng suggests that flow produces different sensations to edgework as 'the flow state produces a loss of self-consciousness', whereas 'edgework stimulates a heightened sense of self' (Lyng 1990: 863). In contrast to Csikszentmihalyi's claim concerning the loss of ego, Lyng explains how edgework generates feelings of self-determination and self-actualisation.

I find both of Lyng's arguments concerning the differences between edgework and flow problematic. Lyng's own data seems to contradict his first point concerning how participants deliberately seek out uncertainty and chaos. Consider the following two extracts:

> Edgeworkers tend to give high priority to the development and use of skills. Sky divers must develop the skill of flying their bodies in free-fall, and mountain climbers must be adept at using their climbing equipment. Even Hunter Thompson's practice of binge drug taking involves the highly developed skills of a veteran substance abuser, that is, knowing how much to ingest of a particular drug, what combinations of drugs are safe, and so on
>
> (Lyng 1990: 871)

[P]lanning is a particularly important part of skydiving. Sky divers spend more time *preparing* for a jump than they do making it. In addition to packing their canopies and checking their equipment, they work out the exact sequence of formations in advance and rehearse the jump on the ground before entering the airplane (in a procedure called 'dirt diving').

(Lyng 1990: 874)

The above extracts demonstrate how skydivers attempt to reduce rather than increase anxiety and chaos. Lyng is very clear about the amount of time and preparation involved in high-risk activities such as skydiving. As he states, skydivers are preoccupied with their skills. He further refers to how individual status within the skydiving community focuses on 'the art of flying one's body in free fall' (Lyng 1990: 859). He also notes how serious injury and even death are seen to be the fault of the individual for not planning and paying attention to 'standard safety precautions' (Lyng 1990: 875). The ultimate challenge of edgework may be to survive an experience that cannot be anticipated, but skydivers are trained to expect the unexpected and to react automatically to a variety of life threatening situations (see Hardie-Bick 2005). Preparing, anticipating, planning and practising new skills and manoeuvres are all part of the overall skydiving experience. Csikszentmihalyi's research also comments on the amount of time participants spend preparing, practising and planning their high-risk pursuits. The amount of preparation involved, he claims, shows how high-risk enthusiasts attempt to 'avoid objective dangers as much as possible' and try to 'eliminate subjective dangers entirely by rigorous discipline and sound preparation'. Rather than seeking out anxiety and chaos, the disciplined training and practice demonstrates that it is 'the sense of *exercising* control in difficult situations' (Csikszentmihalyi 2002: 60–61) that participants find rewarding.

The above discussion suggests the research findings on flow and edgework have more in common than Lyng acknowledges. His second point concerning the different sensations produced by edgework and flow suggest further unacknowledged similarities. First of all, it is important to be clear about Csikszentmihalyi's argument in relation to self-awareness. Csikszentmihalyi argues that as the experience of flow is all encompassing, participants momentarily lose track of time and are distracted from their usual everyday concerns. Intensely focusing on the immediate task at hand combines both action and awareness and the result is a loss of self-consciousness. As Csikszentmihalyi states, 'What slips below the threshold of awareness is the *concept* of self, the information we use to represent to ourselves who we are' (Csikszentmihalyi 2002: 64). The self remains fully functioning but is not aware of itself. Although Lyng claims otherwise, this is also experienced by edgeworkers. The following quote from one of Lyng's informants is particularly interesting in this respect. Here the participant is reflecting on his experience of dealing with a malfunctioned parachute during one of his descents, 'I wasn't thinking at all – I just did what I had to do. It was the right thing to do too. And after it was over, I felt really alive and pure' (cited in Lyng 1990: 860).

This is the experience of self-determination and self-actualization Lyng refers to. The order of the sensations is important. The participant 'felt really alive and pure' *after*, rather than *during*, the experience. During the experience itself the participant claims that he 'wasn't thinking at all' and that he just did what he had to do. Due to the high levels of concentration involved, his perceptual field was narrowed to focusing on the movements, actions and procedures he needed to perform. As Lyng himself states, participants are only aware of 'those factors that immediately determine success or failure in negotiating the edge' (Lyng 1990: 861). As should be clear, this actually supports Csikszentmihalyi's findings. It is only *after* the activity that usual self-consciousness returns and individuals can start to reflect on their disappointments or achievements. As Csikszentmihalyi explains, when 'action follows action in a fluid series ... the actor has no need to adopt an outside perspective from which to constantly intervene' (Csikszentmihalyi 1975: 85).

The reflexive self

Although the similarities between Csikszentmihalyi's work on flow and the edgework perspective are not fully addressed by Lyng or Csikszentmihalyi, both theorists discuss George Herbert Mead's (1967 [1934]; 1982) theory of the self, and Mead's work is certainly a strong influence on both approaches. Mead highlighted the social, reflexive nature of the self, a self that can view itself as both subject and object, but he also recognised that there are occasions where we are not self-conscious:

> When one is running to get away from someone who is chasing him, he is entirely occupied in this action, and his experience may be swallowed up in the objects around him, so that he has, at the time being, no consciousness of self at all. We must be, of course, very completely occupied to have that take place, but we can, I think, recognize that sort of possible experience in which the self does not enter.
> (Mead 1967: 137)

Mead identified two distinguishable aspects of the self which he referred to as the 'I' and the 'me'. Mead referred to the 'me' as the judgemental and controlling side of the self that reflects the attitudes and voices of other members of society while the 'I' is the creative, spontaneous, unpredictable and imaginative side of the self. Lyng argues that Mead's distinction between the 'I' and the 'me' is particularly useful for exploring the phenomenological sensations experienced by edgeworkers. The spontaneous actions of the 'I' capture some of the main characteristics associated with edgework. The conditions of edgework suppress the 'me' phase of the self as the self is responding without reflective consciousness. As Lyng states, 'When the "me" is obliterated by fear or the demands of immediate survival, action is no longer constrained by social forces, and the individual is left with a sense of self-determination' (Lyng 1990: 878–79).

Csikszentmihalyi also draws on Mead's work concerning the dialectical relationship between the 'I' and the 'me'. In activities that induce a sense of flow the 'me' disappears and the 'I' takes over (Csikszentmihalyi 1988: 33). In the most challenging environments participants experience a 'transcendence of the self' due to having to perform actions that are far more complicated than their usual everyday experiences. Numerous empirical studies on the experience of flow show how the the self remains fully functioning but, at the time, is not actually aware of itself (see Csikszentmihalyi and Csikszentmihalyi 1988). As a result of the intense concentration required participants forget themselves, respond automatically and spontaneously without apprehending their movements or reflecting on their actions. Csikszentmihalyi's discussion of Mead is brief, and certainly not as detailed as Lyng's, but he finds Mead's ideas useful for explaining why the self is 'invisible during the flow episode' (Csikszentmihalyi 1988: 33; also see Macbeth 1988; Mitchell 1983, 1988; Sato 1988).

Even though Lyng and Csikszentmihalyi are both influenced by Mead, they reach different conclusions. Lyng argues that edgeworkers do not experience an 'annihilation of the ego' as participation in high-risk activities 'generates a heightened sense of self that subjects describe as self-realization or self-actualization' (Lyng 2008: 119). As I have explained, this difference between their work may not be as substantial as it initially appears. Csikszentmihalyi also argues that participating in these activities can produce a stronger, more vital, sense of self. Even though Csikszentmihalyi explains that a loss of self-consciousness refers to a 'loss of consciousness of the self', he acknowledges that it is often assumed 'that lack of self-consciousness has something to do with a passive obliteration of the self' (Csikszentmihalyi 2002: 64). By providing a more detailed philosophical analysis, it may be possible to have a clearer understanding of both the presence and temporary absence of self-consciousness.

Sartre's existential theory of consciousness has the potential to clarify the changes in consciousness that take place 'at the razor edge of the present' (Lyng 1990: 877). There are similarities between Mead and Sartre (Lippens 2009). Like Mead, Sartre distinguishes two dimensions of the self, which he also refers to as the 'I' and the 'me'. The *I* can be understood as the monitoring part of the self and observes and reflects on the ongoing thoughts and feelings of the *me*. For Sartre (1973, 1998, 2004), the human subject is radically free to transcend their immediate circumstances and question their own actions, beliefs, attitudes, values and desires. The above discussion concerning the absence or 'annihilation' of the self has a particular Sartrean tone. Human subjectivity involves reflecting on the past, contemplating present circumstances and moving beyond itself to imagine future possibilities, but Sartre (2004) also describes situations where the self or ego is annihilated, experiences that are not accompanied by an *I think*. Sartre's existential philosophy provides a detailed phenomenological analysis of consciousness.

Sartre's existential phenomenology

Mead's idea that human beings can take a step back and view themselves as both subject and object is central to Sartre's philosophy (see Hardie-Bick 2011b; Lippens 2009). A core existentialist notion is that human beings have a unique ability to withdraw from themselves so they can contemplate their own behaviour. Human beings can reflect on their surroundings, think about their possible options and make plans about their future. It is only through the ability to 'detatch' from the world and 'nihilate' being that human beings can attach meaning to their existence. Sartre's (1998) ontology makes a distinction between *being-in-itself* and *being-for-itself*. Being-in-itself refers to independent and non-conscious objective reality which is opaque, inert and 'never anything but what it is' (Sartre 1998: xlii). Being-in-itself describes objects in the world that exist without possibility, whereas being-for-itself, or being of consciousness, has no pre-determined essence and, as a consequence, is in a constant state of becoming. Unlike being-in-itself, being-for-itself has the power to 'nihilate being' as it has the potential of 'being what it is not and not being what it is' (Sartre 1998: xli). This distinction between two ontologically distinct types of being allowed Sartre to focus on issues relating to human freedom and to explore how people are free to create, choose, define and contemplate their life projects.

Sartre was influenced by Husserl's (1962) theory of intentionality and argued that 'all consciousness is conscious *of* something' (Sartre 1998: xxvii). For example, if I am concerned or confused, I am concerned or confused about something. If I react, I am specifically reacting to something (see Spinelli 2003). Without the some *thing* for consciousness to be directed towards there would be nothing. Consciousness 'is like a hole of being at the heart of Being' (Sartre 1998: 617), a lack or nothingness devoid of content. This nothingness allows people the freedom to withdraw from themselves, to question their own existence and 'forces human-reality *to make itself* instead of *to be*' (Sartre 1998: 440). Sartre is well known for his distinction between being-in-itself and being-for-itself, but by developing Husserl's work on intentionality, he was also careful to explain the differences between what he termed reflected and unreflected consciousness. This was specifically addressed in *The Transcendence of the Ego* (Sartre 2004) and his ideas developed into his theory of consciousness which Sartre fully elaborated in *Being and Nothingness* (1998). Sartre critically engages with the notion of an inner self that Husserl (1962) posited as necessary for unifying experiences. Rather than the self being conceptualised as an inner entity operating behind the scenes, Sartre's phenomenological analysis claimed that the self should be understood as the product of consciousness.

Two modes of self-consciousness

Sartre argues that Husserl's notion of the transcendental ego, the idea that there is an *I think* that accompanies and is inseparable from our experiences, is based on a misunderstanding of Kant's philosophy. In *The Critique of Pure Reason* (1965 [1781]) Kant claims that it should be possible for the *I think* to accompany all of our representations. As Sartre explains, by suggesting that *it should* be possible he is asserting that there are conscious moments when the *I think* is absent. Husserl's notion of the transcendental ego therefore distorts Kant's philosophy and mistakenly introduces an entirely unnecessary and contradictory entity into phenomenological analysis. Intentionality states that consciousness is always conscious of something. Sartre claims that the notion of a transcendental ego implies that consciousness has contents, rather than being outside in the world. Sartre is particularly critical of Husserl's reliance on the transcendental ego as this supports the theory of internal representations that intentionality aimed to overcome.

Sartre argues that the ego is not an '"inhabitant of consciousness"' at all, but is rather 'outside, *in the world*' (Sartre 2004: 1). To explain how the ego is situated in the world, Sartre argues that the for-itself has two modes of self-consciousness. The first mode is referred to as non-thetic consciousness (of) consciousness. This mode of consciousness is pre-reflective and describes moments of consciousness that are not accompanied by *I think*. Non-thetic consciousness (of) consciousness does not reflect on itself as an intentional object. Sartre argues there is no *I* on this unreflected non-positional level of consciousness:

> When I run after a tram, when I look at the time, when I become absorbed in the contemplation of a portrait, there is no *I*. There is a consciousness of the *tram-needing-to-be-caught*, etc. ... but as for *me*, I have disappeared, I have annihilated myself. There is no place for *me* at this level, and this is not the result of some chance, some momentary failure of attention: it stems from the very structure of consciousness
>
> (Sartre 2004: 13)

The second mode of consciousness is referred to as thetic consciousness of consciousness and describes reflective self-consciousness. Sartre is arguing that the *I* only 'appears on the occasion of a reflective act' (Sartre 2004: 16). Thetic consciousness describes the level of consciousness that reflects on itself and perceives itself as an intentional object. This is not to argue that the *I* fails to appear on the level of unreflected consciousness. The following example highlights how the *I* often appears in everyday conversations without consciousness examining itself as an intentional object:

If I am asked, 'what are you doing?' and I reply, pre-occupied as I am, 'I am trying to hang up this picture', or, 'I am repairing the rear tyre', these phrases do not transport us on to the level of reflection, I utter them without ceasing to work, without ceasing to envisage just the actions, insofar as they have been done or are still to be done – not insofar as I am doing them. But this 'I' that I am dealing with here is not, however, a simple syntactic form. It has a meaning; it is quite simply an empty concept, destined to remain empty. Just as I can think of a chair in the absence of any chair and by virtue of a mere concept, in the same way I can think of the *I* in the absence of the *I*.

(Sartre 2004: 40)

The appearance of the *I* does not necessarily imply the presence of the *I*. However, when the *I* moves from the reflected to the unreflected level, when the *I* is absent, the use of the *I* is degraded and 'loses its intimacy' (Sartre 2004: 40). It is important to note that thetic or reflected consciousness of consciousness is not separate from non-thetic or unreflected consciousness (of) consciousness. As Sartre (2004) explained, the *I* can appear on the unreflected level of consciousness. Without non-thetic consciousness (of) consciousness, thetic consciousness of consciousness would not be possible (Sartre 1998, 2004).

Sartre is asserting that his distinction between the two modes of consciousness of consciousness renders the unifying role of the transcendental ego as 'completely useless'. Contrary to Husserl, Sartre reasons that it is 'consciousness that renders the unity and personality of my *I* possible' (Sartre 2004: 7). The ego, for Sartre, is the unity of states and actions. States such as fear, hatred, love and desire are all transcendent objects available to reflective consciousness. Specific actions such as driving a car, writing a book or jumping out of a plane, together with psychical actions such as meditating, doubting or reasoning should also be understood as transcendent objects. The ego reflects on, structures, interprets and gives meaning to these actions, feelings, thoughts and emotions. The ego is the 'spontaneous unification' of states and actions but the ego is not the 'proprietor' residing within consciousness. The structure of consciousness reveals that consciousness is translucent and completely devoid of content. The ego is transcendent to consciousness and understood as being-in-the-world like other objects that appear to consciousness. The ego is transcendent rather than transcendental and only appears when thetic consciousness of consciousness reflects on itself (Sartre 2004).

Negotiating the edge

Sartre's existentialist philosophy offers particular insights in relation to the sensations described by Lyng and Csikszentmihalyi. The literature on edgework and flow highlights how high-risk experiences demand intense levels of focused concentration, transform spatial and temporal perceptions and provide a sense of existential autonomy. During high-risk activities, participants are forced to ignore stimuli that could distract their attention and understand 'that survival is dependent on complete concentration' (Csikszentmihalyi 1975: 42). As a result participants often describe their experiences of negotiating the edge as 'hyper-real' and 'more real' than their usual everyday familiar routines (Lyng 2005). Csikszentmihalyi's research has highlighted how participants experience a 'loss of ego' or 'loss of self-consciousness' during these activities. In these situations participants become temporarily unaware of their self-construct. The necessary merging of action and awareness allows no time for the critical self-scrutiny that usually accompanies our everyday experiences:

> [T]he merging of action and awareness which typifies the flow state does not allow for the intrusion of an outside perspective with such worries as 'How am I doing?' or 'Why am I doing this?' or even 'What is happening to me?' In the moments of flow the individual does not even consciously acknowledge that he is flowing, much less elaborate and comment on the experience and its meaning. Realization, translation, and elaboration take place when the action has ceased: briefly at a belay stance, when the summit is finally reached, or after the climber is back on level ground. The processual structure of rock climbing not only produces great emotions but also offers regular opportunities to elaborate and solidify the experiences through reflection
>
> (Csikszentmihalyi 1975: 90)

As I have discussed, Lyng argues that high-risk activities produce a sense of self-determination but he distances the 'edgework' perspective from 'flow' activities due to Csikszentmihalyi's notion that flow produces a loss of consciousness (Lyng 1990, 2008). In contrast to flow, Lyng argues, edgework produces a 'heightened sense of self' and creates powerful sensations such as self-realisation and self-actualisation. Sartre's phenomenological work on the structure of consciousness can serve to bridge the gap between these two approaches. Sartre's distinction between reflected and unreflected consciousness not only shows how the *I* should be seen as a product of consciousness, but he also explains how there are activities which are not accompanied by an *I think*. Sartre' phenomenological analysis confirms that there are moments when the *I* disappears. Rather than being an entity that inhabits consciousness, Sartre shows how the *I* only appears as a 'reflective act'. As previously discussed, Lyng cites one of his informants as 'not thinking at all' during the activity and Csikszentmihalyi cites a range of informants who address this issue. The following quotation is taken from a participant who took part in Csikszentmihalyi's research on climbing:

You're so involved with what you're doing [that] you aren't thinking about yourself as separate from the immediate activity. You're no longer a participant observer, only a participant. You're moving in harmony with something else you're part of.

(cited in Csikszentmihalyi 1975: 86)

In high-risk activities any lapse in concentration could have possibly fatal consequences. During freefall, a skydiver needs to be fully aware of her equipment, her actions and her bodily positions in the air. After freefall, when she opens her parachute, she needs to determine whether her main canopy is safe or if she needs to operate the reserve parachute. At the same time she needs to be fully aware of the proximity of other skydivers, her altitude, the location of the drop zone as well as a number of other contingencies that can occur during each decent. When participants are fully emerged in high-risk activities, when they feel as if they are 'participants' rather than 'participant observers', the *I think* is, in Sartre's words, 'annihilated'. As Csikszentmihalyi argues, losing awareness of the self-concept can lead to 'self-transcendence, to a feeling that the boundaries of our being have been pushed forward' (Csikszentmihalyi 2002: 64) and this also explains why edgeworkers claim 'being on the edge is when they feel most alive' (Lyng 2008: 118). It is precisely during these moments of emotional intensity that participants have no time to reflect on the significance of their feelings and their self-concept. It is only after the activity that it is possible to reflect on the accomplishments or indeed the failings of the *I*. Lyng has shown how edgeworkers describe feelings of having an exaggerated or more authentic sense of self when they are negotiating the edge, but these accounts were given by participants who were reflecting on their experiences. This is completely in line with Csikszentmihalyi's research findings. When self-consciousness resumes participants' sense of self can be enriched as they reflect on their personal achievements and the challenges they managed to overcome. In Csikszentmihalyi's words:

> The self becomes more differentiated as a result of flow because overcoming a challenge inevitably leaves a person feeling more capable, more skilled. As the rock climber said, 'You look back in awe at the self, at what you've done, it just blows your mind.' After each episode of flow a person becomes more of a unique individual, less predictable, possessed of rarer skills
>
> (Csikszentmihalyi 2002: 41)

This type of reflection creates a stronger sense of self (Csikszentmihalyi 1988) and as Lyng states, provides a sense of self-actualisation and self-determination.

The necessary involvement required for engaging in high-risk activities overrides an individual's self-awareness and provides a temporary release from conscious constraints such as self-doubt and critical self-scrutiny that accompany many of our experiences (Csikszentmihalyi 2002; Leary 2007). The process of reflecting back and interpreting the significance of their own actions during high-risk encounters has a significant impact on participants' self-concept. Unlike the examples of unreflected consciousness provided by Sartre (such as running for a tram or contemplating a portrait), engaging in high-risk activities provide individuals with a variety of extraordinary and challenging experiences. These are precisely the kind of demanding experiences that are usually absent in our highly routine, mentally detached lives (Lyng 1990, 2008; Mitchell 1983; O'Malley and Mugford 1994). Dangerous activities allow individuals to display courage in highly stressful circumstances. As Lyng argues, these can be viewed as seductive attractions as they provide a powerful contrast to the experiences of living in a highly rationalised and risk averse society. Csikszentmihalyi also recognises that the sensations provided by flow activities are rarely experienced in normative life:

> We are aware of the amount of worry and boredom that people experience in schools, factories, and their own homes. We are concerned about the meaninglessness and alienation in daily activities, and hence the constant efforts we make to get extrinsic rewards which will serve as symbolic counters to compensate for the barrenness of experience. It is for this reason that we have turned to flow activities, to learn from them the mechanisms by which ordinary life could be made more enjoyable.
> (Csikszentmihalyi 1975: 100)

As Mitchell notes, if everyday experiences are constraining, overly structured and invariant then it is understandable why people will 'search out occasions for creative self-expression' (Mitchell 1988: 45). The literature on both flow and edgework demonstrate the benefits of engaging in activities that require a total and complete involvement of both mind and body. These are enjoyable and active experiences that offer a heightened sense of self-determination and provide individuals with feelings of transcendence, self-actualisation and a renewed, authentic sense of self. These are moments of innovation and engagement that provide individuals with an experience they are usually denied: an opportunity for creative and self-realising action (Ferrell 2001, 2005; Lyng 1990, 2005).

Conclusion

Over recent years there has been substantial interest in researching the thrills, excitement and sensations experienced in acts of transcendence and transgression. Lyng's research on edgework has influenced a range of studies that reveal the emotional intensity of a wide range of experiences. Embracing risk is seen as both positive and pleasurable, offering a chance to transcend the 'hyper-banalisation' of everyday life (Hayward 2002) and to experience a more vital sense of self. Whilst edgework has been particularly influential to these debates, Csikszentmihalyi's research on flow remains marginalised within criminological theory, briefly criticised and often dismissed as not being relevant for understanding the behaviour of those attracted to high-risk situations (Lyng 1990, 2008). This chapter has aimed to encourage criminologists to recognise the potential of Csikszentmihalyi's work for understanding the personal rewards of engaging in high-risk behaviour. Both Lyng and Csikszentmihalyi have made important contributions to understanding the attractions of voluntary risk-taking and, as I have tried to show, there are interesting yet unacknowledged similarities between their approaches.

There are important differences between Lyng's focus on how edgeworkers deliberately increase the risks compared with Csikszentmihalyi's findings concerning how participants enjoy the challenge of controlling and minimalizing the risks associated with their activity. I have suggested that these differences may not be as clear as Lyng suggests and future criminological research would benefit from comparing their approaches for understanding the attractions of engaging in dangerous criminal acts. This chapter has also aimed to show how Sartre's existential phenomenology is useful for clarifying both Csikszentmihalyi's claims concerning the absence of the self together with Lyng's focus on how high-risk experiences produce a sense of self-determination. Sartre's distinction between the two forms of consciousness manages to overcome one of the main differences that unnecessarily separate their approaches. Sartre's detailed work on the structure of consciousness confirms how there are occasions where the *I think* is absent, situations in which individuals have no self-awareness. Sartre's theory of how consciousness is both consciousness (of) consciousness and consciousness of consciousness provides a deeper level of understanding of how individuals interpret the significance of their actions and attach meaning and value to the sensations produced by engaging in high-risk experiences.

Losing a sense of self can be a pleasurable and rewarding experience (Csikszentmihalyi 2002; Strenger 2011). In our highly individualised society (Bauman 2001; Giddens 1991) where our minds are 'abuzz with self-chatter' (Leary 2007: 33), disengaging form usual self-awareness provides a powerful temporary form of escape from the familiar concerns, worries and dilemmas that can preoccupy our thoughts. Nevertheless, high-risk experiences offer more than just a temporary escape. Sartre's phenomenology highlights the importance of reflection and interpretation for constructing a sense of self. The reflected act creates the self. As Sartre explains, the self is not something that resides within consciousness. Consciousness itself is empty, the ego is situated in the world and can be reflected on, assessed and evaluated like other objects in the world. Reflecting on the skills required to successfully negotiate the edge provides an unusual and highly rewarding experience. Following Sartre's insights into the very structure of consciousness, it is precisely this type of reflection that serves to create rather than discover the self.

Acknowledgements

The ideas addressed in this chapter stem in large part from discussions with Ronnie Lippens concerning the connections between Sartre's theory of consciousness and the literature on edgework. I would like to thank Ronnie for encouraging me to develop these initial ideas. I would also like to thank Lauren Brooks for providing feedback on an earlier version of this chapter.

Bibliography

Bauman, Z. (2001) *The Individualized Society*, Oxford: Polity Press.
Celsi, R.L., R. L. Rose and T.W. Leigh (1993) 'An Exploration of High-Risk Leisure Consumption Through Skydiving', *Journal of Consumer Research*, 20: 1–23.
Csikszentmihalyi, M. (1975) *Beyond Boredom and Anxiety*, San Francisco, CA: Jossey-Bass.
Csikszentmihalyi, M. (1988) 'The flow experience and its significance for human psychology', in M. Csikszentmihalyi and I.S. Csikszentmihalyi (eds) 1992 *Optimal Experience: Psychological Studies of Flow in Consciousness*, Cambridge: Cambridge University Press.
Csikszentmihalyi, M. (2002) *Flow: The Classic Work on How to Achieve Happiness*, London: Rider Books.
Ferrell, J. (2001) *Tearing Down the Streets: Adventures in Urban Anarchy*, New York, NY: Palgrave.
Ferrell, J. (2005) 'The Only Possible Adventure: Edgework and Anarchy', in S. Lyng (ed.) *Edgework: The Sociology of Risk-Taking*, New York, NY: Routledge.
Ferrell, J., K. Hayward and J. Young (2008) *Cultural Criminology: An Invitation*, London: Sage.
Giddens, A. (1991) *Modernity and Self-Identity*, Cambridge: Polity.
Hardie-Bick, J. (2005) *Dropping Out and Diving In: An Ethnography of Skydiving*, Durham theses, Durham University (online at Durham E-Theses Online, http// etheses.dur.ac.uk/2734/, accessed 2 March 2014).
Hardie-Bick, J. (2011a) 'Skydiving and the metaphorical edge', in D. Hobbs (ed.) *Ethnography in Context*, vol. 3, London: Sage.
Hardie-Bick, J. (2011b) 'Total Institutions and the Last Human Freedom', in J. Hardie-Bick and R. Lippens (eds) *Crime, Governance and Existential Predicaments*, Basingstoke: Palgrave Macmillan.
Hayward, K. (2002) 'The Vilification and Pleasures of Youthful Transgression', in J. Muncie, G. Hughes and E. McLaughlin (eds) *Youth Justice: Critical Readings*, London: Sage Publications.
Hayward, K. (2004) *City Limits: Crime, Consumer Culture and the Urban Expression*, London: Glasshouse.
Hunt, J.C. (1995) 'Divers Accounts of Normal Risk', *Symbolic Interaction*, 18 (4): 439–62.
Husserl, E. (1962) *Ideas: General Introduction to Pure Phenomenology*, New York, NY: Gibson
Kant, I. (1965) [1781] *The Critique of Pure Reason*, New York, NY: St Martin's Press.

Katz, J. (1988) *Seductions of Crime: Moral and Sensual Attractions in Doing Evil*, New York, NY: Basic Books.
Le Breton, D. (2000) 'Playing Symbolically with Death in Extreme Sports', *Body and Society*, 6 (1): 1–11.
Leary, M.R. (2007) *The Curse of the Self: Self-Awareness, Egotism, and the Quality of Human Life*, Oxford: Oxford University Press
Lippens, R. (2009) *A Very Short, Fairly Reasonably Cheap Book About Studying Criminology*, London: Sage.
Lyng, S.H. (1990) 'Edgework: A Social Psychological Analysis of Voluntary Risk-Taking', *American Journal of Sociology*, 95 (4): 851–86.
Lyng, S.H. (1993) 'Dysfunctional Risk Taking: Criminal Behaviour as Edgework', in N.J. Bell and R.W. Bell (eds) *Adolescent Risk Taking*, Newbury Park, CA: Sage.
Lyng, S.H. (ed.) (2005) *Edgework: The Sociology of Risk Taking*, New York, NY: Routledge.
Lyng, S.H. (2005a) 'Edgework and the Risk-taking Experience', in S.H. Lyng (ed.) *Edgework: The Sociology of Risk Taking*, New York, NY: Routledge.
Lyng, S.H. (2005b) 'Sociology at the Edge: Social Theory and Voluntary Risk Taking', in S.H. Lyng (ed.) *Edgework: The Sociology of Risk Taking*, New York, NY: Routledge.
Lyng, S.H. (2008) 'Edgework, Risk and Uncertainty', in J.O. Zinn (ed.) *Social Theories of Risk and Uncertainty: An Introduction*, Oxford: Blackwell Publishing.
Lyng, S.H., R. Matthews and W.J. Miller (2009) 'Existentialism, edgework and the contingent body: exploring the criminological implications of Ultimate Fighting', in R. Lippens and D. Crewe (eds) *Existentialist Criminology*, London: Routledge.
Lyng, S.H. and D.A. Snow (1986) 'Vocabularies of Motive and High-Risk Behaviour: The Case of Skydiving', in E.J. Lawler (ed.) *Advances in Group Processes* 3, Greenwich, CT: JAI Press, pp. 157–79.
Macbeth, J. (1988) 'Ocean Cruising', in M. Csikszentmihalyi and I.S. Csikszentmihalyi (eds) *Optimal Experience: Psychological Studies of Flow in Consciousness*, Cambridge: Cambridge University Press.
Matthews, R. (2002) *Armed Robbery*, Cullompton: Willan.
Mawby, R. and A. Worrall (2013) *Doing Probation Work: Identity in a Criminal Justice Occupation*, London: Routledge.
Mead, G.H. (1967) [1934] *Mind, Self and Society*, Chicago, IL: University of Chicago Press.
Mead, G.H. (1982) *The Individual and the Social Self: Unpublished Work of George Herbert Mead*, edited by A. Strauss, Chicago, IL: University of Chicago Press
Miller, W.J. (2005) 'Adolescents on the Edge: The Sensual Side of Delinquency', in S.H. Lyng (ed.) *Edgework: The Sociology of Risk-Taking*, New York, NY: Routledge.
Mitchell, R.G. (1983) *Mountain Experience: The Psychology and Sociology of Adventure*, Chicago, IL: University of Chicago Press.
Mitchell, R.G. (1988) 'Sociological Implications of the Flow Experience', in M. Csikszentmihalyi and I.S. Csikszentmihalyi (eds) *Optimal Experience: Psychological Studies of Flow in Consciousness*, Cambridge: Cambridge University Press.
Newmahr, S. (2011) *Playing on the Edge: Sadomasochism, Risk and Intimacy*, Bloomington, IN: Indiana University Press.

O'Malley, P. and S. Mugford (1994) 'Crime, Excitement and Modernity', in G. Barak (ed.) *Varieties of Criminology*, Westport, CN: Praeger.

O'Neill, M. and L. Seal (2012) *Transgressive Imaginations: Crime, Deviance and Culture*, Basingstoke: Palgrave Macmillan.

Presdee, M. (2000) *Cultural Criminology and the Carnival of Crime*, London: Routledge.

Reith, G. (2005) 'On the Edge: Drugs and the Consumption of Risk in Late Modernity', in S.H. Lyng (ed.) *Edgework: The Sociology of Risk-Taking*, New York, NY: Routledge.

Sartre, J.-P. (1973) *Existentialism and Humanism*, London: Methuen.

Sartre, J.-P. (1998) [1943] *Being and Nothingness. An Essay on Phenomenological Ontology*, London: Routledge.

Sartre, J.-P. (2004) [1937] *The Transcendence of the Ego*, London: Routledge

Sato, I. (1988) 'Bosozoku: flow in Japanese Motorcycle gangs', in M. Csikszentmihalyi and I.S. Csikszentmihalyi (eds) *Optimal Experience: Psychological Studies of Flow in Consciousness*, Cambridge: Cambridge University Press.

Smith, C.W. (2005) 'Financial Edgework: Trading in Market Currents', in S.H. Lyng (ed.) *Edgework: The Sociology of Risk-Taking*, New York, NY: Routledge.

Spinelli, E. (2003) *The Interpreted World: An Introduction to Phenomenological Psychology*, London: Sage.

Strenger, C. (2011) *The Fear of Insignificance: Searching for Meaning in the Twenty-first Century*, New York, NY: Palgrave Macmillan.

Thompson, H.S. (1967) *Hells Angels*, London: Penguin Books.

Thompson, H.S. (1980) *The Great Shark Hunt*, London: Picador.

Thompson, H.S. (1993) *Fear and Loathing in Las Vegas*, London: Flamingo.

Young, J. (2003) 'Merton with Energy, Katz with Structure: The Sociology of Vindictiveness and the Criminology of Transgression', *Theoretical Criminology*, 7 (3): 389–414.

Young, J. (2009) *The Vertigo of Late Modernity*, London: Sage.

Vanreusel, B. and R. Renson (1982) 'The Social Stigma of High Risk Sport Subcultures', in A. Dunleavy, A. Miracle and R. Rees (eds) *Studies in the Sociology of Sport*, Fort Worth, TX: Texas Christian University Press.

Chapter 9

Criminology and 'criminalisable' legal persons

George Pavlich

Introduction

Even if heterogeneous, criminology embraces an influential 'administrative' approach that consistently predicates itself on versions of crime and criminals as defined by decisions within criminal law (see McLaughlin and Muncie 2001: 6–7; Henry and Lanier 2001: 5ff). Critics of this approach have pointed out how it becomes subordinate to judges' capricious judgments on crime (e.g. Quinney 2001), thus proceeding from legal (rather than scientific) decisions that mostly perpetuate a capitalist order and its inequalities (see Taylor *et al* 1975). Without challenging such critiques, for there is much in them, my aim is a different one; namely, to focus on how criminology has over centuries helped to shape cultures of crime and criminals, thereby enunciating particular subjects as suitable targets for criminal law (Ferrell 1995; Sutherland *et al* 1992: 3ff). Through this cultural engagement, criminology engages a politics of jurisdiction by which changing images of criminal persons are projected and held out as legitimate targets for criminal law's gaze and force. In many cases, this cultural engagement is nondescript, operating in shadows that fix contextual meanings to the elusive – even if jurisdictionally central – idea of person (Dorsett and McVeigh 2012; Naffine 2003; Fagunes 2000–01). Consider, for example, the Criminal Code of Canada's use of the term 'person' as an open placeholder to define the 'offender': '"offender" means a person who has been determined by a court to be guilty of an offence, whether on acceptance of a plea of guilty or on a finding of guilt' ('Definitions' section of the Act). By contrast, Section 16 defines those persons excluded from its gaze:

> (1) No person is criminally responsible for an act committed or an omission made while suffering from a mental disorder that rendered the person incapable of appreciating the nature and quality of the act or omission or of knowing that it was wrong.
> (2) Every person is presumed not to suffer from a mental disorder so as to

be exempt from criminal responsibility by virtue of subsection (1), until the contrary is proved on the balance of probabilities.

(Criminal Code of Canada, Section 16)

In both instances, criminal law's person specifies limits of inclusions and exclusion for its jurisdiction. However, the precise identity of such persons is left open, enabling political fields that define 'appropriate' targets for criminalisation (Dayan 2013; Sutherland *et al* 1992). To the extent that criminology successfully engages this politics of 'criminalisable' persons, it helps to shape the very target, and so jurisdiction, of criminal law.

Without claiming that criminology's jurisdictional contributions to criminal law are necessary, consistent or inevitable in all contexts, it is the case that administrative criminology enjoys a privileged epistemic place in contemporary contexts that, in Simon's (2007) words, 'govern through crime' (see also Garland 2001). That is, within current governmentally organised contexts, some versions of criminology have privileged access to cultural, sub-cultural and disciplinary truth regimes to which agents of criminal law refer to frame up implicit renderings of the criminalisable person (Dayan 2013; Ferrell 1995). Foucault, too, notes criminology's increasingly vital role in modern societies as sovereign law transformed itself to adapt to new political pressures associated with industrial capitalism and the intensified populations of cities:

> One has the impression that it [criminology] is of such utility, is needed so urgently and rendered so vital for the working of the system, that it does not even need to seek a theoretical justification for itself, or even simply a coherent framework
>
> (Foucault 1980: 48)

This utility followed shifts in power that considered crime less a direct challenge to sovereignty (justifying the need for spectacular public vengeance) and more of a matter of individual 'delinquency' (requiring disciplinary reform and correction). In this context judges recognised the need for change to accommodate the latter measures and so increasingly called upon criminologists; that is, 'on those who produce a discourse on crime and criminals which will justify the measures in question' (Foucault 1980: 48).

There are various ways to approach criminology's influence in context. One might, for instance, attend to the precise reception of criminology's discourses within the ratios of particular criminal laws, cases and criminal justice contexts (e.g. Sherman 1992/93). However, this chapter's focus lies elsewhere; namely, on how criminology has defined various instances of the 'criminalisable' person who harbours characteristics requiring the attention of criminal law or justice (see also Rafter 1997; Beirne 1993). That is, without venturing specifically into cloisters of criminal law, the following discussion highlights four criminological conceptions of legitimate targets for criminal law's ratios and punishing force: an early colonial approach that targeted 'categories' of criminal persons within hierarchical social orders; classically framed rational and free willed persons; positivism's character-orientated versions of criminal persons as a 'type'; and an emerging 'biometric' person who extends positivist criminology into increasingly privileged arenas of bio-criminology. By examining how in each case criminology framed images of the criminalisable person, one can chart aspects of a complex politics of recognition and responsibility implicated in criminal law's jurisdictional claims. The contributions of two approaches in this respect – positivist and classical criminology – are especially well known, and so are referenced briefly. By contrast, versions of colonial and biometric persons are sketched in slightly more detail, but all highlight how various criminological discourses provide clues to changing power formations that contour the jurisdictional force of criminal law and justice.

Colonial categories, criminalisable persons and social hierarchy

Although not always framed as 'criminology' *per se*, the colonial foundations of an emergent *logos of crimen* were laid in hierarchy-orientated visions of persons, crime and various conceptions of punishment (Pavlich 2013a, 2013b; Ullmann 2010: chapter 7). One might turn to a specific colonial example where discourses explicitly enunciated which persons to criminalise in law, and how to understand responsibility. In the settler-colonial Cape of Good Hope, *circa* 1795, extraordinarily unsettled socio-political times produced frank discussions on the nature of criminal law and how to rule appropriately through contextual images of persons and punishment. The Cape at this time saw the Dutch East India Company's nearly 150-year rule ended by a British occupation (Giliomee and Mbenga 2007). Early on, an appointed military commander – Craig – had witnessed the cruelties of the law as applied to 'slaves' and requested through formal correspondence that judges of a new Court of Justice (all of whom had served under the conquered regime) re-evaluate such punishment practices (Pavlich 2013b). Their blunt refusal is revealing, as are the justifications they provided for preserving 'distinctions of person' and formulating punishments for crime in relation to such distinctions (see Theal 1897: 303ff).

In an emerging criminological discourse, the judges insisted that any law directed to crime had to distinguish between purportedly different categories of persons that made up the Cape colony's diverse social hierarchy. Revealing an historical prejudice, they considered this hierarchy to reflect different levels of social advancement ('civilization') that each stratum had attained; 'Europeans' at the pinnacle of refinement and 'slaves' as 'uncultivated' subjects at the bottom, with 'others' (e.g. 'burghers', 'hottentots', 'free black men') placed variously in between (Pavlich 2013a). The putatively lower echelons were said to hail from 'rude' nations and climates that had prevented them from mastering – through education and cultured refinement – the animal elements purported within all human beings (Bindman 2002). By this logic, as Esposito (2012: 22) suggests, only full persons were deemed to have mastered the 'animal part' of their natures. Others still had to achieve a 'greater or lesser intensity of deanimalisation' through a capacity to 'master themselves'. The judges transposed such hierarchical thinking to criminal justice arenas by insisting on the need to demarcate clear 'distinctions of person', and to frame notions of crime and responsibility in relation thereto. They argued that since criminal law was to serve a type of justice that upheld a sovereignly sanctioned order (in the Cape case, a 'slave' society for 'his Britannic Majesty'), crime was to be defined in light of the categories of persons projected by that order (Pavlich 2010).

The 'atrocity' or seriousness of a crime was thus formed around the relative social status attributed to victims and offenders, and the threat any act ostensibly posed for the *status quo*. As such, the judges held a similar crime, say murder, committed by a 'slave' on a 'master' to be more 'atrocious' than if the 'master' had murdered the 'slave' (Theal 1897: 304). That is, crimes committed by those considered to occupy lower echelons of the hierarchy (e.g. slaves) against those classified in higher orders (e.g. burghers) were regarded as more serious than the other way around. Similarly, judges argued that law's force had to be unequally unleashed depending on the category of person involved, and the calibrated seriousness of the crime. In context, criminal responsibility centred on the level of 'advancement' supposedly attained by the categories of persons found guilty of crime; the more 'advanced' or 'refined' the person, the more capable that being was deemed able to perceive pain 'internally' (see Theal 1897: 304). By contrast, persons placed in lower echelons were deemed less susceptible to experiencing internal pain. The ruling bigotry considered them as able only to comprehend the pain of extreme violence and torture directed to the body – hence the spectacular public punishments that were designed to broadcast deterrence messages to the entire social body.

In sum, criminal responsibility regimes at the Cape defined crime and punishment in relation to hierarchically conceived social contexts. Of course, such a *logos of crimen* was not unique to the Cape, for it operated in other settler-colonial contexts (Wiener 2009; Kirkby and Coleborne 2001) and imperial regions (Ullmann 2010). Moreover, as Foucault (2000, 1979) suggests, this sort of power-knowledge reflected spectacular models of sovereign power that were gradually supplemented by modern disciplinary, biopolitical and governmental powers. The shifting points of contact between these various models of power and law have undoubtedly developed over the past centuries through the emergence of hybrid sovereign forms (Golder and Fitzpatrick 2009). However, the logic of directing criminal law to specific categories of persons in a social hierarchy remains an embedded legacy in contemporary, advanced liberal criminal justice arenas where one continues to find – despite idioms of equality before the rule of law – different categories of persons disproportionately facing law's force. Wacquant (2009a, 2009b) and Jones and Dlamini (2013) are amongst those who have pointed to the tenacity of a colonial political logic (and associated responsibility framework) that exposes different categories of persons – the poor, people of colour, indigenous people, etc. – to disproportionate and varying intensities of law's force. Perhaps we should not be surprised by this colonial legacy, for it has woven itself into the very fabric of criminal law through a basic version of legal persons. Fagundes' *Harvard Law Review* note on legal persons makes the point this way:

> Courts' treatment of legal personhood communicates anxiety not only about divisive social issues, but also about the operation of law itself. In highly individualistic modern American legal culture, status distinctions seem to be embarrassing remnants of an illiberal past. However, when courts and legislatures engage problems of legal personhood, they are necessarily interpreting and applying very fundamental notions of status. The law of the person, and especially courts' ambivalence about it, exposes the uncomfortable but inescapable place of status distinctions in even the most progressive legal systems.
>
> (Fagundes 2000–01: 1766)

Rational persons, culpability and punishment

Hierarchical frameworks of personhood and responsibility in colonial and medieval discussions of crime provided a backdrop to classical criminological narratives born from modern, enlightenment views of persons, crime and responsibility. As is oft noted, Bentham (2005) and Beccaria (1996) viewed subjects as rational beings innately predisposed to seeking pleasure and avoiding pain. Committed to versions of rationalist utilitarianism, classical approaches aimed at limiting the 'barbarity' of criminal law's spectacular powers, rejecting the assertion that unfettered might was required to demonstrate sovereign strength (Beirne 1993). Their 'humane' reforms assumed the value of rational conceptions of persons, crime and punishment. Consequently, they called for changes to criminal justice procedures that would instil reason into the heart of its assumptions and processes: rational responses to the acts of persons who had clear access to predefined criminal codes; court decisions of guilty based on syllogisms with clearly formulated criminal codes served as the major premise against which criminal actions would be evaluated to arrive at rational decisions; and, reasonably calibrated – rather than extremely harsh – prompt punishments that inflicted minimum pains appropriate to securing specific and general deterrence (Beccaria 1996: 15, 19, 42, 55). The well-known tenets of the approach need not be repeated here (see Rafter 1997; Beirne 1993), but suffice to note that classical criminology adopted a broad rights-based politics of recognition associated with a rational conception of all facets of criminal law.

The latter claimed equally to recognise rational persons by conferring rights and duties, and so ascribed a legal personality. While two classical versions of such persons prevailed (see Naffine 2009: 9), both served as technical legal fictions to define law's jurisdiction. On the one hand, as indicated by Bentham's classical criminology, a 'legalist' position regarded the person as no more than an abstracted fiction (Henry and Lanier 2001). The general point, as Naffine notes, was that 'law *does not* and *should not* operate with a natural conception of the person' (Naffine 2009: 7). Positivist natures were of no consequence to this formulation, since as Smith indicates, 'To be a legal person is to be the subject of rights and duties. To confer legal rights or to impose legal duties, therefore, is to confer legal personality' (Smith 1928: 283).

On the other hand, Beccaria's version of criminology was anchored to 'rationalist' thinking that Naffine (2009: 71) refers to as a 'metaphysical realist' position. In his version of criminology, Becarria argued that criminal law should target persons who have an 'intention' to harm and the ability to make reasonable decisions (Becarria 1996: 65). Both classical criminological views have echoed through the ages, and may be detected in a prevalent strand of thinking which, as Naffine succinctly puts it, continues to frame criminal law around rational beings:

> For these theorists of the criminal law, there exists a fundamental and noble metaphysical truth about what we are ... we are rational beings; it is reason that endows us with a value; and (criminal) law does and should reflect our inherently valuable rational human nature by formally recognizing it and giving it important legal work to do. Criminal law shows its respect for us, as rational agents, as autonomous beings, holding us responsible for what we do. When we wrong another, we can be taken to have chosen our actions; we can be blamed and made accountable
> (Naffine 2009: 71)

Here, classical criminology pitted various images of the rational person, either formal or real, against criminal codes available publicly and followed by all rational persons. The idea of mastery surfaced in a rational guise: reason dictated the most appropriate ways to act and rational persons were expected to follow its precepts. Criminal law was to be developed as a rational endeavour, offering persons 'fair opportunity, as rational agents, to avoid criminal actions'; and when they acted against this law, offenders would be held responsible through rationally calibrated punishment (Naffine 2009: 71–72). Classical precepts imagined autonomous, rational beings that offended (with intent) against codes as criminally culpable. Hence, as with Section 16.1 of the Criminal Code of Canada previously cited, non-rational persons defined by legal tests (such as those related to the famous 1843 McNaughton case; see Lacey 2001a) could be exempted from usual criminal processes; but persons who intentionally transgressed criminal laws were to be variously – but always based on reason – depersonalised as criminals. However, as Morse reminds us, this focus on autonomous individuals who break the law involved only a limited view of rationality:

> The legal view of the person does not hold that people must always reason or consistently behave rationally according to some preordained, normative notion of rationality. Rather the law's view is that people are capable of acting for reasons and are capable of minimal rationality according to predominantly conventional, socially constructed standards
> (Morse 2011: 531)

Within classical precepts, too, rational punishment surfaces as the key measure to hold criminalised people responsible for their offences and to discourage them and others from committing crime in future. Crime prevention and deterrence were key to such notions, as indicated by Beccaria's approach to punishment:

> The purpose can only be to prevent the criminal from inflicting new injuries on its citizens and to deter others from similar acts. Always keeping due proportions, such punishments and such method of inflicting them ought to be chosen, therefore, [on the basis of] which will make the strongest and most lasting impression on the minds of men, and inflict the least torment on the body of the criminal
> (Beccaria 1996: 42)

As is well known, punishment was to apply rationally calibrated pains to deter rational individuals from committing crimes. Under Bentham's utilitarianism, such calibrations entailed a 'hedonistic' or 'felicific' calculus to compute punishments with just enough pain to offset any pleasure gained from a criminal act (Bentham 2005: chapter IV). Notwithstanding notorious problems associated with attempts to so link crime, pleasure and pain, this classical logic has resounded historically in such ideas as maximum and minimum sentences, 'getting tough on crime', the call for 'swift and certain' punishment, zero tolerance policing, 'three strikes' practices, and so on (see Zimring *et al* 2001). In sum, classical images of the criminalisable person call for criminal law to target rational individuals who deliberately break the law with offending action; but criminal law should be governed by reason through publicly accessible codes, procedures and use of proportionate punishment to deter would-be offenders and prevent further crimes.

Persons, characters and corrective reform

An equally well-studied approach, with closer connections to the former than is often granted in the history of criminology (but see Rafter 1997; Beirne

1993; Pick 1989), 'positivist' criminology developed throughout the nineteenth century, achieving particular prominence towards its close. Although somewhat dispersed, its discourses tended to focus on discovering an identifiable 'character' attributed to the criminalisable person (Rafter 2008; Lacey 2001a; Wiener 2009). Attached to fluid empirical 'sciences' at different times during the nineteenth century, positivism in criminology defined various images of criminal character, typically framed around biological, bodily, mental, and social causes. Its emphasis on empirical observation cloaked 'findings' in idioms that purported neutrality, but emerged through moralising frames that described criminal beings as having 'character defects', inclining them towards criminal behaviour. As Wiener notes:

> It was less the actions than the characters of offenders on which attention came to focus ... crime was essentially seen as the expression of a fundamental character defect stemming from a refusal or inability to deny wayward impulses or to make proper calculations of long-run self-interest
> (Wiener 1996: 46)

Character-deficient, criminal types were also often viewed as having failed to check an underlying animality by not mastering their passions, as might be expected from persons of good character and habit (Pavlich 2010; Rafter 2008, 1997). Esposito's genealogy of concepts defining a person also indicates that it was used to describe (largely) 'men' with an inability to master 'the more properly animal part of his nature', recognising that, 'not everyone has this tendency or disposition to de-animalize' (Esposito 2012: 22).

Within positivist criminology, those with a limited capacity to 'de-animalise' were variously cast as lesser persons with insufficiently developed characters, and identified through such labels as 'moral degenerate', member of the 'dangerous classes', 'sinful men', 'asocial', 'incorrigible criminal', 'habitual criminal', and so on (Pavlich 2010). Later, this focus on character was revised in scientific attempts to observe differences between criminals and non-criminals: Gall's criminal head shapes, Galton's composite portraits of 'criminal types', Lombroso's hereditary criminals, various versions of 'criminal personalities' and so on (see Wetzell 2000: 17–31; Beirne 1993). When such thinking was attached to versions of social evolution, as evinced by Lombroso's famous 'atavist', criminal characters were deemed incapable of embracing the rapidly changing demands of modern, industrial society (Pick 1989: 120–21). As this character type supposedly possessed habits that inclined them towards criminal behaviour, a new kind of criminalisable persons emerged around the mid-nineteenth century: a discrete type that 'habitually' committed crime (Pavlich 2010). This type was later recast as having biological (eugenic), psychological and/or social predispositions, continuing a line of thinking that tied criminality to physiognomy, phrenology and images of a 'dangerous' or 'criminal class' of people (Wiener 1996).

In short, positivist formulations of the criminalisable person targeted subjects said to possess a specific nature that disposed them towards criminal action. Criminal justice demanded less a rational calibration of prompt, rational punishment than corrective measures directed somehow to reclaiming specific individuals (see Rafter 2008; Beirne 1993; Pick 1989). According to this reasoning, if science discovered the variables that caused criminality, it could also predict and manipulate behavioural outcomes. Biological, psychological, eugenic and social tenets were fused with character-based understandings to assert a distinctively deficient character to criminalisable persons requiring some or other form of 'treatment', 'correction', and 'rehabilitation' (Pavlich 2010). The legacy of this criminology through the twentieth and twenty-first centuries is hard to overestimate, having embedded itself in the very criminal law that focuses on individuals and unleashes its force through vast correctional regimes designed to rehabilitate offenders. Behind such trends lies a positivist image of the person over whom criminal law might legitimately stamp its jurisdiction.

Criminal responsibility, biopolitics and the biometric person

Closely related to positivist criminology's scientific hues, one can identify the rise of 'criminalistics' and 'criminal anthropology' that mounted biologically construed identities of the criminalisable person (Pavlich 2009). While both approaches involved a biopolitics of recognition, the former emerged as a specific response to the problem of reliably identifying repeat offenders who tried to escape the label of a 'habitual criminal' – and associated harsher punishments – by masking their appearances. Bertillon's anthropometry could be taken as an exemplar – it carefully measured bodily attributes, recoded dimensions on index cards and developed elaborate classification systems for retrieving stored metrics to compare against the bodies that presented before technicians (Cole 2001). His success laid the foundation for biometric technologies and these were initially only targeted to 'persistent' offenders, but have since become ubiquitous in a biopolitics of recognition that contours contemporary societies (Agamben 2011). By contrast, Galton's criminal anthropology was more concerned with photographs and fingerprints. He put such biometrics to work as potential predictors of criminal behaviour (Pavlich 2009). This discourse helped to found a merciless moment in criminology that sought to identify criminalisable persons as determined, 'degenerate' persons who were destined to lives of crime (Pick 1989: 37ff). Leading to disastrous forms of social engineering (e.g. eugenic exclusions and genocides, gas chamber exterminations), such approaches were centred on new biometric technologies that purportedly identified and recognised criminalisable persons through biomechanical instruments (Rose 2007).

Agamben (2011) helpfully notes how biometric identifications of both approaches have pervaded everyday cultures, threatening to destabilise conventional understandings of person by transferring a centuries-old recognition function from social processes to policing technologies. As he puts it:

> In the second half of the 19th century, techniques used by the police undergo an unexpected development, which involves the decisive transformation of the concept of identity. From this point identity no longer has, essentially, anything to do with recognition and the person's social prestige. Instead, it responds to the necessity of ensuring another part of recognition: that of the recidivist criminal by the police officer
> (Agamben 2011: 48)

The effects of such a change on a surrounding politics of recognition are profound because biometric technologies – from pass-codes that admit or deny entry, retinal scans at airports, face recognition tools from CCTV data, fingerprints, passwords that give access to ubiquitous electronic devices – replace social with mechanistic (digital) patterns of recognition (Cole 2001). We might note that as such technologies develop, so the persons to be targeted for criminal law are re-imagined, with consequential implications for law's quests to hold them responsible. For Agamben, these biometric identities are so dangerous precisely because they reduce persons to biological data, and so destroy social forms of enunciating persons (Agamben 2011: 51). Thus, the infiltration of biometric identification suggests a profound change:

> For the first time in the history of humanity, identity was no longer a function of the social 'persona' and its recognition by others but rather a function of biological data, which could bear no relation to it. Human beings removed the mask that for centuries had been the basis of their recognizability in order to consign their identity to something that belongs to them in an intimate and exclusive way but with which they can in no way identify. No longer do the 'others', my fellow men, my friends or enemies, guarantee my recognition. ... This is something with which I have absolutely nothing to do ... naked life, a purely biological datum.
> (Agamben 2011: 50)

Further, Agamben argues that as the numbers and digits of biometric identification reduce persons fully to their biology, to 'naked life', so a politics of recognition with eerie overtones of the consummate reductions of Nazi death camps surfaces:

> The reduction of man to a naked life is today such a fait accompli that it is by now the basis of the identity that the state recognizes in its citizens. As the deportees to Auschwitz no longer had either name or a nationality, and were by then only the numbers that had been tattooed on their arms,

so the contemporary citizens, lost in an anonymous mass and reduced to the level of potential criminals, are defined by nothing other than their biometric data ... their DNA

(Agamben 2011: 52)

He detects in recognition practices bereft of social contact the rise of a digitally targeted 'identity without person'. Such an elimination of persons would radically challenge the auspices of criminal law, with the possible – and for him potentially positive – effect of rendering criminal law inoperable from within (see also Parsley 2010: 32). Whether or not the latter is so, his work here raises a basic point: if reduced to the mere life of biological precepts, can anyone be held politically responsible or culpable for his or her crimes? Worse yet, does this eliminate the very idea of a person, the jurisdictional basis of modern criminal law?

Notwithstanding the importance of his worry about the extreme dangers of a reduction to biologism, I wonder about Agamben's view that biometric identification technologies have eliminated (or are 'without') the person. To be sure, the rise of biometric technologies is extraordinary, and they are likely to have even greater effects on the criminal justice domains from which they surfaced. However, the notion that biometric identification is 'without' person suggests that there is an *a priori*, or fixed, quality to persons that permits their conceptual demolition. Yet, his own insistence on the instability of historical concepts of person, as products of various recognition politics, suggests otherwise. One could argue, by contrast, that biometric identification has not so much emaciated *as redefined and fractured* other versions of the person in criminal law. A new (biometric) politics of recognition has certainly emerged, but it has not done so by emaciating previous versions of personhood – indeed it grew out of positivist formulations thereof. It may well have generated new images of the person, just as previous ways of identifying categorised persons, or bad character, or even intentional acts shaped different versions of personhood. As such, a modern politics of recognition and identification might well be changing fundamentally with biometric techniques, but it is doing so by redefining – rather than eliminating some static image of – the person. And criminology is again involved with the unfolding jurisdictions of criminal law: the criminalisable person is being refashioned as a biological datum and defined, or referenced, by biometric identification technologies (Rose 2010).

One may detect here, as does Lacey, a 'revival of character' in patterns of criminal responsibility that verge, 'on forms of character essentialism and character determinism which sit uncomfortably with the liberal values which twenty-first-century criminal justice purports to protect' (Lacey 2001a: 175). The discomforts of this 'revival' signal social dangers brought by a return to biology, which – for Rafter – will only increase as the dominance of a new 'biocriminology' plays out:

> In the years ahead, biological explanations are likely to play an increasingly prominent role in efforts to understand criminal behaviour. Just as, according to predictions, the 21st century will be 'the century of biology,' so too, on a more specific scale, is it likely to be a century of biocriminology
>
> (Rafter 2008: 240)

But she insists such a renewed turn to biology in criminology is unlikely –given the atrocities of its predictive use over the twentieth century – to emulate the crude reductions associated with earlier positivist and eugenic criminology. The latter's new attachments to biology, for her, fully accepts indeterminate – often social or cultural – components that reject strong predictive logics of the kind found in previous versions of biological (eugenic) criminologies (Rafter 2008: 214).

For example, strands of criminology may embrace a cresting intellectual wave of 'neuroscience' that in more perfunctory formulations promises to discern brain activity to predict aggressive and/or criminal action (see Freeman 2011; Rose 2010). But current versions of neuroscience, genetics and bio-social criminology increasingly acknowledge an indeterminism afforded by, say, the 'plasticity' within neuroscience (Malabou 2010, 2008), epigenetics, or the biological role accorded to the 'environment' (including social, cultural and economic factors) of persons that turn to crime (Rose 2010; Rafter 2008). Even so, Rafter's sanguine view may not appease Agamben that biocriminology will escape the dangers akin to those of Nazi, or eugenic, reductions of persons to biology, or indeed that – as she seems to suggest – sociology can counter the rhetorical power of predictive determinism in science-obsessed cultures. If not, then biocriminology may well project, rather than counter, the very biological reductions of persons that Agamben fears, but with potentially significant effects on the very persona of the criminalisable person, the processes for deciding on criminal guilt, and the responsibility objectives of criminal law.

With this in mind, one might allude to emerging debates and trends to illustrate the sorts of changes that predefined biometric persons bring to criminal law. In short, can criminal offenders be held responsible if their genes, brains, the environment, or combinations thereof determine them? A simple negation will not do because criminal responsibility in criminal courts centred around culpability for rational, autonomous decisions of individuals was never wholly at odds with determinists formulations – biological, social or psychological elements were after all assumed in notions of free will, choices and so on. As Morse reminds us:

> The truth of determinism is not inconsistent with the view that mental states matter to the causation of behaviour and that human beings are capable of being guided by reason, including the law's commands.
>
> (Morse 2011: 544)

While taking his point, we might nevertheless expect courts, when specifically considering how to hold biometric persons responsible, to embrace new management forms less concerned with depersonalisation through criminalisation alone. As these management forms expand, criminal courts may well seek to broaden what they manage as 'known' criminogenic variables within biometric persons. The result would likely involve a diminishing juridical focus on questions of guilt, innocence and punishment (correction), and a greater emphasis on the most suitable ways to manage the perceived risks of newly framed biometric persons. In such contexts, crime prevention has already assumed particular significance (see Blomberg and Cohen 2012), as have alternatives that 'divert' selected persons from courts to face different – often mediation-based – genres of accusation and restorative justice (Pavlich 2005). In addition, as court management responds to biometric information specifically considered to be potentially criminalisable, so it may face new procedural challenges when managing biologically charged persons through 'drug courts', 'therapeutic jurisprudence' and so on (McIvor 2009; Madden and Wayne 2003). Juridical decisions here appear to require a change in genre – from prescribed legal verdicts to informed judgement about how best to manage biometrically framed at-risk persons. No doubt, the emphasis on stratifying the risky echoes a colonial emphasis on 'distinctions of person', but now a biopolitics enlisted to recognise criminalisble persons through digital means finds fertile administrative ground.

As criminalisable persons are increasingly identified through biometric technologies, so a biopolitics of recognition is likely to concentrate criminological discussions at the gateway to criminal justice institutions, emphasising criminal identification and accusation processes (Pavlich 2009). Digitised processes of criminal accusation may still refer to transcribed and sworn testimonies of firsthand witness, police or justices of the peace; but increasingly they are likely to be informed by data from biometric databases and 'profiles' (in turn generated from data collected about 'known' events and persons as a way to predict future problems). Surveillance-based, digital accusations are already part of a biometric politics of recognition that predicts, classifies and streams criminal 'suspects'. Criminal accusations that use such methods to identify targets for criminal law rely on an inductive, actuarial logic through an elusive, virtual process: on one side of an imagined gate to criminal justice stand vast databases with their accumulations of digital analogues of biometric persons; on the other, refigured profiles, groupings of biometric variables, are accumulated into criteria that simulate biometric identity profiles deemed to require, in probabilistic terms, some form of criminal justice intervention. In between lie unseen comparative algorisms of specifically designed computer programs – the sovereign's virtual gatekeepers – with their Boolean logic whose digital 'gates' ply a reductive biometric trade that knows complexity only as it is framed through ones, zeros, ons, offs, ins, outs, etc. In the end, this logic of gates either flags suspects through or not in digital accusatory paths. Decisions about who or what to admit and hold criminally responsible are embedded in this virtual biopolitics of recognition. Responsibility patterns lie embedded in a virtual logic of biometrics, profiles, comparison and actuarial categorisation, located at the thresholds of entry to criminal justice processes. The prejudices of such categorisations lie buried in simulated profiles, echoing elements of both criminological positivism and the logic of persons in colonial criminal responsibility.

In short, as criminal accusation forms around the predictive logics of biocriminology, 'criminalisable' persons are increasingly imagined as wanting criminal justice interventions in advance of ever having committed an offence (Rafter 2008). Echoing elements of positivist criminology's claim to predict crime through some or other bio-type, with all the attendant dangers, new predictions tap into genetics, social-psychology and neuroscience (Rose 2007, 2010). These approaches are seldom posited without equivocation or without clear warnings to guard against the view that persons are fully determined. Uncertain environmental (social, cultural, etc.) factors are usually inserted into the very biology of biometrically-conceived persons (Freeman 2011; Rafter 2008). Even so, they are proffered as scientifically credible ways to identify biometric persons at risk of committing crimes. Persons charged with predefined combinations of biological, psychological and social traits deemed as criminogenic are now prime targets for criminal justice responses, often in the name of crime prevention strategies. Through such endeavours, criminal responsibility follows the logic of thwarting profiles claimed to be conducive to lives of crime.

Conclusion

In reflecting on changing criminological discourses and how these variously define the persons deemed worthy of criminal law's attention, the previous discussion has indicated how the former shapes the very jurisdiction of the latter. Criminology's understandings of a criminalisable person enunciated through hierarchical categories, rational autonomy, distinct and observable characteristics, and/or biometric technologies in virtual labyrinths, have variously enabled regimes of criminality and responsibility within criminal justice horizons. In concert, criminology's power-knowledge complexes have helped to shape criminal law's persons in different historical contexts, and its cultural contributions are tied to a politics that frames law's jurisdiction over criminalisable persons. With this in mind, one might allude to various possible implications of the previous discussion.

First, focusing on how criminological discourses shape the jurisdiction of criminal law enables one to highlight an oft-overlooked terrain. It also suggests possibilities for wider, more synoptic, reflections on the politics of recognition and responsibility directed at persons framed as foci for criminal law and justice. Understood thus, the preceding analysis reaffirms Fletcher's

(1978) and Lacey's (2001a, 2001b) sense that different 'patterns' of criminality and responsibility co-exist in given criminal justice horizons, complementing their respective philosophical and socio-legal discussions with an analysis of criminology's contributions to defining the criminalisable person in criminal justice domains. It also develops their implicit challenge to those who might consider criminal law a homogeneous domain, with a singular political logic advancing along a progressive path to greater degrees of justice. If the analysis points to the salience of legal pluralism in criminal justice arenas, and even a global legal pluralism (see Isiksel and Thies 2013; Berman 2012), it also shows how four co-existing criminological approaches to the criminalisable person enable heterogeneous political rationalities within legal domains. These help to forge hybrid responsibility arenas that claim to underpin, say, social order, rational just deserts, corrective rehabilitation and crime prevention/risk reduction strategies. By attending to diverse contributions and legacies of criminological thinking around the criminalisable person, a plural politics of recognition and accountability behind the laws that claim jurisdiction over criminal justice domains is brought into bold relief.

Second, despite criminology's changing images of criminalisable persons, an enduring problem surfaces through the legacy hierarchies associated with colonial 'distinctions of person', with its overtly racist expression in criminal anthropology and eugenics. If these formulations exposed contextually categorised persons to variable criminal practices and disproportionate intensities of law's force, one may note the tenacity of what appears to be a systemic logic that continues to administer – under new pretexts – such force unevenly to specific categories of persons (Wacquant 2009a). Of course, much may have changed, including transformations yielded by classical calls for equality before the law. Yet the sheer persistence of these disproportions suggests the resilience of a logic that categorises, processes and punishes persons enunciated through unequal and historically framed social strata and hierarchies. The previous discussion may not tackle the matter head on, as others have done (e.g. Wacquant 2009b), but it does point to certain race-based outcomes of colonial and positivist criminologies that have yet to be expunged from the identifications of persons targeted as subjects for criminal law's gaze. It is well to focus attention on the political and cultural arenas of recognition that frame criminal law's jurisdiction. For in these may lie consequential ways to resist unexamined categorising practices that usually translate into disproportionate punishment regimes.

Lastly, the preceding notes how specific bundles of data comprise the biometric person of emerging virtual crime control contexts. Yet, as indicated, biometric data do not discover *a priori* beings: they create a new version of the criminalisable person. Despite biocriminology's appeals to 'new' and 'better' science, it is important to recall that the creation of legal persons is never, ultimately, a matter of discovery or necessity. Criminological discourses that submit to ruling policy frameworks have little appetite for questioning the foundations of systems upon which their science depends, and from which they derive their authority. No doubt, such foundational critique is better suited to increasingly marginalised realms of ethics and politics that embrace –rather than eschew – those radically undetermined and incalculable terrains that shape history, that bring questions of justice to the fore. In such terrains, Agamben is right to worry about reductions of identity to biology that disavows the indeterminacy of social recognition, and a dynamic politics that has for centuries defined different persons. If reduced to a determined biology whose 'naked life' is identified only through biometric technologies, persons would seem to be purged of a capacity to bring interdeterminate action into being. Should we be reassured by Rafter's (2008) optimism that biocriminology will create social openings via 'environmental' factors at the foundation of biology? I think not. Agamben's fear about biologically reduced subjects that approximate the bare life of concentration camps is unlikely to vanish with biocriminology's limited and biologically-centred versions of indeterminacy. And why would critical criminology challenge the determinations – even if attenuated to biology's sanctioned 'environments' – of a now privileged Leviathan of *bios*, of life? In short, because foundational challenges to determinist thinking, opening permanently to its always limiting horizons, are all that we have to resist totalitarian socio-legal closure. Perhaps we would be well advised to recall this warning: such totalising thinking contoured criminology's bleakest moment when it paraded eugenic versions of a criminal type as a relatively fixed being only then, blithely, to sanction its elimination.

Acknowledgement

The author would like to acknowledge the Social Science Centre in Berlin for providing a congenial context for the initial formulation of this chapter.

Bibliography

Agamben, G. (2011) *Nudities*, Stanford, CA: Stanford University Press.
Beccaria, C. (1996) *Of Crimes and Punishments*, New York, NY: Marsilio Publishers.
Beirne, P. (1993) *Inventing Criminology: Essays on the Rise of Homo Criminalis*, Albany, NY: State University of New York Press.
Bentham, J. (2005) *An Introduction to the Principles of Morals and Legislation*, New York, NY: Oxford University Press.
Berman, P.S. (2012) *Global Legal Pluralism: A Jurisprudence of Law Beyond Borders*, Cambridge: Cambridge University Press.
Bindman, D. (2002) *Ape to Apollo: Aesthetics and the Idea of Race in the 18th Century*, Ithaca: Cornell University Press.
Blomberg, T.G. and S. Cohen (2012) *Punishment and Social Control*, New Brunswick, NJ: Transaction Publishers.

Cole, S.A. (2001) *Suspect Identities: A History of Fingerprinting and Criminal Identification*, Cambridge, MA: Harvard University Press.
Dayan, C. (2013) *The Law is a White Dog*, Princeton, NJ: Princeton University Press.
Dorsett, S. and S. McVeigh (2012) *Jurisdiction*, New York, NY: Routledge.
Esposito, R. (2012) *The Third Person*, Malden, MA: Polity.
Faguntes, D. (2000–01) 'What We Talk About When We Talk About Persons: The Language of a Legal Fiction', *Harvard Law Review*, 114: 1746–55.
Ferrell, J. (1995) 'Culture, Crime and Criminology', *Journal of Criminal Justice and Popular Culture*, 3 (2): 25–42.
Fletcher, G.P. (1978) *Rethinking Criminal Law*, Boston, MA: Little, Brown.
Foucault, M. (1979) *Discipline and Punish: The Birth of the Prison*, New York, NY: Vintage Books.
Foucault, M. (1980) *Power/Knowledge: Selected Interviews and Other Writings, 1972–1977*, New York, NY: Pantheon Books.
Foucault, M. (2000) *Power*, New York, NY: The New Press.
Freeman, M. (ed.) (2011) *Law and Neuroscience: Current Legal Issues*, Oxford: Oxford University Press.
Garland, D. (2001) *The Culture of Control: Crime and Social Order in Contemporary Society*, Chicago, IL: University of Chicago Press.
Giliomee, H. and B. Mbenga (eds) (2007) *New History of South Africa*, Cape Town: Tafelberg.
Golder, B. and P. Fitzpatrick (2009) *Foucault's Law*, New York, NY: Routledge.
Henry, S. and M. Lanier (eds) (2001) *What is Crime?*, Lanham, MD: Rowman & Littlefield.
Isiksel, T. and A. Thies (2013) 'Changing subjects: rights, remedies and responsibilities of individuals under global legal pluralism', *Global Constitutionalism*, 2 (2): 151–59.
Jones, M. and J. Dlamini (eds) (2013) *Categories of Persons: Rethinking Ourselves and Others*, Johannesburg: Picador Africa.
Kelsen, H. (1945) *General Theory of Law and State*, New York, NY: Russell and Russell.
Kirkby, D.E. and C. Coleborne (2001) *Law, History, Colonialism: The Reach of Empire*, New York, NY: Manchester University Press
Lacey, N. (2001a) 'The Resurgence of Character: Responsibility in the Context of Criminalization', in R.A. Duff and S. Green (eds) *Philosophical Foundations of Criminal Law*, Oxford: Oxford University Press, pp. 152–83.
Lacey, N. (2001b) 'In Search of the Responsible Subject: History, Philosophy and Social Science Theory', *The Modern Law Review*, 64 (3): 350–71.
Lacey, N. (2007) 'Space, Time and Function: Intersecting Principles of Responsibility across the Terrain of Criminal Justice', *Criminal Law and Philosophy*, 1 (1): 233–50.
Madden, R. and R. Wayne (2003) 'Social Work and the Law: a Therapeutic Jurisprudence Perspective', *Social Work*, 48 (3): 338–47.
Malabou, C. (2008) *What Should We Do with our Brain?*, New York, NY: Fordham University Press.
Malabou, C. (2010) *Plasticity at the Dusk of Writing: Dialectic, Destruction, Deconstruction*, New York, NY: Columbia University Press.

McIvor, G. (2009) 'Therapeutic Jurisprudence and Procedural Justice in Scottish Drug Courts', *Criminology and Criminal Justice*, 9 (1): 29–49.
McLaughlin, E. and J. Muncie (eds) (2001) *The Sage Dictionary of Criminology*, London: Sage.
Morse, S. (2011) 'Lost in Translation: an Essay on Law and Neuroscience', in M. Freeman (ed.) *Law and Neuroscience: Current Legal Issues*, Oxford: Oxford University Press, pp. 529–65.
Naffine, N. (2003) 'Who are Law's Persons? From Cheshire Cats to Responsible Subjects', *Modern Law Review*, 66: 346–67.
Naffine, N. (2009) *Law's Meaning of Life: Philosophy, Religion, Darwin, and the Legal Person*, Portland, OR: Hart.
Parsley, C. (2010) 'The Mask and Agamben: the Technics of Legal Regulation', *Law, Text, Culture*, 14 (1): 12–39.
Pavlich, G. (2005) *Governing Paradoxes of Restorative Justice*, London: GlassHouse Press.
Pavlich, G. (2009) 'The Subjects of Criminal Identification', *Punishment & Society*, 11 (2): 171–90.
Pavlich, G. (2010) 'The Emergence of Habitual criminals in 19th century Britain: Implications for Criminology', *Journal of Theoretical and Philosophical Criminology*, 2 (1): 1–62.
Pavlich, G. (2013a) 'Cape Legal Idioms and the Colonial Sovereign', *International Journal for the Semiotics of Law*, 26: 39–54.
Pavlich, G. (2013b) 'Sovereign Force and Crime-Focused Law at the Cape Colony', *Journal of Historical Sociology*, 26, 3: 318–38.
Pick, D. (1989) *Faces of Degeneration: A European Disorder*, Cambridge: Cambridge University Press.
Quinney, R. (2001) *The Social Reality of Crime*, New Brunswick, NJ: Transaction Publishers.
Rafter, N.H. (1997) *Creating Born Criminals*, Urbana, IL: University of Illinois Press.
Rafter, N.H. (2008) *The Criminal Brain: Understanding Biological Theories of Crime*, New York, NY: New York University Press.
Rose, N. (2007) *Politics of Life Itself: Biomedicine, Power, and Subjectivity in the Twenty-First Century*, Princeton, NJ: Princeton University Press.
Rose, N.S. (2010) '"Screen and Intervene": Governing Risky Brains', *History of the Human Sciences*, 23 (1): 79–105.
Sherman, L.W. (1992/93) 'Influence of Criminology on Criminal Law: Evaluating Arrests for Misdemeanour Domestic Violence', *Journal of Criminal Law and Criminology*, 83 (1): 1–45.
Simon, J. (2007) *Governing Through Crime: How the War on Crime Transformed American Democracy and Created a Culture of Fear*, New York, NY: Oxford University Press.
Smith, B. (1928) 'Legal Personality', *The Yale Law Journal*, 37 (3): 283–99.
Sutherland, E.H., D.R. Cressey and D.F. Luckenbill (1992) *Principles of Criminology*, Oxford: Rowman & Littlefield.
Taylor, I., P. Walton and J. Young (1975) *Critical Criminology*, London: Routledge & Kegan Paul.
Theal, G.M. (1897) *Records of the Cape Colony, from February 1793 to 1801*, vols 1–3, London: Printed for the government of the Cape Colony (by W. Clowes and Sons).

Ullmann, W. (2010) *The Medieval Idea of Law as Represented by Lucas de Penna*, London: Routledge.
Wacquant, L.J.D. (2009a) *Prisons of Poverty*, Minneapolis, MN: University of Minnesota Press.
Wacquant, L.J.D. (2009b) *Punishing the Poor: The Neoliberal Government of Social Insecurity*, Durham, NC: Duke University Press.
Wetzell, R.F. (2000) *Inventing the Criminal: A History of German Criminology*, London: University of North Carolina Press.
Wiener, M.J. (1996) *Reconstructing the Criminal: Culture, Law, and Policy in England, 1830–1914*, New York, NY: Cambridge University Press.
Wiener, M.J. (2009) *An Empire on Trial: Race, Murder and Justice under British Rule, 1870–1935*, Cambridge: Cambridge University Press.
Zimring, F.E., G. Hawkins and S. Kamin (2001) *Punishment and Democracy: Three Strikes and You're out in California*, New York, NY: Oxford University Press.

Chapter 10

The pursuit of a general theory of crime and the indeterminacy of human experience

David Polizzi

Introduction

From its very inception, criminology has sought to construct itself as an 'objective' science capable of providing an explanatory system by which to study the phenomenon of crime and criminal behaviour. Included in this methodological endeavour has been the desire to instill a degree of 'scientific' predictive certainty, which in turn has helped to legitimise the conclusions that this type of objectified disciplinary explanation has strived to achieve (Einstadter and Henry 2006; Walsh 2014; Wortley 2011). Whether this 'certainty' has been focused upon those 'objective' economic, political or sociological factors or variables present within a given culture or within the 'rational' and 'objective' decision-making process employed by rational actors involved in various modes of criminality, these conclusions have failed to achieve what appears most desired by the field, that is, a general theory of crime (Einstadter and Henry 2006).

However, rather than question the philosophical foundation of these failed Cartesian or positivistic-objective strategies, greater focus has been given to quantitative innovation or the reintroduction of a type of biological determinism, which has rendered much of the same results (Buss 2012; Durrant and Ward 2012; Einstadter and Henry 2006; Hall 2012; Owen 2012; Pakes and Winstone 2007; Walsh 2009, 2014; Wortley 2011). The conclusion should be obvious: an objective approach to criminology will neither deliver a general theory of crime nor tell us what we need to know about crime construction or the phenomenology of criminal behaviour. Crime and criminal behaviour, as a subjective enterprise, must be viewed from a theoretical frame of reference that is able to take up the subtle and nuanced realities of human existence without concern for the actuarial requirements demanded by generalised and objectified methodological agendas.

Such a theoretical refocusing of the project of criminology would require not only the conceptualisation of criminality as a subjective enterprise, but would by necessity need to include how all subjective experience is inseparably situated within a social world that is equally implicated in the creation and experience of crime. Numerous examples exist within the social sciences of an 'objectified subject' who more or less exists side by side an objective world. In fact, many within the field of criminology would readily agree with such a formulation: the event of crime is caused by a specific set of biological or genetic factors or perpetrated by a rational actor(s) who is viewed as being categorically separate from the social world (Einstadter and Henry 2006; Gadd and Jefferson 2007; Hall 2012). This approach shares some basic philosophical underpinnings with one whereby the focus is shifted to the social structures of a given society and their role in the production of crime.

Within these formulations of crime, the criminal act becomes viewed as an epiphenomenal artifact emerging from a variety of deep structural processes that are formulated as the determining consequence or cause behind the act of offending. From these perspectives, criminal behaviour is manufactured or produced by the presence of various manifestations of existing structural inequalities, be these economic, political and social or located within an integrated variation of the same that are ontologically implicated within these cultural contexts. As a result, human potentiality or choice is overwritten by these larger structural demands, thereby nullifying or over-determining one's ability to adequately respond to these marginalising processes of human control. That is the fabrication of the social self (Polizzi et al 2014). From these perspectives, the potential meaning for human experience is defined relative to these structurally derived and overly-determined social contexts.

In response to these positivistic formulations of crime and criminal behaviour, a variety of theoretical approaches have emerged to address and critique the positivism of the discipline, which has become widely accepted by the field (Arrigo and Milovanovic 2009; Arrigo Milovanovic and Schehr 2005; Ferrell 2004; Gadd and Jefferson 2007; Hall 2012; Hardie-Bick and Hadfield (2011); Henry and Milovanovic 1996; Katz 1988; Quinney 2000). In clear opposition to these more objectified approaches to the study of crime, a more subjective or constructionist frame of reference has emerged which seeks to reconfigure the place of human experience within these larger social contexts that provide both meaning and potentiality. As such, the demarcation between individual action and social influence becomes blurred given that no clear separation between individual and world is philosophically recognised or methodologically privileged. Although the reality of the social world is not denied or reduced to a category of solipsistic extension, neither is it privileged in a way that would effectively undermine the role of human participation in its constant unfolding.

Subjective or constructionist approaches to crime and criminal behaviour, in their rejection of 'objective' criminology and its positivist philosophical foundations, seek to reconfigure human action and social world. From this perspective, the artifact of criminal behaviour specifically or the production of crime generally, emerges from this participatory interaction between individual and social world, which is predicated upon the specific point of reference from which this interaction takes places (Arrigo and Milovanovic 2009; Hall 2012; Hardie-Bick and Hadfield 2011; Herman 1995; Polizzi 2011a, 2011b; Ryals 2014; Unnever and Gabbidon 2011). For example, from this understanding of crime, the reality of one's social existence as this relates to a variety of socially imposed economic, political and social structures is inseparably implicated in every aspect of human intention, motivation and perspective.

The attempt to integrate criminology

What becomes fairly obvious is that the field of criminology is a divided discipline, which according to Agnew tends: '… to focus on different types of crime, employ different explanations for these crimes, test their explanations using different methods, and make different recommendations for controlling crime' (Agnew 2011: 2). Agnew continues by observing that the philosophical depth of this disagreement within the discipline of criminology is so wide that it is unlikely that any integrative accommodation could ever be reached that would have the theoretical breadth to incorporate in any coherent way these differing epistemologies and incompatible ontologies. Regardless of the integrative challenges facing such a project, Agnew offers an integrative model by which he hopes to resolve these seemingly irreconcilable differences.

In his attempt to resolve the fractured state of criminological discourse, Agnew focuses upon the conceptualisations of agency and determinism, the nature of society, and the nature of reality itself. The targets of Agnew's critical exploration may seem odd for a criminology text, but are actually essential to this discussion insofar as the process or method, by which one constructs the meaning of crime, still remains a human enterprise that must attempt to confront the complexities of its subject. How does human agency get implicated in the criminal act? What role, if any, is there for a conceptualisation of agency when human experience is defined as the backward tracing of behaviour to neuro-transmitters, to genomic systems, and ultimately reducible to the movement of Newtonian objects (Kauffman 2008: 13)? If human agency or subjectivity is essential to this project, how does the fact of our undeniable biology get legitimately recognised within this discussion without conflating human being into untenable reductionism (Kauffman 2008: 10–18)?

Agnew, in his important text *Toward a Unified Criminology: Integrating Assumptions about Crime, People and Society*, makes the following observation toward the end of that text, which powerfully configures the real depth of the issues he attempts resolve:

> There is reason to believe that behavior is influenced by both subjective views and objective reality. Individuals base their actions on their views, even if such views are mistaken. But at the same time, the real world

imposes constraints on action and influences individuals in ways that they are unaware of or misperceive.

(Agnew 2011: 186)

What this quote conveys is a privileging of 'objective' reality, which seeks to recognise and 'correct' the errors of subjective existence or perception, or at the very least, describes how subjective existence occurs as a parallel to objective reality. Within this context, the 'objective' or the recognition of objective reality is constructed as a separate philosophical category that exists external to or 'alongside' the subjective, which is also identified as a distinct philosophical category that may be influenced by this objective reality, but is somehow not included within it. Such a positivistic or Newtonian rendering of objective reality (Mead 1967; Wendt forthcoming, 2014) and subjective experience has become the corner stone for an objective criminology and with it, the desire to formulate a general theory of crime. Agnew goes on to state that:

> For example, many social learning theorists argue that crime is a function of both its *perceived* costs and benefits and its actual costs and benefits (with actual costs often influencing perceived costs). And strain theorists focus on the importance of both objective strains and the subjective perception of those strains. Other perspectives, however, argue that subjective views *or* objective reality is the primary determinant of behavior. But even here, a good case can be made that both subjective views and objective reality are important and should therefore be considered when explaining crime.
>
> (Agnew 2011: 186)

However, what this observation fails to recognise is that such a conceptualisation of subjective perspective and objective reality not only drastically hinders any possibility for an integrated theory of crime, but renders the subjective viewpoint as being epiphenomenal to that reality. For example, the distinction made above between the perceived and actual costs of crime is not located within the relationship between human perspective and objective context or by the philosophical privileging of one view of reality over another. Rather, it reflects the incongruence of these two competing 'subjective' points of view that construct the act and 'costs' of crime from two very different socially situated perspectives. The meaning of the criminal act rendered by the perceiving subject is really no different from the act of crime perceived from the perspective of the law: each brings with it a specific point of view, which in turn evokes a very specific meaning relative to the social construction of crime and criminal behaviour that in turn evokes a very different construction of its 'value'.

In critiquing the Behaviourism of his day, Mead maintained that it was a mistake to '… conceive of society as a merely historical and cultural phenomenon, which as an external bond holds together human individuals who are by their nature isolated. Instead, he conceives of human nature itself as essentially social' (Joas 1997: 113). In describing his understanding of the social act, which certainly must include criminal behaviour, Mead (1967) makes the following observation. 'The social act is not explained by building it up out of stimulus plus response; It must be taken as a dynamic whole – as something going on – no part of which can be considered or understood by itself …' (Mead 1967: 7).

Taken from this perspective, the experience of criminal behaviour must be viewed as an aspect of this 'dynamic whole' that cannot be viewed within the context of isolated ontologies (Moore 2014: 88–92; Unnever and Gabbidon 2011: 4–6). As such, criminal behaviour, the social construction of cultural institutions, the process of adjudication as reflected in criminal law or the theorising offered by the discipline of criminology and criminal justice proper, do not exist in separately constructed realities identified by their objective and subjective qualities. Rather, all come to represent various points of reference within this larger dynamic whole. Objective criminology fails in large part due to its inability to recognise this basic reality of human existence. It then exasperates this failure by relying upon the objectification of certain 'factors' or 'variables' that are then identified as the philosophical cornerstones of criminological theory. But if a truly objective criminology is impossible and with it, a general theory of crime or criminal behaviour, where do we go from here?

If the above observation is correct, then perhaps we must begin not with a general theory of crime, but with a clarifying description of what it means to be human. Such a refocusing of the criminological project will require a general understanding of the ontological grounding for human existence and its relationship to the social world. Crime or the criminal act represents a single response to one's engagement with the social world. If we are truly to understand the phenomenon of crime, we must also be able to recognise how this specific human action unfolds within the premise confines of the social world that is directly related to its construction.

In Chapter 3 of Agnew's text, *Toward an Integrated Criminology*, the concepts of determinism and agency are discussed. Agnew introduces his topic by asking the following question: 'In particular, what causes individuals and groups to intentionally harm others without legitimate justification or excuse, to risk public condemnation, and/or risk state sanction? Related to this, what actions can be taken to reduce such behavior' (Agnew 2011: 44)? It is important to note that how a question is phrased is equally as important as its answer. The either or formulation of the question establishes the philosophical contours that the answer will likely follow. By objectifying and isolating the external environment from an equally objectified and isolated conceptualisation of human agency, our answer becomes determined by either an external or individually formulated positivism that must either conflate the one into the other or ignore its existence all together.

Crime or the production of crime has been generally understood as either a deterministic response to environmental conditions that exist outside the immediate control of the individual or the product of a rational free will which chooses to pursue criminal behaviour as a legitimate act of agency. From the deterministic perspective, crime is inevitable due to the certainty of various types of environmental or physiological influences; where as a purely agentic understanding of criminal behaviour is the result of free will, which is both capable of pro-social action, as well as capable of recognising the deterrent effect of possible punishment for law-breaking behaviour. Unfortunately, neither of these philosophical perspectives is able to provide a convincing account of the complexities involved in the act of criminal offending.

If crime is a process that is beyond human control, human agency fails to exist and becomes little more than an epiphenomenal artifact to externally derived cues found in the environment. If crime is the result of a rational free will that is in no way directly influenced by the external environment, then the social world becomes irrelevant for the simple reason that the individual exists somewhere outside this reality. In either example, the process by which crime is constructed becomes an isolating event that fails to recognise the inseparable quality of human existence and social world. The retreat to these untenable philosophically reductive accounts of criminality, if nothing else, helps to illuminate the complexity of the topic under study. How then do we reconcile this disjointed foundation between human existence and world that we regularly witness in criminological discourses?

Although the continued attempt to arrive at a general theory of crime seems unlikely given the undeniable complexity of human existence, this failure should not imply that a more thorough conceptualisation of crime and criminal behaviour is not possible. Such a conceptualisation of crime would need to include the role of the recessive human body – that is, the biological, genetic and neurological aspects of human behaviour – as well as the place of legitimate human agency or consciousness as this relates to individual intention and action. Add to these the various ways in which the ontological characteristics of human existence manifest or presence within very specific social contexts that are inseparably implicated in the creation of human subjectivity or the human self, and it becomes difficult to imagine how such a pursuit could be successful. It would also be difficult to conceptualise such a possibility within the reductionist approaches employed to solve this problem.

Although Agnew's text offers perhaps the most theoretically sophisticated attempt towards the construction of a unified theory of criminal behaviour, it fails in its inability to sufficiently distance itself from the reductionist underpinnings that still seem central to much of the logic of his discussion. Agnew rightly aims his focus on the topics of human agency and determinism, the nature of the human animal and the nature of reality itself; all of which are clearly implicated not only in the meaning of human existence, but the meaning of the social world and the recognition of the real, which in turn makes possible the production of crime. Any attempt to bifurcate the fact of human experience from its biological reality or any theoretical approach that seeks to isolate the individual from the inseparable influences of social interaction, must result in failure or at the very least, leave us with an answer that is hopelessly incomplete.

Biological indeterminacy

If the possibility for a general theory of crime is to be rejected, what then becomes the strategy for an appropriate study of crime? As has been argued above, any such attempt must be capable of reconciling the seemingly incapable realities of human biology and human agency. It must also be able to adequately address the various ways in which human existence and social world evoke an inseparable bond that implicates both human actions along with the reality of existing and emergent social structures, as this relates to the meanings which emerge from these encounters. Lastly, and most importantly, it must be able to recognise the irreducibility of human existence, and the participatory aspect of human lived-experience as this situates social life in all of its various manifestations and contexts. As such, the following attempt to provide an indeterminate phenomenology of crime and criminal behaviour will call upon the philosophies of Martin Heidegger, Giorgio Agamben and the theoretical biologist Stuart Kauffman. I will begin with a brief discussion of the work of Stuart Kauffman.

Kauffman in his influential text, *Reinventing the Sacred: A New View of Science, Reason and Religion*, begins with the following powerful observation concerning the role of reductionism in both the natural and social sciences:

> In brief, reductionism is the view that society is to be explained in terms of people, people in terms of organs, organs by cells, cells by biochemistry, biochemistry by chemistry, and chemistry to physics. To put it even more crudely, it is the view that in the end, all reality is *nothing but* whatever is 'down there' at the current base of physics: quarks or the famous strings of string theory, plus the interactions among these entities.
> (Kauffman 2008: 10–11)

He argues that not only is it scientifically incorrect to reduce biology to physics, but also maintains that Darwin's theory of evolution represents an equally irreducible process of natural selection that can neither predict or prestate the totality of possible evolutionary variations within the biosphere, which would of course need to include the predictability of criminal behaviour. Although Kauffman's argument goes far beyond the scope and space of this discussion, his focus on the irreducibility of Darwin's theory of evolution and adaptation is particularly salient to the current discussion, insofar as it provides a natural scientific perspective by which the biological may be incorporated into the discussion of criminal behaviour, without any reliance on reductive theoretical explanations. One such avenue is found in Kauffman's description of Darwin's concept of pre-adaptation.

Pre-adaptation relates to the existence of an unstated biological function that has no 'selective significance' in one environment, but may in another. 'By "preadapted" Darwin did not mean that some intelligence crafted the pre-adaptation. He simply meant that an incidental feature with no selective significance in one environment might turn out to have a selective significance in another' (Kauffman 2008: 132). As such, the predictive accuracy of more traditional theoretical attempts to explain and predict criminal behaviour become highly questionable given their inability in advance to calculate the infinite possible configurations of a 'selective environment'. Neither is it possible to isolate human behaviour in such a way that would exclude or underestimate the role played by the environment in the creation of this more long term or more spontaneous environmental adaptations:

> The profound implication of this is that virtually any feature or interconnected sets of features of an organism might, in the right selective environment, turn out to be a preadaptation and give rise to a novel functionality. Thus the evolution of the biosphere is radically often unprestatable and unpredictable in its invasion of the adjacent possible on the unique trajectory that is its own biological evolution.
> (Kauffman 2008: 133)

One of the central concepts offered by Kauffman's new theory of biology is the introduction of what he identies as the adjacent possible. The adjacent possible is described as:

> ... that set of specific and immediate possibilities available to an evolutionary system at any particular moment of its duration. As a system evolves – biologically, economically, politically – it not only passes from particular state to state but also develops intrinsically within shrinking or expanding zones of what kinds of events might subsequently occur, the possible steps the system might take.
> (Gangle 2007: 225)

Such a holistic conceptualisation of this evolutionary system immediately recognises the irreducibility of human adaptive variation and the variation of a given environment. From this perspective both human adaptation and environment are viewed as indeterminate in their productive capacities, evoking both passive and active interactive influences that are not reducible to objectified conclusions. A similar degree of variability is witnessed within Heidegger's concept of the ontological structure of being-in-the-world.

Being-in-the-world

For Heidegger, being-in-the-world reflects the fundamental or ontological characteristics for human being. Included within this ontological 'structuring' of human being are the specific ways in which human existence finds itself within the social world. This ontological structure, also identified as care, is made up of three different aspects of being-in-the-world: existence, facticity and falling. 'Care represents the way in which being-in-the-world seeks to remain open to its own potentiality to be, as well as the being of others' (Polizzi 2011b: 132). Existence reflects that aspect of being that is ahead of itself as it takes up its potentiality and pursues its projects. Facticity or thrownness reflects the various ways I find myself thrown into certain contexts or situations, which places limitations on my ability to be; and falling represents the ways in which truth is concealed within daily affairs (Richardson 2012: 111–12; Zimmerman 1981: 65).

As such, the care structure situates these differing aspects of being-in-the-world within a temporal frame of reference (Zimmerman 1981: 62–68). Existence as a projective possibility is future focused, whereas thrownness is concerned with the past and the limits this places on human experience and falling describes the current condition of being-in-the-world (Polizzi, 2011b: 132) Whereas the ontological qualities of being-in-the-world are those characteristics most fundamental to what it means to be human, the ontic manifestation of those possibilities is always inseparably and invariably situated within the contextual possibilities offered to human experience. For example, all human beings are confronted by the inescapable fact of their own morality, but the time, place and circumstance of that fact will always be ontically determined.

Just as all human beings must ultimately confront the inevitably of their own deaths, so too must they confront the conditions of their own existence. As existence seeks to take up the pursuit of its own projects it is continually confronted by the thrown and fallen aspects of being-in-the-world. The ontic manifestation of facticity or thrownness reveals or calls forth the specific conditions which being-in-the-world must confront relative to everyday existence. Included here would be those specific manifestations of culture, economics, politics and the ordering of social existence that we must take up as an everyday task of daily living. The fact of one's economic marginalisation or the presence of stigmatising impositions concerning ethnicity, gender, sexual orientation, mental illness, etc. all evoke a specific set of challenges to those confronted by these thrown realities. However, the thrown quality of human existence does not end here.

Thrownness must also include the fact of our biological and neurological framework that is always implicated in being-in-the-world's ability to be like others are allowed to be. However, this recognition of our physiological facticity is not grounded in any reductive theoretical frame of reference and is theoretically compatible with Kauffman's conceptualisation of biological indeterminacy. From this perspective predisposition or pre-adaptation reflects the openness of being-in-the-world's potentiality that is recognised as possibility and not destiny. Although these physiological structures of human existence cannot be denied, such recognition does not inevitably require a reductive rending of this functionality.

It is also important to note that the specific conditions of one's social reality not only impose very specific and identifiable limits to the potentiality of being-in-the-world, but may also greatly determine the very ability to be. The act of crime or the possibility of being-in-the-world-as-criminal reflects a specific encounter with the realities of this thrown existence that are fundamentally implicated in its construction. A positivistic rendering of this encounter, either as the consequence of one's genetic or biological destiny or as the result of objectified social structures, fails to recognise the fundamental quality of the sociality of human existence. However, because this thrown reality for being-in-the-world reflects merely a specific type of social comportment, it is always possible for it to reveal other possibilities of being-with that this thrownness seeks to deny.

Perhaps most important to this quality of thrownness is the way in which being-in-the-world finds itself within the current conditions of its existence. As fallen, being-in-the-world attempts to cover over the truth of its being, the reality of its thrownness and seeks to conform itself to the averageness imposed by 'the they'. Heidegger describes the they-self in the following way:

> In its being, the they is essentially concerned with averageness. Thus, the they maintains itself factically in the averageness of what belongs to it, what it does and does not concern valid, and what it grants or denies success. This averageness, which prescribes what can and may be ventured, watches over every exception which thrusts itself to the fore.
> (Heidegger 2010 [1953]: 123)

When applied to the conceptualisation of crime and criminal behaviour, Heidegger's configuration of the they-self has important implications concerning the reality of crime.

From this perspective, the they-self prescribes for being-in-the-world that which will be validated and 'granted' success and that which will not. Within this fallen acquiescence to the demands of the they, criminal behaviour is identified as the exclusive realm of the offending individual who must be viewed as other, who is not like me. It renders invalid any attempt to implicate those conditions of being-in-the-world that would require the re-formulation of the meaning of crime or the structuring of the social order. After all, it is the they-self that validates those explanations of the 'criminal other', which recognises those people, those genes, those biological systems, and those adaptations for the creation and ultimate ethical responsibility for the production of the act of crime.

Heidegger, in describing his conceptualisation of others, observes, 'Others' does not mean everybody else but me – those from whom the I distinguishes itself. Others are, rather, those from whom one mostly does not distinguish oneself, those among whom one also is' (Heidegger 2010 [1953]: 115). Within this context, these others are identified by the they-self as those who are not criminal, are not mentally ill, are not poor and are not dangerous. Once this relationship to the they-self has been established and validated, it becomes much easier to reject any aspect of this otherness that does not reflect the individual that I am. Explanations of crime, which identity a specific individual or specific group as criminal or in some other way deficient, become that which I am not, become that which may be denied success by the they.

Heidegger's understanding of 'Others', also applies when situated within the context of criminal behaviour or any behaviour that helps to reflect the type of being that I also am. The individual involved in various types of street crime, for example or other types of officially sanctioned acts of corruption, as exemplified by the Enron scandal, establish being-in-the-world's relationship to a specific manifestation of the they-self. Agnew's distinction between the actual and perceived costs of crime similarly reflects differing and competing manifestations of the they-self that often exist within the very same social context. I have argued elsewhere how the experience of subjective strain is always in relation to a specific manifestation of the they-self, which greatly influences the meaning of that event for that individual (Polizzi 2011a). However, being-in-the-world finds itself situated within the confluence of competing manifestations of the they-self, each of which seek to impose that which will be validated and that which will not.

It is important to recognise, therefore, that this interaction with the they-self reflects a layered encounter with competing meaning generating contexts. Just as the act of criminal behaviour is made meaningful from a variety of manifestations of the they-self, this same focus needs to be applied to the way in which our theorising about crime also reveals this same type of relationship. The averageness maintained by the relationship of academics to this 'professional' they, reflects the same leveling down of being-in-the-world that is generally present in any variation of our fallen existence. The epistemological demands often required by this academic they-self, determine ahead of time that which may be ventured and that which may not.

Those theories that seek to challenge the basic foundations or assumptions of 'accepted' epistemological beliefs are either rejected out of hand for failing to adhere to the tenants of the faith or ridiculed and caricatured as antiscientific speculation not worthy of further consideration. Such required orthodoxy, whether consciously intended or accidently achieved, reflects a strong relationship to this they that easily identifies those that are most like me and those that are not. Such a dynamic, which specifically validates a group of theoretical approaches as the 'legitimate' discourse by which to study the phenomena of crime, reflects what Foucault and Agamben have conceptualised as the apparatus.

The apparatus

In describing his conceptualisation of the apparatus, Foucault makes the following observation:

> ... an apparatus is essentially strategic, which means that we are speaking about a certain manipulation of relations of forces, of a rational and concrete intervention in the relations of forces, either so as to develop them in a particular direction, or to block them, to stabilize them, and to utilize them. The apparatus is thus always inscribed into the play of power, but it is also always linked to certain limits of knowledge that arise from it, and to an equal degree, condition it.
>
> (Foucault 1980: 195)

From this perspective, the they-self of social experience, which validates certain possibilities for being-in-the-world, and invalidates and marginalises others, or the process of theorising crime or criminal behaviour, which validates specific approaches relative to the explanation of crime and denies success to others, reflects this play of power that Foucault describes. In either of these examples, what emerges is what I have identified elsewhere as the fabricated self of the criminological rehabilitation machine (Polizzi *et al* 2014: 239–44). 'Within this process, the apparatus of the correctional/rehabilitative machine produces what Agamben identifies as a new I that is calibrated by the techniques of correctional practice' (Polizzi *et al* 2014: 238).

However, it is important to recognise that Agamben's conceptualisation of the apparatus goes beyond Foucault's initial description of this concept. In describing this re-formulation of the apparatus, Agamben states:

> I wish to propose to you nothing less than a general and massive portioning of beings into two large groups or classes: on the one, living beings (or substances), and on the other, apparatuses in which living beings are incessantly captured.
>
> (Agamben 2009: 13)

He continues by stating:

> Further expanding the already large class of Foucauldian apparatuses, I shall call an apparatus literally anything that has in some way the capacity to capture, orient, determine, intercept, model or control, or secure the gestures behaviours, opinions, or discourses of living beings.
>
> (Agamben 2009: 14)

Agamben completes his description of the apparatus by including what he defines as a third category, identified as subjects, 'I call a subject that which results from the relation and, so to speak, from the relentless fight between living beings and apparatuses' (Agamben 2009: 14). The emergence of the subject is the result of the in-between 'space' that the struggle between living beings and apparatuses evokes. Much like the struggle of being-in-the-world that must confront the reality of its thrown and fallen existence, the subject appears as an indeterminate presencing of this dialogical process. However, when confronted by the realities of the apparatuses of social prejudice or economic inequality and marginalisation, living beings can be easily overwhelmed by this struggle, making it difficult to find a place where this subject may dwell. One of the artifacts of this process is the fabrication of the social corpses of the criminological/rehabilitative machine (Polizzi *et al* 2014: 239–40).

Within this context, living beings are manipulated by the power imposed by the apparatus of the they-self. Given that the fact of criminal behaviour remains contained under the exclusive domain of the individual actor, any and all aspects of the social world that may be implicated in its construction are either minimised or rejected outright. What remains is the fabrication of these docile social selves that are required to 'adapt' to these environmental social realities without any possible recourse to their change or transformation. Those who attempt to confront this process of 'pacification' are labeled as resistant or unwilling to address the 'social risks' their needs impose on social existence. When the process of criminological theorising becomes overly focused upon an objective rendering of criminal behaviour and its causes, the possible manifestations of this emerging 'theoretical' subject are similarly limited.

Such approaches to theorising reject the aspect of the apparatus that is fundamentally implicated in its conclusions. To reduce living beings to the function of biological networks not only invalidates the potentiality of living beings, but also lessens the possibility for the emergence of the subject. Included in this formulation is the specific ways in which the emerging subject of this type of theoretical approach is also held beholden to the manifestation of the apparatus of the professional they-self.

Just as the constructing power of social apparatuses attempt to direct and control living beings and their potential to be subjects, criminological theorising imposes the same manipulating influence upon those explanations concerning the causes and consequences of criminal behaviour. It is also necessary to recognise that much like the manifestation of competing they-selves, the subject, which arises from the conflict between living being and apparatus, is also indeterminate and variable and often context specific. Some of these examples may be as mundane as one's involvement with a supportive university or department or one's involvement within the context of liked minded scholars. Although it may be 'easier' to acquiesce to the demands of the apparatus, to what they say, the adjacent possible and all that it represents is also situated within this conflict. How these competing possibilities emerge will remain the unstatable possible that is an 'artifact' of the total gestalt of existence and world.

Conclusion

In closing, it is necessary to point out that the they-self can never represent a singular meaning generating process for being-in-the-world and neither can Kauffman's biological indeterminism or Agamben's conceptualisation of the apparatus. For example, Heidegger's conceptualisation of the they-self must be context specific to reflect the variety of variability within and across these specific localities for the presencing of being-in-the-world. Although it may be possible to identify a dominant narrative within a given thrown context, it is very likely that other competing manifestations of the they-self will also be present to challenge, these more "privileged" constructions. Agamben's notion of the apparatus reflects an ever present struggle with living beings that will always be in some way contingent on the potentiality of the emerging subject. Kauffman's formulation of the adjacent possible reflects the presence of these unprestatable contingencies, found both within the self and environment, which recognises the possibility for both adaptive and unanticipated human potentials.

Such theorising of human existence and human potential must reject any and all attempts to continue to embrace reductive formulations of criminological theory and the potential policy implications such conclusions invite. Although such recognition does foreclose the possibility for a general theory of crime or criminal behaviour, it still offers a conceptual reference that is capable of incorporating the fact of our biology, the power of human agency and the issues confronted by our situated interaction with various manifestations of the social world.

The purpose of this reflection has been to offer an introductory and decidedly incomplete exploration of those issues underlying any discussion of crime and criminal behaviour. The theoretical sketches offered above need a much more thorough exploration that is simply not possible here. The need for Cartesian and Newtonian certainty, however, continues to plague the 'scientific' foundations of the field of criminological theorising and must continue to be rigorously critiqued. The possible recognition of the indeterminate reality of human behaviour and social world seems to evoke such disciplinary anxiety that its presence invites the pursuit of the next wave of deterministic theorising.

Although a more indeterminate approach to these issues, whether related to human being generally, or criminal behaviour specifically, pose a much more complicated set of questions that offer no easy answers, they also provide us the opportunity to honestly embrace the complexity of human existence.

Our desire to simplify this search may provide some relief to this uncertainty, but it really does not answer the questions that need to be answered and may inappropriately manipulate this conversation in ways that take us further from, and not closer to, its resolution.

Bibliography

Agamben, G. (2009) *What is an Apparatus? And other Essays*, Stanford, CA: Stanford University Press.

Agnew, R. (2011) *Toward an Integrated Criminology: Integrating Assumptions about Crime, People, and Society*, New York, NY: New York University Press.

Arrigo, B. and D. Milovanovic (2009) *Revolution in Penology: Rethinking the Society of Captives*, Lanham, MD: Rowman & Littlefield Publishers.

Arrigo, B., D. Milovanovic and C. Schehr (2005) *The French Connection in Criminology: Rediscovering Crime, Law, and Social Change*, Albany and New York, NY: SUNY Press.

Buss, D. (2012) 'The Evolutionary Psychology of Crime', *Journal of Theoretical & Philosophical Criminology*, Special Edition, 4: 90–98.

Durrant, R. and T. Ward (2012) 'The Role of Evolutionary Explanations in Criminology', *Journal of Theoretical & Philosophical Criminology*, Special Edition, 4: 1–37.

Einstadter, W.J. and S. Henry (2006) *Criminological Theory: An Analysis of its Underlying Assumptions*, 2nd edn, Lanham, MD: Rowman & Littlefield.

Ferrell, J. (2004) 'Scrunge City' in Ferrell, J., Hayward, K., Morrison, M., and Presdee, M. (eds.) *Cultural Criminology Unleashed*, London, England: Glasshouse Press, pp. 167–179.

Foucault, M. (1980) *Power/Knowledge: Selected Interviews and Other Writings, 1972–1977*, edited by C. Gordon, New York, NY: Pantheon Books.

Gadd, D. and T. Jefferson (2007) *Psychosocial Criminology: An Introduction*, Los Angeles, CA and London: Sage.

Gangle, R. (2007) 'Collective Self-Organization in General Biology: Gilles Deleuze, Charles S. Peirce, and Stuart Kauffman', *Zygon*, 42, 223–39.

Hall, S. (2012) *Theorizing Crime & Deviance: A New Perspective*, Los Angeles, CA and London: Sage.

Hardie-Bick, J. and P. Hadfield (2011) 'Goffman, Existentialism and Criminology', in J. Hardie-Bick and R. Lippens (eds) *Crime, Governance and Existential Predicaments*, London and New York, NY: Palgrave Macmillan, pp. 129–55.

Heidegger, M. (2010) [1953] *Being and Time*, translation by J. Stambaugh and D. Schmidt, Albany, NY: State University of New York Press.

Henry, S. and Milovanovic, D. (1996) *Constitutive Criminology: Beyond Postmodernism*, Thousand Oaks and Los Angeles, CA: Sage Publications Ltd.

Herman, N.J. (1995) *Deviance: A Symbolic Interactionist Approach*, Lanham, MD: General Hall.

Joas, H. (1997) *G.H. Mead: A Contemporary Re-examination of his Thought*, Cambridge, MA: MIT Press.

Katz, J. (1988) *Seductions of Crime: Moral and Sensual Attractions in Doing Evil*, New York, NY: Basic Books.
Kauffman, S. (2008) *Reinventing the Sacred: A New View of Science, Reason, and Religion*, New York, NY: Basic Books.
Mead, G.H. (1967) *Mind, Self, & Society: From the Standpoint of a Social Behaviourist*, edited by C. W. Morris, Chicago, IL and London: Chicago University Press.
Moore, D. (2014) 'Theorizing Criminal Subjectivities: Narrating Silenced Identities', in D. Polizzi, M. Braswell and M. Draper (eds) *Transforming Corrections: Humanistic Approaches to Corrections and Offender Treatment*, Durham, NC: Carolina Academic Press, pp. 83–98.
Owen, T. (2012) 'The Biological and the Social in Criminological Theory', in S. Hall and S. Winlow (eds) *New Directions in Criminological Theory*, London: Routledge, pp. 87–97.
Pakes, F. and J. Winstone (2007) *Psychology and Crime: Understanding and Tackling Offending Behaviour*, Cullompton and Portland, OR: Willan Publishing.
Polizzi, D. (2011a) 'Agnew's General Strain Theory Re-considered: A Phenomenological Perspective', *International Journal of Offender Therapy and Comparative Criminology*, 55 (7): 1051–71.
Polizzi, D. (2011b) 'Heidegger, Restorative Justice and Desistance: A Phenomenological Perspective', in J. Hardie-Bick and R. Lippens (eds) *Crime, Governance and Existential Predicaments*, London and New York, NY: Palgrave Macmillan, pp. 129–55.
Polizzi, D. (2014) 'Developing Therapeutic Trust with Court-ordered Clients', in *Transforming Corrections: Humanistic Approaches to Corrections and Offender Treatment*, Durham, NC: Carolina Academic Press, pp. 303–33.
Polizzi, D., M. Draper and M. Andersen (2014) 'Fabricated Selves and the Rehabilitative Machine: Toward a Phenomenology of the Social Construction of Offender Treatment', in B. Arrigo and H. Bersot (eds) *The Routledge Handbook of International Crime and Justice Studies*, London and New York, NY: Routledge, pp. 233–55.
Quinney, R. (2000) 'Socialist Humanism and the Problem of Crime: Thinking about Erich Fromm in the Development of Critical/Peacemaking Criminology', in K. Anderson and R. Quinney (eds) *Erich Fromm and Critical Criminology: Beyond the Punitive Society*, Urbana and Chicago, IL: University of Illinois Press, pp. 21–30.
Richardson, J. (2012) *Heidegger*, New York, NY and London: Routledge.
Ryals, J. jr. (2014) 'Offender Objectification: Implications for Social Change', in D. Polizzi, M. Braswell and M. Draper (eds) *Transforming Corrections: Humanistic Approaches to Corrections and Offender Treatment*, Durham, NC: Carolina Academic Press, pp. 57–82.
Unnever, J.D. and S.L. Gabbidon (2011) *A Theory of African-American Offending: Race, Racism, and Crime*, New York, NY and London: Routledge.
Walsh, A. (2009) *Biology and Criminology: The Biosocial Synthesis*, London: Routledge.
Walsh, A. (2014) *Criminological Theory: Assessing Philosophical Assumptions*, Boston, MA: Anderson Publishing.
Wendt, A. (2014) *A Quantum Social Science* (manuscript in preparation).

Wortley, R. (2011) *Psychological Criminology: An Integrative Approach*, London and New York, NY: Routledge.

Zimmerman, M.E. (1981) *Eclipse of the Self: The Development of Heidegger's Concept of Authenticity*, Athens, OH: Ohio University Press.

Chapter 11

Critical realism, overdetermination and social censure

Colin Sumner

Introduction

Critical realism became popular in philosophy in the 1990s at a time when the world reflected on the mess it had been driven into by the uncritical unrealism of free-market economics. With its delusions of rational choice, efficient markets, de-regulation of financial institutions, and the reduction of welfare benefits, neo-conservatism left behind the empirical solid world of mutual assurance societies and, melting into air, ventured boldly where no one should go, into the fantasy land beyond the Glass-Steagall Act, of sub-prime investing, leveraged trading, credit default swaps and other means of mass wealth-destruction. The lords of the financial rings had inflated the definition of 'assets' to include all manner of liabilities, wild guesses and plain old bad bets.

The fanciful idea that inequality generated economic growth crash-landed into the harsh reality that sharply polarising levels of wealth destroys any illusion of human or financial growth for billions of human beings. The Bhopal disaster of 1984 illustrated this ugly truth, with its obscene combination of irresponsible negligence and mass mutilation (Pearce and Tombs 2012). Contrary to the guesswork of Alan Greenspan, with his desire to liberate the rich from any restraint, the crimes, anaesthetics, underground economies and suicides of the many reiterate the fact daily that capitalism is not meritocratic, does not generate equality, is not rational in most senses of the word, and does not advance human progress that much spiritually. Criminology should, therefore, be a discipline full of critical or at least social realists. But it is not, and indeed so much of it seems fairly ignorant of the philosophy of social science.

Philosophy in criminology

Many philosophical matters are odd in criminology. The so-called positivists, or administrative criminologists, with their commitment to 'hard science' are really often anti-realists or instrumentalists (conventionalists who think that truth is constructed either through conventions, like the one that supposes that state categories are indices of crime, in both content and rate, or that truth is merely the product of the instruments used to measure it, like statistics). That is, they view the unobservable as non-existent or not proven, except to the extent it can be measured by its surface manifestations or indicators. They know the crime statistics are political in content and use, based on policy and choices, but believe, in true anti-realist or instrumentalist style, that this is their point and inner validity. The positivists of the nineteenth and early twentieth centuries may well have believed in causal sequences and worked hard to correlate antecedent conditions with criminal outcomes, but my guess is that today's administrative criminologists and 'police scientists' could not care less about epistemological issues, devoting themselves to integrating their observations of surface patterns within the political needs and parameters of their funding agencies and what they would see as the necessary political authority.

This makes so-called 'witchcraft' as good a bet as relying on official statistics as indicators of crime rates or of the distribution of 'evil'. Indeed, when working in developing countries, I discovered the value of calling those numbers the officials' statistics. Policing is a political instrument: it may or it may not 'work', depending on what exactly is the objective, but if it does work then few will worry about its rationality or moral validity. I once asked a Zambian woman, from the Bemba community, why she used Western fertility drugs, as well as rubbing certain twigs on her bare arm as advised by the African ('witch') doctor, and her answer on the question of the rationality in believing in either was simply: 'whatever works'. She did not need a belief in either, just a baby. In almost exactly the same manner, the orthodox grant-getting criminologist might say that their criminology 'works' – because it gets funding, it gets published as criminology, it wins prizes and the state treats it as scientific criminology. Even though reading your horoscopes and watching *Luther* or *The Wire* might give you as much if not more insight into crime, if it looks like criminology, pays like criminology and is called criminology, then it is criminology.

Instrumentalist criminology, however, actually requires unacknowledged or closet theory. The so-called 'hard' truths about so-called criminal behaviour absolutely depend on the rules used, the correspondence or translation rules, theoretical entities, to translate observable patterns into meaningful or 'realistic' statements that a government or authority might be paying to receive. For example, crime itself is unobservable – because it is an evaluative category (e.g. killing is observable but it could be heroism in war) – and requires a rule to translate it into empirically measurable forms. Normally, the assumption or correspondence rule used is that crime manifests itself as, and is measured by, convictions for correctly adjudicated and signed-off infractions of the criminal law of the state. How convenient is this, since the state is also the employer, grant-giver or money-provider for such research.

State-friendly criminology would be using or assuming a rule supposing that there is a reliable and accurate correspondence between crime and convictions, implying that there are no significant problems or disruptions with this rule. Yet that glosses over many well-known significant problems with the rule: the criminal law is made by state politicians representing vested interests more than the collective good, law is selectively enforced for many differing reasons by the agencies of law enforcement, the police and authorities commit crimes themselves in the course of their employment, the worst offences against the basest human morality are rarely prosecuted successfully within international criminal law, and, of course, the patterns of reporting and recording of crime reveal huge variations depending on many issues irrelevant to the logic of the criminal law.

The conventionalist, or instrumentalist, and the positivist in criminology relies on the convention that crime is defined by the state and committed by the poor, and that this is not theoretically significant, or a theory. This is a state of denial, driven by politics and vested interest. It expresses itself in the most bizarre claim, or psychological projection, that it is the criminological opposition that is driven by partisan interest, politics and ideology. RealPolitik thus portrays its critics as unrealistic when the only reality is decreed by the state. Power equals rationality and knowledge; critique equals irrationalism and ideology.

However, being in denial of the philosophical opposite in criminology afflicts the various forms of radical conventionalism too. Such philosophies suppose, for example, that knowledge is defined by power, or by situated individuals with 'cultural' biographies. All too frequently in doing research, the interpretive sociologist or the Foucauldian has to rely on or suppose given facts or data, or else their output becomes a mere string of subjectivities mapping out some other subjects' string of subjectivities, and so gives no reason to be compelled by it, other than as an intuitively attractive graphic. This was the problem of decoding ideology that I explored at length in *Reading Ideologies* (Sumner 1979): we appear to be trapped within a hermeneutic circle where there seems little justification for our reading that crosses the space between it and the discourse being read. The post-Foucault generations of genealogists and discourse analysts are openly conventionalist in philosophical terms, in supposing that all truths are reducible to terms within discourses, supported by institutional practices, and thus can bear no relationship to any social reality outside the discourse. Unfortunately, this lack of a commitment to scientific truth is probably what leaves both their histories and their social analyses open to the charges of selectivity of data and amoral or disingenuous descriptiveness – as exemplified at its worst by Foucault's feeble comments in *Discipline and Punish* (1975) that disciplinary power appears to be 'concomitant' with capitalism, and to develop around the same time, whilst denying the use of relevant and known social realities and other scholars' well-established research on the same subject.

Most standpoints in criminology are underdeveloped philosophically, frequently requiring to do in research exactly that which their philosophical beliefs are against. But if we look at the research method of ethnographies, this will move us forward. The value of ethnographic work is undermined (and of course improved) by interest, sympathy or group 'membership' of the ethnographer. Yet we also know that there are 'bridges' in ethnography: language, knowledge of others' cultures, forms of sentience such as intuition and empathy, insider/outsiders who share information, and of course commonly shared or recorded information or collective histories. These bridges are the very foundations of critical realist knowledge in social science.

Critical realism in general

Probably because of its links with Marxian analysis, critical realism, and output based on its premisses, has been regularly avoided by criminology. Yet if one had to pick one multidisciplinary subject area that most needed a unified theory of science, it would be criminology, with its components ranging from law and medicine through psychoanalysis and psychiatry to sociology and cultural studies. Without such a thing, as we all once agreed at a Cambridge Institute staff meeting, criminology would just be a group of disparate souls stood under the umbrella definition of the subject of people studying crime and justice, some doing scholarship, others trying to help the damaged or lost, others seeking to legislate behaviour, some wanting to build a consistent legal system, and some trying to change society.

Critical realism is succinctly defined in *Wikipedia*, and outlined very well in Keat's and Urry's classic text *Social Theory as Science* (1982 [1975]). In its central form in the early work of Roy Bhaskar (1975, 1989), science is concerned to detect and outline the generative mechanisms or internal structures of phenomena that explain their surface manifestation; the roots, photosynthesis and stems that give rise to surface flowers; the damaged personality that gives rise to bad behaviour. This is a notion of science that is not just based on natural sciences but transcends that limit and copes with the rigours of the social sciences, where research subjects talk back and accommodate themselves to the researcher. It supposes a unity of scientific method whose essence 'consists in the movement, at any one level of enquiry, from manifest phenomena to the structures that generate them' (Bhaskar 1989: 19). That method is aimed at 'an analysis of causal laws as expressing the tendencies of things, not conjunctions of events', and at scientific inferences 'that must be analogical and retroductive, not simply inductive and/or deductive' (Bhaskar 1989: 19). So, in the social sciences, the critical realist sees that: '[H]istorical things are structured and differentiated (more or less unique) ensembles of tendencies, liabilities and powers, and historical events are their transformations' (Bhaskar 1989: 19).

Causal relationships, especially in the human sciences, are never reducible to constant surface correlations but are constantly moving and changing sets of conditions of existence, mediating supports and generative mechanisms. In critical realism, the Popperian falsificationist instances and statistical correlations of positivism are not rejected, but merely seen as surface manifestations in need of explanation. In its form in the social sciences of critical naturalism, critical realism is acutely conscious of social change, that most social processes are in a state of flux, that today's world can be seen as an accelerated hyper-modernity that is 'always on' and always rapidly reconfiguring around certain fundamentals, and that any realistic social science must see movement and its internal contradiction as a key principle, even in the analysis of fundamental structures and processes. Last but not least, the critical realist researcher in the social sciences must always be aware that the subjects of this research are very aware of their researchers and adapt their behaviour and statements to them. The Higgs boson might stay the same but people deflect, lie, spin and rationalise.

The classic examples of critical realist work are, of course, Marx and Freud. Both suppose that the generative mechanism lies inside the subject matter, that it only functions under certain conditions of existence, that it has internal contradictions which always threaten to bring it to a halt, that it produces counter-tendencies which sustain it, that it produces layers of self-justification and social protection, and that its counter-tendencies, self-justifications and protective structures feedback or revert into the core structure to such an extent that they become integral parts of its mature forms. Important subject matter, such as the capitalist mode of production or psychopathology, is in this way overdetermined. Both Marx and Freud find a core interest in, and take as their starting points, important contemporary phenomena that are subject to overdetermination and are thus highly symptomatic of the whole system in question, either the society or the personality. In the case of any would-be critical realist criminology, the equivalent would be crime, and the task would be to unpack its generative structures and mediating conditions of existence.

With Marx, for example, capitalism only emerges on the condition that there is free labour, or that there is labour that can be freed, and an economic surplus, either internally generated or brought in from the outside. The inner mechanism, that both explains capitalism's *modus operandi* and its rationale, is described in the theory of surplus value; namely, that in private ownership of the means of production, with all else on one side, the labourer will in a day's work produce enough value to cover his/her costs and also a surplus value for the owner, providing s/he can unlock that surplus by later selling the product. This mechanism has its own internal contradictions or tensions, notably between capital and labour, one wishing to maximise the surplus through intensification of labour or the development of better technology, the other wishing to maintain parity between wages/salaries and the cost of living. Importantly, the whole capitalist operation also has counter-tendencies: so the general tendency of the rate of profit to fall in the long run is countered by the expansion of capital, usually overseas, into territories with low labour costs.

This ever-moving and ever-growing matrix, or social formation, has several self-justificatory mechanisms and ideologies, such as the commercial mass media and the doctrine of the free market, and of course it develops a huge protective shell in the form of the state, with its armies, surveillance technology, destructive weaponry and geo-political treaties and alliances. All in all, for the critical realist, Marx's account of capitalism describes not just a mechanism, like a clock, but a multi-layered empire, an overdetermined social formation, revolving around a generative core, each layer with its own conditions of existence, each part of each layer also, and each layer linked with the other; a Star Wars-style ship so encrusted with its new technologies, its counter-products, barnacles and protections that they become integral to its make-up. No revolution would happen unless change (or Luke Skywalker) could fly into the centre and transform the generative core, although blowing the whole thing up does not actually help future generations who would all die unless they were Luke's offspring, a point sometimes overlooked, or even worse, desired by would-be revolutionaries.

In Freud, we can see a similar analytic structure in his *The Interpretation of Dreams* (1976 [1900]). The relationships in dream formations between the dream-content and the dream-thoughts drawn from to constitute the dream are complex, and selective absence or displacement of certain dream-thoughts is one of the key movements (Freud 1976: 82–105, 383–413). One of the key processes in Freud is multiple determination. Groups of ideas coalesce, which 'makes it easier for an element to force its way into the dream-content' (Freud 1976: 402). Just as superstructural products or effects become embedded within the base in Marx, so for Freud the overall dream is very much a *condensation* of interconnected dream-contents, underpinned by layers of underpinning but often contradictory dream-thoughts, guided by the individual's unconscious desire to find approximation, similarity or consonance between the dream and memories. Without tackling the question of the mechanism which drives a subject to dream, we can see that a thorough critical realist analysis like Freud's makes no concession to any easy, linear, superficial cause-and-effect. There are drivers, conditions of existence, feedback loops, coagulations or condensations, parallels and tendencies to consonance or approximations to progress, order and direction. There is often an overdetermination of key phenomena which needs decoding, unpacking and laying bare, but, as Althusser and Balibar clarified (1970: 243–47), always in a sequence or series of evolutions or movements amounting to a legible succession of forms.

Ultimately, critical realism, in Marx's terms, aims to rescue the rational core from the mystical shell (Nicolaus, in Marx 1973: 43). For Marx, that meant his analysis or breakdown of capital had to begin with the commodity, not the history of modes of production. It had to begin with 'the category which occupies a predominant position within the particular social formation being studied' (Marx 1973: 37). The beginning has to be, as Nicolaus, paraphrasing Marx of the *Grundrisse*, puts it, not an eternal abstraction asserted like a *deus ex machina*, but a concrete, material embodiment of all the contradictions in the political economy: 'the concrete ... the concentration of many determinations, hence unity of the diverse' (Marx 1973: 101). The contradictions, Marx argued, should not be excluded from the outset by asserting some abstract universal, such as population, as the starting point and centre of the analysis:

> Bourgeois society is the most developed and the most complex historic organization of production. The categories which express its relations, the comprehension of its structure, thereby also allows insights into the structure and the relations of production of all the vanished social formations out of whose ruins and elements it built itself up, whose partly still unconquered remnants are carried along with it, whose mere nuances have developed explicit significance within it etc
> (Marx 1973: 105)

Commodity had to be the starting point for the analysis of the capitalist mode of production. It expressed the themes that are now well-known to Marx scholars after the detailed enunciation of them by Althusser and Balibar in *Reading Capital*, and by Stuart Hall in his essay on Marx's method (Hall 1973): the overdetermination of key elements, historical traces, relative autonomy of individuals, institutions and levels, succession of forms in uneven development, and of course the crucial unity of opposites generating their progeny. Although Hall grasped it most elegantly in that and other papers, the key to a critical realism is taking the historic categories as we find them in their most common usage, respecting their integrity and specificity, and deconstructing their social and historical meaning and components from their detail. As Marx expressed it, again in the *Grundrisse*:

> In the succession of the economic categories, as in any other historical, social science, it must not be forgotten that their subject – here, modern bourgeois society – is always what is given, in the head as well as in reality, and that these categories therefore express the forms of being, the characteristics of existence, and often only individual sides of this specific society ...
> (Marx 1973: 106)

The impact of this philosophy for a sociological criminology is this: as we try to understand the moral culture of our social world, the starting point has to be the social censures of crime in practice, or concrete criminalisations. Not social censure in general; not crime in general; but rather the specific social censures of crime in an epoch or period as expressed in the vernacular in their contexts in use. Criminology must begin with crime, but not with such crude and politically loaded an abstract idea of crime as a 'behaviour' but crime as a condensed, overdetermined, situated and motivated social censure containing signifier, intended referent, historical traces or antecedents, and context or conditions of existence.

Realism in criminology

Realism in philosophy holds that our 'reality' is independent of the concepts and research methods we use. It has its own ontology or internal constitution, and is irredeemably separate. For a realist social scientist, the establishment of any social truth must bear some relationship to the full social reality it purports to describe or explain. This could be a relation of correspondence describing the key conditions of existence of some social process, a mirroring of that reality's inner workings, an intuitive-empathic grasp of how a subject's motivations produced the actions or effects to be explained within a given situation, or a logical explanation of its how its internal mechanisms produce its external manifestations. Realists argue that whatever we believe now is only ever an approximation of reality.

Without supposing we can ever be the undisguised object of our own enquiry or perfectly bridge the gap between our perceptions and the life-worlds of others, the critical realist, like the good ethnographer, uses 'bridges' and believes that some knowledges really are more accurate than others and that there are bridging research methods, and levels of analytic approximation, that move us forward towards provisional and conditional statements about tendencies, patterns, forms and mechanisms that command widespread assent as explanatory and meaningful descriptions of people, events, sequences and their causal mechanisms. For example, the critical realist might well hold that a good and solid starting point is crime – as an event expressing and denoting the practical social censures of crime, or criminalisations, in enforcement practice, and that the task of explanation is to account *inter alia* for the aggregate patterns of those criminalisations. The critical realist in criminology therefore is interested in both accurate descriptions of surface patterns and events as well as explanations of those patterns, and indeed in the mediating institutional and cultural forms which link and blend the two. A full account not only produces an explanatory theory, but it ascertains data and constructs links between macro- and micro- that amount to the joined-up thinking that delivers the reasons why the structure produced its manifestation at that time and in that place.

The fact is that criminology is precisely one multidisciplinary subject area where reality is rarely what it seems, and indeed the fact that the man holding the smoking gun is not always the killer is the joy of many movies and television dramas. It is also the cause of political embarrassment and subsequent jail sentences for whistle-blowers, when the killer turns out to be US military in a helicopter mowing down unarmed men in Iraq and the video is released by *Wikileaks* to a horrified public. Surface manifestations do not often betray their roots, genealogies, causes or underlying mechanisms. Indeed, where politicians are involved, the aim is to stop the surface being held to reveal underlying reality: for example, nobody wants to publicise the correlation between economic recession and rising official crime rates or to accept that the government commits war crimes.

Unsurprisingly, perhaps, once the post-war fantasy welfare consensus wore off and the neoliberal fiscal state-welfare deconstruction kicked in, academic observers in philosophy and criminology turned to various kinds of realism: critical, left, Marxian, structuralist. Some of these realisms emphasised the power of the deep structure to deliver, create, express, underpin, explain and form the manifest conflict on the surface (Hall *et al* 1978). Others focused more on the obscenity of everyday violence, and its accompanying cultural baggage (Winlow and Hall 2006). Within criminology, there were substantial differences and antagonisms between left realism and critical realism; between the right of the socialist movement and the left. The former restored moral outrage to criminology by emphasising that crime damaged people and divided communities. It emphasised the fact that crime often occurs within and against the local working class or ordinary urban communities. Critical realist work focused more on the big structures of capitalist society, the state and economy, and the way that these, via various cultural and institutional mechanisms, translated into major violence in wars, killing fields, death squads, and alternative economies in both the metropolitan streets and the rural peripheries. Writing in 2014, the differences between left and right in the labour movement seem irrelevant and minor compared to genocides, the problems of globalised polarisation of wealth and life prospects, the return of slavery and mass unemployment, post-colonial cultural issues, continuing gender unfairness, the destruction of the environment, and the shrinking relevance of nation states.

A properly realist position accepts that all we can try to do is move towards closer and closer approximations to the object of our enquiry through deeper and deeper immersion into the subject matter. Manifest reality often deceives, especially in the arts, humanities and social sciences where people and their behaviour are involved, both as researchers and research objects. The critical realist tries to decipher, to decode, to take off masks, to recognise the underlying faces, and to connect up the dots in the bigger picture.

Awareness of both the surface obscenity of serious crime *and* the dark deep, often 'normal', structure of social pathology brought any realist criminology to the point in the 1990s where it had to recognise a combination of things: that criminal acts could be very damaging to innocent people and romantic defence of them often concealed darker practices, that criminal acts were often also an effective underground economy to which the community turned a knowing blind eye or even openly supported, that the state itself committed some crime and/or often worked hard to conceal the crimes of its friends and sponsors, that criminology had to work with politicians or political activists towards social justice, and that crime control was not something we could do without but was also too-often counter-productive, being only targeted at the poor or those censured as deviant and so a warped punishing of marginality and failure (see Taylor 1981, 1999). Philosophical realism required us to move beyond Merton and the Chicago School to a deeper appreciation of the amount and range of crime that was embedded within normal society, its institutions and practices, and was not 'innovation' so much as conformity.

Contrary to the impression given by the laid-back labelling theorists of the 1960s and 1970s with their emphasis on discriminatory labels of 'deviance', the criminalisation of victimless activities, and the growth of heavy-handed policing in the West generally, crime had now grown a new seriousness. The texts of left realism too often took us back to urban decay and the exotica, pathological or otherwise, of working-class subcultures, back to the Chicago School and Merton, insufficiently questioning the pathology of social normality and/or the anti-social behaviour of the rich and powerful. From the 1990s onwards, those criminologists whose work was or could be rooted in critical realism were focusing on the big structures, the 'higher immoralities' (C. Wright Mills), the imperial roots of urban gangsterism, the global relations between crime and underdevelopment, and the reluctance to recognise that conformity too could breed 'crime' and 'administrative irregularities that are easily rectified' (or the non-censure of middle and upper-class 'anti-social behaviour').

In passing, we can see that the recent 'cultural criminology' revived an older notion of culture as difference (see Bauman 1999 [1973]), rarely breaking with the older, cruder, culturalism of Merton and the Chicago School. Criminology has, in fact, been very 'cultural' since the early 1930s (see Sumner 2013 [1994]: chapters 2 and 3), in the sense of preferring to focus in various ways on working-class culture as the cause of crime rather than looking at the pathology of a boom-and-bust capitalism. In trying to explain coal scavenging or the rise of organised delinquent gangs or drug addiction, the likes of Sellin, Wirth, Lindesmith and Shaw in the 1930s and 1940s had all used a notion of culture as difference (Sumner 2013 [1994]: chapters 2 and 3). In doing so, they challenged the colonial or master perception of the Other as a strange and exotic species, and almost freed themselves from its clutches when seeing the sins of the terminally unemployed as all-too-human. Sellin and Wirth in particular were so clear about the importance of culture and ideology, and their links to social structure, that they laid down one of the foundations for uncoupling criminology from the capitalist state, towards a criminology which could critically assess both the economic-political roots of practices censured as crime and the (sub-)cultural character of their (mis-)representation in legal and media discourses. All too often since that time criminologists have assumed that the key or only subcultures were working class. Insofar as left realism and cultural criminology have moved beyond the Chicagoans and Merton, into, for example, the impact of consumerism or unemployment on motivation there is forward movement in the theoretical grasp of contemporary formations (see Hall *et al.* 2008; Winlow and Hall 2006; Hall and Winlow 2012; Sumner 2012; Hayward 2004).

Criminological theory today should be assessed, from a critical realist standpoint, to the extent that it has begun to deconstruct the most concrete and important of contemporary terrains within the analysis of crime and deviance, in sociology, criminology and politics, namely the recalcitrance of a criminogenic capitalism, and its expansion on a world scale, the pathological impact of globalisation and its driving imperialisms on indigenous social practices and cultures (Sumner 1982). This requires forms of thought and research that integrate deep structures into the theorising of surface expressions; to explain the well-springs and conditions of existence of contemporary social censures and pathologies.

The breakthrough in *Policing the Crisis*

There were a few voices in criminology that stood for a critical realism, both philosophically and politically. We took crime as seriously as the left realists. Indeed, we also took teaching criminology or the sociology of crime and deviance very seriously. These voices included the late Stuart Hall. The success of a collectively written study of the moral panic around black crime in a disintegrating early 1970s Britain, appropriately called *Policing the Crisis* (Hall *et al* 1978), was testimony to the importance of a critical realist approach in social science research. My own writings on social censure (Sumner 1990, for example), and even my critique of that book (Sumner 1981), were based on such a philosophy of social science.

The realism embedded in the awareness of the obscenity of some crimes, including the vicious mugging at the heart of *Policing the Crisis*, sat alongside the equally realistic views that most of the serious crimes globally were rarely prosecuted and that the spin-off from British imperial decline included the crimes of urban, British, black sons and daughters of immigrants from the Caribbean as well as the constitutional disintegration and reconfiguration of the UK. What *Policing the Crisis* did philosophically for criminology was to recognise the relative autonomy and uneven co-existence of different levels of explanation, and to work through the complex ways that deep structure was mediated by institutions and culture before it delivered surface patterns. True, the work is not fully theorised or systematic or explicit about its own commitments, but it is not difficult to recognise a complex 'structure-in-dominance' within the account, or, if you like, levels of determination which unevenly combine and interact to produce an overdetermined censure of mugging as the key index of a hegemonic crisis.

The critical realist philosophy implicit throughout *Policing the Crisis*, and explicit in my own analysis of social censures, is long overdue a full articulation within critical criminology or sociology of crime and deviance. Many criminologists sneer at what they call 'theory'. Some imagine it can do without much theory. But, as my ex-colleague Nigel Walker once so wisely observed: the *explicans* must always explicate the *explicandum*. When it does not, we cease to be doing good science; where science means an attempt to produce a knowledge that has an inner integrity and contains a close approximation to or grasp of the phenomena it is attempting to explain. Of course, criminology, by its very DNA, is tied to the state and therefore tends to steer away from explanation, preferring its conclusions baked in advance to enable or at least not prevent the re-election of politicians. The only explanations seemingly worth discussing in state and orthodox criminologies surround antiquated concepts of the bad individual, the rotten apple in the healthy barrel, the emotional or animal *id* springing free of its restraints, the biological defect, insanity and unreason (Foucault 1967), and the 'criminal mind'. Explanations that focus upon relationships, social structure, the invisible, multiple and layered social conditions of existence and interactional triggers of violence or other behaviours that disgust, the overlapping causes of pathological situations – that might suppose that society is the patient not the doctor (see Frank 1948) – tend to be deflected as too woolly, socialistic, abstract, impractical, 'sociological', 'hypothetical', unmeasurable and 'theoretical'.

Policing the Crisis broke the mould of social science research into crime and deviance in 1978 by starting with a specific social censure of crime or at least anti-social behaviour – mugging – and analysing the cultural and historical traces and elements condensed within its overdetermined form.

Already, we have seen that in critical realist work there are levels of explanation, theories of evolutionary sequences or theorised histories, and a sense that a simple social phenomenon may be a condensed expression of multiple, overlapping social relationships and events. But some social manifestations are more emblematic, symptomatic or representative of the tensions of a period of development than others. Stuart Hall and his team set out to show how the brutal and apparently meaningless mugging of an elderly gentleman by three black teenagers came to be represented as a symptom of a society in crisis, weakened by immigration, undermined in its authority over the 'affluent' young, disintegrating at the very heart of its constitution as a 'United Kingdom', and desperately in need of a new moral-political consensus or settlement. The book then tries to pay full respect to all the levels of determination: the borrowing of the category of mugging and its racial significance from the American media, the logics involved in the social production of news, the political representation of post-war immigration as a threat to the British constitution, and the successive challenges to the hegemony of the post-war social-democratic consensus. It is true that one further crucial level was under-researched, namely the deterioration of police-black relations in the UK and in Birmingham in particular, and that my own research on the British press in 1972–73 shows that actually the censure of political demonstrations was much more frequent and much more important (see the essay on the censure of political demonstrations in Sumner 1990). But these are not decisive points, for although the censure of 'the demo' was probably more significant in 1972–73, the point must surely be that the whole moral map of the UK at that time was being renovated, reconfigured and recalibrated in line with what was undoubtedly a watershed in our political economy around 1970. New censures emerged and others dimmed during the period, as the culture re-organised itself to re-present, contain and stifle the oppositions to authority of power and capital.

What a critical realist approach had especially brought to the research table were: (a) the concept of an overdetermined censorious ideological form that compacted many of the social contradictions of the period; and (b) a sense of the importance of levels of determination, levels of causal analysis with their own relatively autonomous dialectics. The moral panic around mugging was revealed as the condensation of multiple layers of determination and constitution, each with their own relation to the final form. A contemporary social censure was shown in detail to represent the contradictions and anxieties of its age. Ideology was demonstrably not simply a complex system of thought or belief-system, but very much a generic term for multiple and hybrid forms of consciousness operating in an integrated way, rooted in several forms of social practice and driven by the needs of a contested political hegemony. Social censures could easily be seen as compacted, contested and fragmented ideological formations, with no single source or logic. Overlapping practices, each with their own tensions or contradictions, produced these composite or hybrid ideologies, loaded with a variety of inflections, debates and readings.

Criminology could and would never be the same again. The 'causes of crime' gradually lost its meaning and value as an intelligible research agenda, being replaced, at least in principle, by two new seminal research programmes that go hand in hand: (a) the historical etymology and structural elucidation of the social censures of crime; and (b) zemiology, the study of social harms and the way societies selectively neglect some and punish others. These programmes in tandem will eventually move us beyond the behavioural concept of crime forever. The moral-political component of orthodox or state criminologies had been revealed and there is no going back. In years to come, even though we will probably still be struggling with questions of what to criminalise, and how, we will smile at the very idea that the state categories of crime dominated our moral compass and governed our criminology for so long.

Critical criminologists have begun to plough this furrow, without necessarily being conscious of their philosophical position, and much good work has been done already that never even mentions critical realist philosophy. The study of corporate and state crime is now being funded and advanced; the culturally specific character of moral censures is being revealed; and many now know that, globally, the gulf between the application of the criminal law and the moral integrity of the people is huge. The weight of social censure has been thoroughly uncoupled from the tariffs of punishment. Women who resist being forced into marriage are threatened with execution, yet corporate executives and bankers who manipulate markets and whole governments and destroy the financial futures or even the health of millions are rarely even morally censured. When law and morality are so far apart, there is a need for criminology to be considerably more philosophical, more critical and more realistic.

Bibliography

Althusser, L. and E. Balibar (1970) *Reading Capital*, London: New Left Books.
Bauman, Z. (1999) [1973] *Culture as Praxis*, London: Routledge & Kegan Paul.
Bhaskar, R. (1975) *A Realist Theory of Science*, Leeds: Leeds Books.
Bhaskar, R. (1989) *The Possibility of Naturalism*, New York, NY: Harvester Wheatsheaf.
Foucault, M. (1967) *Madness and Civilization: A History of Insanity in the Age of Reason*, translation by R. Howard, London: Tavistock Publications.
Foucault, M. (1975) *Discipline and Punish: The Birth of the Prison*, translation by A. Sheridan, London: Allen Lane.
Frank, L.K. (1948) *Society as the Patient: Essays on Culture and Personality*, New Brunswick, NJ: Rutgers University Press.
Freud, S. (1976) [1900] *The Interpretation of Dreams*, Harmondsworth: Penguin.
Hall, S. (1973) 'Marx's notes on method', *Working Papers in Cultural Studies*, 3, and (2003) *Cultural Studies*, 17 (2): 113–49.
Hall, S., C. Critcher, T. Jefferson, J. Clarke and B. Roberts (1978) *Policing the Crisis: Mugging, the State, and Law and Order*, London: Macmillan.
Hall, S. and S. Winlow (eds) (2012) *New Directions in Criminological Theory*, London: Routledge.
Hall, S., S. Winlow and C. Ancram (2008) *Criminal Identities and Consumer Culture*, Cullompton: Willan.
Hayward, K. (2004) *City Limits*, London: Cavendish.
Keat, R. and J. Urry (1982) [1975] *Social Theory as Science*, London: Routledge & Kegan Paul.
Marx, K. (1973) [1857] *Grundrisse*, Harmondsworth: Penguin.
Pearce, F. and S. Tombs (2012) *Bhopal: Flowers at the Altar of Profit and Power*, North Somercotes: CrimeTalk Books. Available as an ebook from YPD Books.
Sumner, C.S. (1979) *Reading Ideologies*, London: Academic Press.
Sumner, C.S. (1981) 'Race, crime and hegemony', *Contemporary Crises*, 5 (3): 277–91.
Sumner, C.S. (ed.) (1982) *Crime, Justice and Underdevelopment*, London: Heinemann.
Sumner, C.S. (ed.) (1990) *Censure, Politics and Criminal Justice*, Milton Keynes: Open University Press.
Sumner, C.S. (2012) 'Censure, culture and political economy: beyond the death of deviance debate', in S. Hall and S. Winslow (eds.) *New Directions in Criminological Theory*, Cullompton: Devon., pp. 165–180.

Sumner, C.S. (2013) [1994] *The Sociology of Deviance: An Obituary*, North Somercotes Crime Talk Books.
Taylor, I. (1981) *Law and Order: Arguments for Socialism*, London: Macmillan.
Taylor, I. (1999) *Crime in Context*, Cambridge: Polity Press.
Winlow, S. and S. Hall (2006) *Violent Night*, Oxford: Berg 3PL.

Index

affecting bodies 15–17
Agamben, G. 127, 167–9, 174, 189–90, 191
agency: and determinism 180, 182–4; schema QD 66–7n, 77; *see also* collective action
Agnew, R. 180–1, 182, 183–4, 188
Akram, S. 125–6
Amatrudo, A. 108
Andrieu, B. 17
anxiety and edgework 145–7
Aristotle 48
art: and aesthetics 55–8; and rhetoric 52
Austin, J. 63

Beccaria, C. 163, 164, 165
being and being-with 38
being-in-the-world 186–9
Bergson, H. 17–21, 27, 71, 73, 78; critique of 21–3
Bhaskar, R. 198
biological indeterminacy 184–5
biopolitics and biometric identity 167–72
black crime *see Policing the Crisis*
bodies: affecting 15–17; creativity 17–21
boundaries/dividing lines *see* edgework; image of the line
Bratman, M. 106, 112, 118–20
Busemeyer, J. and Bruza, P. 73–4, 75
Butler, J. 124

Canada, Criminal Code of 159–60, 164–5
Cape of Good Hope 161–2
capitalism (late): conservative and 'liberal left' perspectives 122–6, 128; development of 130–3; harms 126–8, 129; Master and Slave recognition 129–30; politics of aetiological revival 126–8; subjectivity and special liberty 128–30, 134; transcendental materialism 133–7
capitalism (Marxist) 199–201
chaos and edgework 145–7
'chaosmic' ethics 61–2, 63
character typologies and corrective reform 165–7
circularity (theoretical framework) 86–8
collective action 111–14; addressing reductive theories 111; central problem 107–11; compositionality criteria and individual possession 114–15; *Going to New York Together* 118–20; Law Commission Report 117; personal desert criteria 117–18; plural subjects theories 113–14; team preference approach 111–12; we-action theories 112, 115–17; we-intention theory 113, 118–19
collective bodies 17
colonial categories and social hierarchy 161–3
compositionality criteria 114–15
conformity and non-conformity 90–2
consciousness/self-consciousness: fabulations 19–21; loss of 146–8, 152–4, 155; phenomenology and existentialism 21–6, 148–50; two modes of 150–1
control: myth and 'communal' mode 53–4; pseudo-pacification process 130–3; theory 35–6
Cover, R.M. 53–4
creativity 17–21
Crewe, D. 33, 36, 42, 43
crime: discourse: theme and variations 48–55; and law 37, 94–6; subjective experiences of 142

crime theory and human experience 178–80, 191–2; apparatus 189–91; attempt to integrate 180–4; being-in-the-world 186–9; biological indeterminancy 184–5; challenges to 'objective' criminology 178–80
Criminal Code of Canada 159–60, 164–5
'criminalisable' legal persons 159–61, 172–4; biopolitics and biometric identity 167–72; character typologies and corrective reform 165–7; colonial categories and social hierarchy 161–3; rationality, culpability and punishment 163–5
criminological classification: character typologies and corrective reform 165–7; gangs 106–7; modernity/violence nexus 35–7
Critchley, S. 43
critical realism: breakthrough in *Policing the Crisis* 205–8; in general 198–202; and philosophy in criminology 195–8; and realism in criminology 202–5; and social censure 201–2, 205, 206–8
Csikszentmihalyi, M. 143–4, 145, 146, 147, 148, 152–4, 155
culpability: and collective action 107–11; rational persons 163–5
'cultural criminology' 204–5

Damasio, A. 16, 17
Darwinian/evolutionary perspective 17–18, 184–5
Delanda, M. 67, 68, 71, 73, 74–5, 76
Deleuze, G. 16, 17, 55, 74–5, 79; and Guattari, F. 18, 21, 53, 55, 56, 63, 67, 68–9, 71, 74, 75, 79
deliberative collective action 110–11, 116–17
democracy 49–50
depressive hedonia and soft narcosis 137
Derrida, J. 49–50, 62, 63
Descartes, R. 34, 38–9
desert theory 117–18
determinism: agency and 180, 182–4; biological 184–5
difference (theoretical framework) 88–90
dissociation 134
Douzinas, C. 47

edgework 141, 154–5; anxiety, chaos and uncertainty 145–7; criminology and transgression 141–3; existentialist phenomenology 149–50; modes of self-consciousness 150–1; negotiating 151–4; reflexive self 147–9; sense of flow 143–5, 152, 154
'élan vital' (creativity) 17–21
Esposito, R. 162, 166
ethics 15–16, 40–1, 42; chaosmic 61–2, 63; and growth of markets 131, 132; moral-political component of criminology 207–8
ethnographic research 198
evolutionary/Darwinian perspective 17–18, 184–5
existentialism, phenomenology and 21–6, 148–50
experience *see* crime theory and human experience; subjectivity

fabulations 20–1; images and 17–21
Ferrell, J. 143
flow, sense of 143–5, 152, 154
Foucault, M. 55, 160, 189, 197, 206
freedom and normative constraint 40–1
Freud, S. 199, 200

Gabor, D. 71, 73, 76
Gangle, R. 185
gangs 36–7; and individual agency *see* collective action; UK treatment and typologies 106–7
Gaut, B. 57, 58
Gilbert, M. 114, 115
Gioia, T. 58, 59, 61
God/Nature 14, 15, 16
Going to New York Together 118–20

Hall, Steve 122, 126, 127, 128, 130, 135, 136; Winlow, S. and 123, 127, 128, 203
Hall, Stuart 201; *Policing the Crisis* 205–8
Hancock, H. 61–2
harms 126–8, 129
Heidegger, M. 186, 187, 191
Hess, H. and Scherer, S. 92–4
Hirsch, A. von 117
Hobbes, T. 34
Holland, E. 67, 68, 71, 79
holographic theory 72–3
Husak, D. 53
Husserl, E. 23–4, 25, 38–9, 43, 149, 150

ideology, symbolic systems and 135–6, 197

image of the line: affecting bodies 15–17; constitution of the world 23–6; images and fabulations 17–21; phenomenology and existentialism 21–6; Spinoza and neo-Spinozism 15–21; two perspectives 13–15, 26–8; wholeness 29, 32–4
individuals and groups *see* collective action; gangs
intentionality 38–9, 43; and consciousness 23–6, 150–1; and protected legal rights 95–6
inter-subjectivity 38, 40, 42

jazz: art and aesthetics 55–8; 'chaosmic' ethics 61–2, 63; counterpoint 59–61, 62; and different sense of criminology 62–3; roots 58–9
Johnston, A. 134–5

Kant, I. 87, 88, 96, 97, 150
Katz, J. 142
Kauffman, S. 184–5, 191

labelling theory 78
language 38–9, 51–2; and art/aesthetics 56, 63; narratives 53–4; unexamined statements 76
law: crime and 37, 94–6; crime and science 50–5; moral-political component of criminology 207–8; values 91–2; *see also* 'criminalisable' legal persons
Law Commission Report: *Participating in Crime* 117
left: 'liberal left' 122–6, 128; realism and 'cultural criminology' 204–5
legal personality 51
legal persons *see* 'criminalisable' legal persons
Levinas, E. 33, 39, 40, 41, 42–3
liberalism 136–7; 'liberal left' 122–6, 128; *see also* neoliberalism
lines of division/boundaries *see* edgework; image of the line
Lippens, R. 141, 148
Luhmann, N. 85, 89, 91, 99
Lyng, S.H. 141, 142–3, 144, 145–7, 148, 151, 152, 154, 155

Marx, K. 199–201
Master and Slave recognition 129–30
Mead, G.H. 147, 148, 181–2
Merleau-Ponty, M. 27

Messner, C. 47, 51, 52, 54, 55, 57, 63
minimal individualism theory 115
modernity: law, crime and science 50–5; subject of 32–5
modernity/violence nexus, criminological classification and 35–7
Morse, S. 165, 170
Murrow, G. and Murrow, R. 17

Naffine, N. 164
Nature/God 14, 15, 16
neoliberalism 124–5; totalitarian 127–8
neuroscience 16–17
nomadology *see* quantum, holographic affirmative nomadology
non-conformity, conformity and 90–2
non-violent crime 131–2
normative constraint: control myth and 'communal' mode 53–4; freedom and 40–1
nothingness 21–2, 25–6

object (theoretical framework) 84–6; circularity 86–8; difference 88–90; reality 90–2; theory 92–4; what is the case and what is behind it? 96–8
'objective' criminology, challenges to 178–80
obligation and responsibility 42–3
Other 34–5, 39–40; freedom and normative constraint 40–2; inter-subjectivity 38, 40, 42; post-criminological perspective 43–5; responsibility to and for 42–3, 44–5; and they-self 188

Participating in Crime (Law Commission) 117
Pavlich, G. 161, 162, 166, 167, 171
personal responsibility *see* 'criminalisable' legal persons; responsibility
phenomenology 14–15; and existentialism 21–6, 148–50
Plato 48
plural subjects theories 113–14
Policing the Crisis 205–8
political catastrophism 127
political perspectives: biopolitics and biometric identity 167–72; moral-political component of criminology 207–8; *see also* capitalism
Polizzi, D. 186, 188; *et al* 179, 189, 190
polyphony 60, 62

positivism: character typologies and corrective reform 165–7; conventionalism and instrumentalism 195–8
post-criminological perspective 43–5; 'post-modern' subject and 37–42
power relationships 93, 95
pre-adaptation 185
primal trauma theory 124; and late capitalism 135–7
prisoner's dilemma 109–10
pseudo-pacification process 130–3
punishment: desert theory 117–18; rational persons, culpability and 163–5

quantum, holographic affirmative nomadology 71–9; comparative methodologies 66–8; and normal science 68–71

Rafter, N.H. 169–70, 172, 174
rationality, culpability and punishment 163–5
realism 202–5; capitalist 136; see also critical realism
reason and action 97–8
reductionism 111, 184–5
reflexive self 147–9
responsibility: and collective action 117–18; obligation and 42–3; to and for Other 42–3, 44–5; see also 'criminalisable' legal persons
risk, edgework as 145–7
'rogues' 49–50
'rule-breaking' 62, 63

Said, E. 62
Saramago, J. 92, 99
Sartre, J.-P. 21–3, 24–6, 27, 39–40, 41, 42, 148–51, 152, 155
Schinkel, W. 35, 37
science: biology see biological indeterminancy; biopolitics and biometric identity; law, crime and 50–5; neuroscience 16–17; physics see quantum, holographic affirmative nomadology; see also positivism
self-consciousness see consciousness/self-consciousness
Sibley, F. 56–7
Smith, A. 34
Smith, B. 164

social censure 201–2, 205, 206–8
social communication, manipulation of 88–90
social hierarchy, colonial categories and 161–3
soft narcosis, depressive hedonia and 137
sovereignty 27–8
special liberty 128–30, 134
Spinoza, B. de 13–14, 34; and neo-Spinozism 15–21
state of exception 127; see also special liberty
statistical crime, decline of 125
strain theory 36
subject: and apparatus 190; of modernity 32–5; 'post-modern' 37–42
subjectivity 123–4; experiences of crime 142; inter-subjectivity 38, 40, 42; and objectivity 180–4 (see also object (theoretical framework); and special liberty 128–30, 134
sublimated aggression 132–3
Sumner, C.S. 106, 197, 204, 205
Sutherland, E.H. 48
symbolic systems and ideology 135–6, 197

team preference approach 111–12
they-self 187–8; apparatus of 189–91
Thompson, H.S. 142, 145
throwness 186–7
totalitarianism 127–8
transcendental ego 150, 151
transcendental materialism 133–7
transgression, edgework and 141–3

victim movement 28
'vital current' (creativity) 17–21

we-action theories 112, 115–17
we-intention theory 113, 118–19
Weber, M. 91, 98
White, J.B. 51, 52
wholeness 29, 32–4
Wiener, M.J. 166
Wilber, K. 29
Winlow, S. and Hall, S. 123, 127, 128, 203
Wittgenstein, L. 38, 51, 56, 57, 59

Young, J. 70, 123

Žižek, S. 123–5, 127, 134–5

CPSIA information can be obtained
at www.ICGtesting.com
Printed in the USA
JSHW011319201219
3107JS00002B/15